This book is dedicated to the memory of Chris Martens

WORLD WRESTLING INSANITY

The Decline and Fall of a Family Empire

JAMES GUTTMAN

ECW Press

Published by ECW PRESS
2120 Queen Street East, Suite 200, Toronto, Ontario, Canada M4E 1E2

Library and Archives Canada Cataloguing in Publication

Guttman, James, 1977–
World Wrestling insanity : the decline and fall of a family empire / James Guttman.

ISBN 1-55022-728-9

1. McMahon, Vince. 2. World Wrestling Entertainment, Inc. 3. McMahon family.
4. Wrestling—United States. 5. Wrestling promoters—United States— Biography. I. Title.

GV1196.M35G88 2006   796.812'0973   C2006-900490-0

Editor: Michael Holmes
Typesetting: Gail Nina
Cover and text design: Tania Craan
Cover photo: James Guttman

PRINTING: Marquis

DISTRIBUTION

CANADA: Jaguar Book Group, 100 Armstrong Avenue, Georgetown, ON, L7G 5S4
UNITED STATES: Independent Publishers Group, 814 North Franklin Street,
Chicago, Illinois 60610

PRINTED AND BOUND IN CANADA

ECW PRESS
ecwpress.com

CONTENTS

Acknowledgements

I want to thank the following people for all they did to help me make this book become a reality: My wife Jaimee, Michael Holmes and everyone at ECW PRESS, Derek Burgan, Mallory Mahling, Matt "Dawgs" Aponte, Tom Prichard, the entire staff at WorldWrestling-Insanity.com for all the amazing work they've done, Stu Saks, Dave Scherer, the Pro Wrestling Torch, Samer El-Khawam, Monterey Monger, all the people who I can't thank by name but know I wish I could, my brother and parents, Terry Funk, Elix Skipper, Aaron Aguilera, Jim "Kamala" Harris, Missy Hyatt, D-Lo Brown, the Honky Tonk Man, Lanny Poffo, Amy Weber, Charlie Haas and all the readers of my work through the years. Thank you for making all this possible.

Alright, hold up. Before we begin, there are a few things that need to be made clear. First and foremost, this is not a book that sets out to unfairly slam World Wrestling Entertainment and the McMahon Family. My goal here isn't to say that everything they've done in their entire lives has been wrong. Vince McMahon, along with many others, helped to create a unique piece of American pop culture and for that, they deserve our respect.

They've done plenty of things right on their ride to the top. For every employee who cried unfair treatment after leaving, there's two to say things were jellybeans and rainbows during their WWE tenure. Some of those former employees are quoted in this book. The company has been a staple of American society for so long that it had to be doing something right. I don't ignore that fact. I present it. Then again, I examine the other side too. Lately, there's been a bit too much of "the other side." You'll read all about it soon.

Here's the issue. Wrestling is an often overlooked segment of our society. People don't watch it. They also make sure people know they don't watch it. I realized that when I told people about this book. I'm not talking about family or friends, but acquaintances, friends of friends, distant relatives and barbers. I'm talking about people who have no idea what I write about. They don't know Triple H from Triple A. They don't know Vince McMahon from Ed McMahon. They don't know Johnny Ace from Jonny Quest. This is fun, but I digress. Where was I? Oh yeah, telling people about the book.

Someone would bring it up and they'd ask me what I was doing with myself. With a big smile, I'd say, "I'm working on a book." Inevitably, they'd respond, "Oh, what's it about?" That's when the fun began.

I tried many different ways to say it. I tried, "It's about World Wrestling Entertainment." That was usually met with a cold stare because most people still think it's the World Wrestling Federation. Then I'd have to go into the whole story about how they had issues with the World Wildlife Fund and explain the lawsuit. It became a hassle. Plus, they didn't give a damn in the end anyway. Another five minutes of my life wasted.

After trying to find imaginative ways to explain what this book was about without coming off like Captain Wrestling Fan Weiner of Planet Doofus, I figured to hell with it. I just said it like it is. They asked what it was about, I said "professional wrestling."

The response I was met with most? "Oh, I don't watch wrestling."

Now, keep in mind I didn't say I was writing a flyer to pass around for free at the supermarket. This is a real book. People buy it. It's in stores. It's a pretty cool thing. None of that mattered though — it's about wrestling.

Seriously, I could tell these people that I'm a writer, but I write a free newsletter on Post-it notes and stick them on my bathroom mirror. If the subject matter of the Post-it notes was football or stock picks, they'd be impressed. The fact that it's wrestling negates anything good about it in some people's eyes. Folks who can only name about five wrestlers off the top of their heads. They know Jimmy Snuka, The Rock, Hulk Hogan, Steve Austin and Rocky Balboa. Then they realize that Rocky Balboa wasn't a wrestler, but a movie boxer and the number drops to four.

That's the sad fact. However, wrestling is a huge empire with money flowing in that most corporations would kill for. It's a part of our society. It's something anyone who's grown up in any decade since the '50s can relate to. How could something with so much perseverance be scorned by so many?

It's this scorn that has allowed professional wrestling to exist in a bubble for years. No one notices what happens on WWE programming. It's almost as if I'm the only person on the planet who gets *Monday Night Raw* and *Smackdown* with my cable package. Many nights I've witnessed insane and unbelievable television moments that would knock the world on its ass if *ER* had done it. Sadly, it's WWE and no one seems to care.

This is a scary thought. Do you realize that currently there's one major wrestling promotion in the United States and it's owned by a man that no longer has to worry about competition? Vincent Kennedy McMahon, along with his family and colleagues, is sitting pretty. It's the scariest predicament that most professional wrestlers could have ever imagined. A strong-willed promoter with unchecked power running amok and going haywire at the drop of a hat. What could be worse? There's no way out. It's like an episode of *The Twilight Zone.* I expect Rod Serling to show up at any moment and take us all away from this. Then again, if he did, Vince would take ol' Rod and make him join the "Mr. McMahon Kiss My Ass Club" on live TV.

You don't know what the Kiss My Ass Club is? Oh, you're in for some fun. You're gonna get a lot out of this book. Basically, Mr. McMahon went through a phase where he enjoyed making employees kiss his exposed ass on television. Yeah. Let that soak in. Imagine these situations in your own life.

Picture working for an owner who no longer has to worry about losing you in a bidding war to another company. Imagine how grateful you'd have to be to that boss in order to not lose your job. Sure, he was loving you six years ago when you threatened to jump to a rival company. Now that company is dead. In fact, there's pretty much no other rival at all. Either stay at this insane office and allow the boss's son-in-law to unplug your computer every time you're just about to finish your report or else you have to go to Japan to find work. Sucks, huh? Welcome to World Wrestling Insanity — where up is down. Down is up. And you're thankful just for a chance to be on the show.

Maybe you do know what the Kiss My Ass Club is. Great. You're gonna get a lot out of this book too. There's plenty here for everyone. I have inside stories and thoughts on wrestling philosophy from some of the industry's most well-known names. There's analysis and then analysis of that analysis. Then we analyze that analysis until we all have headaches. Don't worry, there's plenty of sarcasm, wise-ass skits and parody. Not to mention those delightful doctored photos that have made me a favorite in the McMahon household for years.

Also, let it be known that this book doesn't reflect the views and opinions of any other writers, my friends, my family or anyone else. I doubt that anyone else blames Triple H for as much as I do anyway. What I'm saying is that I wrote this alone and didn't run it by anyone except the good folks over at ECW PRESS. Everything I say here is something I myself believe. That's it. If I didn't believe it I wouldn't write it. Watch I'll show you:

There really is a Santa Clau . . .

See, couldn't finish writing it. Why? I don't believe it. See how that works? Good.

As I said earlier though, this isn't an anti-McMahon book. This stuff is all straight shooting. I don't play devil's advocate. I never provoke debate just so I can argue. I have no agendas and don't set out to piss off Vince, Stephanie, Shane, Johnny Ace, Triple H or anyone else just for the sake of pissing them off. If I anger WWE it's not because I'm taking a cheap shot. It's because I'm pointing out something insane about their product. Hopefully they'll correct it. It's constructive criticism. Sure, I can be a jerk about it, but whatever.

People claim that wrestling writers (and the media in general) enjoy taking a negative view on the stories they cover in order to sell more books, newspapers or magazines. This book isn't negative. Or positive. This book is true. It's the way I see the industry. It's the observations I've made through conversations with different people in the wresting business, watching the product on television and viewing it live. I don't apologize if you find it to be cynical. I don't get giddy over the thought that you might find it uplifting. It's reality. That's all.

In fact, my goal has always been to see the wrestling industry flourish. When I first began writing about the business, I sent in résumés to World Wrestling Entertainment in hopes of helping them craft the shows. Time marched on though, and as it did, I learned more about the industry. It didn't take long before the position seemed less and less appealing and I stopped checking the jobs section of their website.

Now even though I don't want to script terrific WWE programming anymore doesn't mean I don't want someone else to do it. It's the exact opposite actually. I want someone to do it. Anyone. Please! No wrestling fan wants the business to be in a slump. Who wants their favorite form of entertainment to seem like a chore every week? You? Do you? Answer me. I didn't think so. I don't either.

This industry is complicated and too many people write it off as "a male soap opera" or "phony baloney." They shouldn't be so quick to judge. After all, it's something that their parents probably watched and their parents before them. Explain to me how "phony baloney" can survive so long if so many people are supposedly too classy to watch. Sure thing. I guess it's just me. All by myself, I made Vince McMahon twenty mazillion dollars. That was all me and me alone. Yeah right.

So you're watching. You may not be watching now, but you've watched at one point in your life. Guess what? I watch too. You want to talk about it? Well then read on. Go on. It's OK. No one's looking. Read the wrestling book. I won't tell your high-class friends.

CHAPTER 1

Looking for Fault in
All the Wrong Places

There's an old adage when it comes to the world of professional wrestling: For those who enjoy it, no explanation is needed. For those who don't, no explanation will do.

The world of sports entertainment remains a mystery to those who choose to shun it. In many ways, it also remains a mystery to those who follow it. The intrigue behind wrestling is so complex that it's almost impossible to explain without going into detail. While someone who enjoys television sitcoms is someone who enjoys comedy or someone that watches action movies strays toward excitement, professional wrestling isn't so black and white. The industry as a whole wears many hats. It can appeal to those who like anything from comedy to drama, athleticism or romance and every other genre imaginable. For the most part, there's something for any taste within the confines of the squared circle. Chances are even if you've never watched a wrestling program in your life, there's something that's been done somewhere at some time that you would enjoy.

That's not to say that sports entertainment succeeds in each and every case. In fact, sometimes it falls flat on its face. In the last few years, it seems to constantly be falling on its face.

Why? Well, that's not so easy to blame on one thing. It's a cavalcade of errors that have all lead to the slow sinking of World Wrestling Entertainment's ship.

What's World Wrestling Entertainment? That's WWE. World Wrestling Entertainment? Still have no idea what I'm talking about? I'm talking about the WWF. It changed its name. Ohhhhhh. Now you get it.

Most people have no idea that it's no longer the World Wrestling Federation. A 2004 article in *The Source* magazine actually sported the huge headline, "Is Hip Hop the Next WWF?" It featured this headline two years after WWE had changed its name.

In a MTV news brief awhile later, pop singer and on-again off-again nutcase Mariah Carey repeated this headline, complete with the "WWF." It became apparent that this whole name change thing didn't take so well.

With the World Wildlife Fund forcing a name change, Vince McMahon had no choice but to alter his long-standing company's initials. When doing so, he adopted the phrase "WWE — Get the F Out." It was witty. Sadly, most of its audience took the advice and decided to do just that. They started to get the F out . . . in droves.

So now that we know the name of the company we're talking about, let's talk about its problem. Is it nepotism? Is it ego? Is it lack of competition? Is it gremlins? What can we blame the rise and fall of World Wrestling Entertainment on? There's a ton of possibilities, many of which will be explored in the upcoming pages.

Before doing so, though, it's important to understand the excuses that WWE gives for its woes. It's also important to point out why those excuses don't hold any water. After all, you can't find something's real problem until you clear the air of fake reasons spun to keep people with egos from taking a fall.

It's always amazed me how WWE can spout off so many reasons for why its business is down. For some reason, it always gives the same answers when people complain about its product. There's a ton of phony reasons, and fans, eager to find an explanation as to why the industry they love doesn't excite them anymore, are lining up and taking numbers to buy the lies. Step right up. Let's hear 'em:

WWE Excuse: It's hard to come up with six hours of original television each week. No one else has to do this. Other shows do half an hour. We do six. Off our case, Pizzaface.

That's a classic World Wrestling Excuse. It has to do six hours of TV every week. The number ranges, but always hovers well above two. WWE tells us to be understanding. Filling that much time is tough. This, of course, begs one question.

Well, who the hell told you to do six hours of original television each week? What kind of backward mentality is that? I don't recall people petitioning for six hours of new wrestling programming each week, do you?

It's as if I decided to write a 200-page book every day for a year. I burn myself out in a big way trying to fill all the pages and come up with original material. Inevitably, I would hit creative pitfalls. It's natural. There's no possible way to write award-worthy material each time you sit at a keyboard, no matter who you are. That's understandable.

Yet, if people complained, I wouldn't turn around and scream, "Do you know how hard it is to come up with 200 pages of original work each day? Other writers don't have that luxury! They don't write that much! Just me!"

This would of course be followed up with, "Well, uh, why the hell do you do 200-pages of original work each day?"

The answer, of course, would be that I want to make more money. If I do 200-pages of writing a day, I have 200-pages a day of new stuff to sell. That's why WWE does so much television each week. They don't do it because someone passed a law mandating they produce more TV time than sitcoms and reality shows. They don't do it because they have such an abundance of creative thought that they need to get it out. They don't do it because they like you.

WWE does it because they want to sell us as much as they can. So they write as much as they can. Of course, they hit creative pitfalls. When they do, they lash out. You people are so demanding! Our stories aren't exciting, but that's because we're working overtime to fill paper so you buy more stuff! We could do less and make it more exciting, but then you won't give us as much money! That's why we're doing six hours each week! Do you people know how hard it is to provide six hours of filler so that we can sell more ad space? God, people want everything nowadays!

We should mention that this company, which complains about the frequency of the shows it has to script, emails out *two* company newsletters each week.

One, entitled *Between the Sheets*, consists of your regular old company stuff. It has a section that recognizes top employees as "WWE Champions" each week. It spotlights featured office workers and lists various info about the current on-air product. No big deal. It's what you'd expect.

The other is called *The Weekly Buzz*. This one includes information on competing television programs, business news and current hot products in their target demographic. Uh . . . OK. Gotcha. It makes sense really. When scripting storylines about gay rape and necrophilia, it's important for the writing team to know what type of sneakers the young people are wearing.

Is there anything wrong with two weekly newsletters? No. I'm just saying that if you can't handle the workload with television writing each week, just cancel the newsletters. That's five less pages each week right there. Now you can focus on things like making sure your shows don't put me to sleep.

> **WWE Excuse:** The business is cyclical. It goes in cycles. There's up cycles and down cycles. It happens every few years.

This is my least favorite excuse by World Wrestling Entertainment. The wrestling business apparently has these "cycles." During these time periods, fan interest can be either up or down. It's unavoidable. According to many buck-pushers in the industry, these cycles are as much a part of the wrestling business as the rings are.

It's a monster. The cyclical monster that devours our form of entertainment every few years cannot be stopped. It's relentless and won't stop no matter what you do. You shouldn't say its name three times. You shouldn't get it wet, and whatever you do, don't feed it after midnight.

It can last anywhere from 18 months to six years depending on how smart the person telling you about it wants to appear to be. It's the cycle. We're in a down cycle now. We'll be in an up cycle next week. Cycle. Cycle. Cycle.

Let's say all this is true. Wrestling goes through periods of exciting and non-exciting times. On the surface, this all makes sense . . . well, kind of. If you look at the past twenty years, the "cycles" are off tremendously.

There was a big boom from 1984–1988. That lasted four years. Following that was about six years of "downtime." In 1996, things perked back up for about three and a half years. It's been downhill from there.

Seems cyclical, right? After all, business went up and then went down. How else do you explain it? How else can you possibly rationalize that an entertainment company, devoted to writing stories and promoting wrestling, can fall off the charts every few years?

Well, that's it. Right there. If wrestling were truly cyclical, vulnerable to Father Time's fickle finger of fate, all wrestling would look the same. You could pop in a videotape of WWE from 1999, its hottest period, and 1995, one of its lamest, and not see a difference. The show quality would be similar, and the only reason why one year would be better than the other is because of these "cycles." It would have nothing to do with the fact that 1999 featured some of the industry's greatest gimmicks and stories while 1995 featured such WWE-created characters as Xanta Klaus — the "Evil Santa," Barry Horowitz and King Mabel.

You can use cycles to explain a dip in revenue. You can point to cycles as the reason behind a drop in T-shirt sales or falls in ratings. You can't, however, use it to explain away your stale stories and poor company direction. It's a defeatist attitude from a company that prides itself on being anything but. If the industry really goes up and down on its own while Vince McMahon remains helpless, then why do we need him? Why do we need any office people in WWE? Fire everyone. Keep a handful of wrestlers and let everyone else go home. It doesn't matter anyway. Business will be up in a few years no matter what you do.

Ooma. Ooma. Aaaaahhhhhoooooommm. Long live the cycle monster. Amen.

WWE Excuse: It's the economy, stupid!

That's got to be it. Anytime you hear a wrestling critic bring up the downturn in business, those on the other side will scream and yell about the economy. It's hitting us all hard.

I might actually agree with this argument . . . if WWE CEO Linda McMahon didn't already squash it. In April of 2001, McMahon was asked by *Slam! Wrestling* whether or not downturns in the economy would have an impact on wrestling popularity. When she was asked how it had affected the WWE so far and whether or not she expected it to be a problem she replied:

> Haven't seen an impact yet. Don't know if we'll see one in the upcoming economy. Traditionally, when there is a slight downturn in the economy, entertainment revenues hold because it's not something you do every week. It's usually special, like our events would come to some areas only twice a year. . . . We think we are reasonably priced in the marketplace. It's something we play close attention to, particularly in markets that we frequent often, because you don't want to burn out the public. You always want them to feel they got great value for their dollar.

Man. That would have been a good argument too. They could have blamed the economy. I probably would have bought it. It sure sounded better than that cyclical thing. Too bad Lindy Mac killed it.

Even better than WWE's excuses for business problems is the way it deals with those who voice frustration and valid criticism over their product. World Wrestling Entertainment answers their critics unlike any other company in the world. How does it answer them? Simple. It disregards them. How does it disregard them? Well, with reasoning that's far more flawed than that used to come up with excuses. What do I mean? This is what I mean:

> The Internet/dirt sheet writers only complain because that's what sells. If they weren't negative, no one would buy their newsletter/website.

This is a statement that remains a favorite of WWE kingpin Vince McMahon. In fact, it's something he's told his employees.

World Wrestling Entertainment holds something called "Ask the Chairman." It's considered a benefit of working for the McCompany. Each employee is allowed to submit anonymous questions to be answered directly by Vince. The questions and answers are video-taped, broadcast throughout the offices and kept on file for future reference. In the 2005 installment of The Vinnie Mac show, an employee asked about his feelings regarding website and newsletter reporters.

His answer was the same as you read above. He feels, and has always stated, that journalists are negative because that's what sells. They're just like supermarket tabloids . . . only about wrestling.

Interesting analogy, guys. Wrong — but still interesting none-theless.

You see, tabloid gossip is just that — tabloid gossip. The entire job of the *National Enquirer* or whatever is to delve into the scan-dalous private lives of stars. They don't exist to report on the on-air happenings of TV shows. They don't analyze the current TV trends or systematically break down each movie and television episode the stars make. They simply dish the ish on Joe and Mary Hollywood's private life. That's it. They save the real entertainment news for the other entertainment magazines. Their job is gossip.

Wrestling newsletters and websites have much more ground to cover than a tabloid. For starters, there's no wrestling newspaper or industry magazine to report timely "news." That job falls on the shoulders of the newsletters.

In fact, many times the personal lives of wrestlers and employees are kept personal while wrestling journalists turn their attention to analyzing storylines or crowd reaction. I myself have been told many things about many wrestlers that would be considered scandalous. I haven't reported it, because that's not why I'm here. I'm here to tell you how I feel about WWE's product. Good, bad, indifferent, it does-n't matter. I'm here to tell you the truth.

The fact of the matter is that we don't sell more when we com-plain. Why? Well, when business is down, so are we. You think more people are lining up to read people rant about how Triple H is hurting the industry than those that read about Steve Austin and The Rock revolutionizing it? Does it impress my friends more when I'm writing a book about wrestling at a low point than it does at a high point? No. In today's dilapidated wrestling landscape, do you honestly feel we're being negative to make more money off newsletters? Maybe people are being negative because the quality of the on-air product bites the big one.

> Go back in time to 2000 and on any given Monday night there were 10, 12 million people watching wrestling between *Nitro* and *Raw*. Fast forward to 2005 and there's been 2 1/2 million people watching. So where did 9 1/2 million people go? They all didn't just get up and die. They turned the channel. — **D'Lo Brown**

WWE also tried to discredit the "dirtsheets" by claiming that their sources are "bitter employees with an ax to grind." Well, let me ask you, if a point is valid, does it make a difference if the source is bitter or not?

OK, another favorite sentiment is frequently echoed by Vince's son-in-law, "The Game," Triple H. It's this little gem:

> Internet writers are a bunch of kids using their parents' computers. They comment on an industry they never competed in. Besides, Internet fans only make up a small percentage of the audience.

Wow. Wow. Wow. Let's tackle this bit-by-bit, shall we?

First of all, not all wrestling writers are kids using their parents' computers. But, let's pretend that they are, just for the sake of playing the game, let's say that a law was passed and you're not allowed to talk about wrestling online unless you're under the age of 15 and don't own your own laptop. Good? Good.

OK, well isn't WWE's target demographic young teenage males? Isn't that why I have to sit through half naked women having lingerie pillow fights? Isn't that why fans are encouraged to chant "slut" and "show me your puppies" at female wrestlers? Are these segments written for middle-aged men? No. Middle-aged men may join in, but it's written with a younger audience in mind. It's the same audience that Trips condemns for commenting on his wife's daddy's company.

If they are all 14-year-olds, shouldn't you listen to them? Shouldn't you hear what your fans have to say about your product? It's as if Martha Stewart said that her critics don't matter because they're just a bunch of housewives. No shit, Skeeter. That's your audience, baby.

She wouldn't say that, because she's not stupid. Triple H says it because . . . well, you have to ask him.

As for the second half of his statement, that too is flawed. Apparently we can't judge the on-air product until we've created it. Saying that wrestling journalists need to compete is like saying that baseball writers need to play professional baseball. I can offer a more ridiculous example if you'd like. Here goes:

> *President Bush, how do you answer the critics that say you invaded Iraq without justifiable cause?*
>
> You know something, those journalists have never been president, have they? They never even ran for president! I'm the president. They have no right to comment on anything I do. Until they walk the campaign trail, kiss babies and work in the Oval Office, they can't say a damn thing.

Sound dumb? That's because it is dumb. So, the wrestling writers who only "make up a small percentage of the audience" need to compete in the biz in order to understand. Sure. Fine. You know, this is even dumber when you consider that in the same breath, Hunter Hearst Helmsley and others will condemn the Internet for giving away "secrets and results" prior to TV airings. Triple H, while promoting his *Blade 3* cameo, wondered in an interview how it was fun to know the outcomes ahead of time. According to Hunter, that Internet sure ruins the business.

I thought we only made up a small percentage of the audience, Gamy. Who cares what a small percentage of the audience does? There's a ton of fans who would have stopped watching the product by now had it not been for newsletters that help them recognize a section of the industry they'd have otherwise never known.

So, whatever. We give away results. We ruined the business. We told the world it was fake. Oh wait, that wasn't us. That was Vince McMahon.

Big Mac labeled his promotion "sports entertainment" long ago. He used the ambiguity of this new genre to avoid scrutiny from state athletic commissions and fully embraced the era of exposed secrets. Historically, however, it dates back even further.

In 1985, Vince McMahon was facing problems regarding a 20/20 interview where performer David Schultz slapped reporter John Stossel for asking if the industry was fake. Also around that time, McMahon finally went public with the predetermined nature of his product. After bearing his secrets to the Athletic Commission, Vinnie told the *LA Times*, "It really doesn't matter to me whether someone believes that wrestling is fake or not."

After that, WWE hired a publicist to put a spin on the whole fake or real debate. The McMahon-hired publicist actually released this statement: "You'd have to be brain-damaged to think this stuff is real."

That's someone who was contracted by World Wrestling Entertainment. Wow. So, if it's not real and WWE has been admitting to that for over 20 years, why not report on it? I guess brain-damaged people won't buy the newsletters, but other people will. After all, don't you want to know more about the product you enjoy?

It's as if you loved the television show *Seinfeld*. You're going to buy the DVDs, right? You want to see behind-the-scenes footage included, right? Why? You want to ruin the magic? You want to expose yourself to these people outside their characters? Kramer isn't really Kramer. He's Michael Richards. If you see him out-of-character, you'll ruin the magic. Don't buy the DVD! For the love of God! Don't buy it! You'll see all the things you weren't meant to see! What fun is that?

Plenty. Fanatics of entertainment like to read and know as much about it as possible about the shows and artists they love. It doesn't ruin their experience, it enhances it. That's why people buy *Entertainment Weekly*, read online commentary regarding new movies and backstage TV notes, and get the Super Duper Special Edition of their favorite DVDs. By reading about wrestling's behind-the-scenes doings, that doesn't make wrestling fans like the shows less. It makes them like it more.

It's like that with any form of entertainment. If WWE is so intent on calling itself an entertainment company, you'd think they'd know that. Wouldn't you?

Yeah. Me too.

So who are the people that help to create these excuses? What are the names, ranks and serial numbers of the people responsible for the real downturns in wrestling? What did they do? Tell me more! Tell me more!

Calm down, kiddo. All in due time. Sit back and grab some hot cocoa. I'll take you back to January of 2005 and introduce you to the man behind the curtain. The puppet master, the yellow suit wearer and the Genetic Jackhammer himself — Vincent Kennedy McMahon. After all, he's the mad scientist with the big office. Might as well start there.

CHAPTER 2

All Hail the Quad King

It was a chilly January night and Kevin Dunn, WWE's head producer, was freaking out in his office. His voice could be heard throughout the studio.

The reason? World Wrestling Entertainment's annual Royal Rumble was coming to a close. Each year, WWE holds a pay-per-view centered around the Rumble concept. There are 30 participants. Each draws a number. Numbers one and two start off against one another and every two minutes (or in the 2005 case, ninety seconds) another man enters. At the end of the match, the last man to avoid being tossed over the top rope wins. It's always one of the most anticipated pay shows, featuring most of the roster in one match. Good stuff.

The finale of the 2005 Rumble was supposed to see Dave Batista, the freshly turned hero from *Monday Night Raw*, dump out John Cena, the Marky Mark hero from *Thursday Night Smackdown*, over the top rope and win the contest in a very convincing manner. Unfortunately, it didn't happen like that. Instead, Dave slipped while holding Cena in the air. They both tumbled over the top rope and landed on the ground. Uh oh.

To their credit, WWE covered the blunder beautifully. They had two referees argue over which man had won. One official raised Batista's hand, while the other raised Cena's. It was a finish that the Rumble had seen before and most fans thought that all was going to plan. No one knew it was a mess-up . . . well, except grumpy ol' Kevin Dunn.

Now here's the problem, how does the match continue? Since it involved wrestlers from both *Raw* and *Smackdown*, they couldn't send one of the general managers out to settle the squabble. They needed to send the chairman, the Genetic Jackhammer, the Lord and Master of Time and Space, Vince McMahon. Without him, the referees would just be holding hands up and down forever!

So Vinnie Mac emerged ready to react. He almost wobbled to the ring with his trademark swagger, which always becomes more pronounced at important, high-profile events. He rushed the ring and slid in underneath the bottom rope — slamming both his thighs on the edge of the canvas, and tearing both quadriceps in the process.

If Dunn was so critical of Batista's slip, I wonder what he'd say about what his boss did. Oh wait, it's his boss. He'd probably say nothing. Nevermind.

So Vince got into the squared circle and tried to confront everyone. He didn't realize that his legs didn't work, so they buckled and he crashed to the mat live on pay-per-view.

What followed is both a testament to Vince McMahon's manhood and one of the funniest visuals in wrestling history. Despite being in tremendous agony, Mr. McMahon didn't show any pain on his face. That's the manhood part. The funny visual was that he demanded the match continue and reprimanded both referees . . . while sitting on his butt with his legs stretched out and his hands on his hips. He looked like four-year-old listening to the story of *The Hungry Caterpillar*. I kept picturing him with his hand raised saying, "Umm, I spilled my juice!"

So the match continued and all went fine from there. No one noticed the screw up of the original Rumble ending and thought it all was smooth from that point on. They didn't understand that Vince was injured either. His tear, while serious and painful, didn't look like anything major on television. It looked like he slid into the ring and then decided to relax for a bit.

> I know Vince has a lot of respect in this business. I just have the utmost respect for him. . . . For him to tear both his quads and then wait for all the wrestlers to leave the building because he didn't want anyone to see him in a wheelchair, that just shows you what kind of heart and what kind of man he is. He never wants his employees to see him down, you know? To me that's so cool. No matter if you work for a computer company or a construction company, you look to your boss for leadership. — **Aaron "Jesus" Aguilera**

If there's one characteristic about Vince McMahon that's never doubted, it's leadership. McMahon has the uncanny knack of being seen as a strong figure physically, mentally and in a business setting. He stands tall, looks confident and doesn't think twice about telling you where you can "stick it, Pally."

The day after the Rumble, Linda McMahon filled all of WWE's employees in on the situation by sending out this e-mail:

> I just wanted to give you a brief report on an accident that happened to Vince on Sunday night at the PPV.
>
> First of all, he is fine. He did, however, have to have surgery to repair torn quad tendons in both legs. James Andrews, who is one of the foremost orthopedic surgeons in the country, performed the surgery. Dr. Andrews has operated on several of our Superstars, as well as many other sports figures.
>
> We flew to Birmingham, Alabama, on Monday for the surgery. I expect he will be in the health facility here for about 4–5 days and then return to Connecticut for rehabilitation. Other than being totally annoyed at himself, he is fine.

Fine? He's fine? A 59-year-old man slides into the ring and tears both of his quads, yet he's fine? Whatever works, I guess.

The visual of Vinnie tearing his legs apart was funny in that it was so strange. Many are still laughing over the mad dash, slide and plop maneuver that took him out of action. It was embarrassing. What a strange way to hurt yourself in the ring. A few years earlier when injury prone Kevin Nash tore his quad while running across the ring, everybody was laughing so hard they were puking.

Vince knew it was embarrassing too. After all, he tried to put a positive spin on the whole damn thing. In a March 2005 interview with the *Wall Street Journal*, he put it like . . . well, like this:

> Seven weeks ago, I severed both of my quadriceps tendons doing a stunt in the ring. I wasn't warmed up, I didn't stretch and that unfortunately is major surgery. My character, his time has come and gone. I'll be 60 in August. I'm better utilized from a resource standpoint not being a performer.

Yeah. Running and sliding into the ring was a stunt. He should have stretched before he ran to the ring. Sadly, he just wasn't warmed up enough to step on the canvas. Ring announcer Lillian Garcia must have to do Tae Bo before she gets in there to introduce the wrestlers.

First there's the issue of calling it all a "stunt." Come on. Mick Foley tossing himself from the top of a cage through a table and nearly killing himself is a "stunt." Jeff Hardy plummeting from a ladder through a table is a "stunt." Lowering someone in a feathered cape from the rafters by bungee chord is a "stunt." You? You got in the ring, Vince. Come on.

Secondly, and decidedly more unsettling, is the fact that Vince openly lied to the *Wall Street Journal* without fearing he would get caught. He was so secure in the fact that the person interviewing him didn't watch wrestling that he outright lied. Vince had no fear the interviewer would say, "You're a liar! You weren't doing a stunt! I saw the Royal Rumble!"

The interviewer didn't see the show. He wasn't worried that he would be called on the carpet and look stupid. Not only that, but he wasn't worried about any of the *Wall Street Journal* subscribers reading it and saying "Hey! You're a filthy liar! Liar!" Apparently he was assuming that they didn't order the show either.

No. They weren't watching the Royal Rumble. McMahon knew

that. Seems disconcerting, no? The owner of World Wrestling Entertainment is so secure in the fact that wrestling is in a downward spiral, he has no fear of spinning the truth in his favor, even if it's a downright fib. The thought that the reporter actually watched his show didn't even enter the equation. It was a given that no one in the mainstream was watching WWE pay-per-views. Even the owner knew it. What type of message does that send to his employees?

During all this, Vince began an insane workout and rehab regimen. He was intent on being able to walk at *WrestleMania*, merely three months away. He was pushing himself to the max and people were skeptical. The ego of the chairman may have finally caught up to his physical limitations. Ain't no way that Mr. McMahon is getting himself to *Mania* in anything but a wheelchair.

It didn't happen. *Mania* came and went and we all knew he wouldn't make it. After all, there were only 64 days between the Royal Rumble and *WrestleMania*. Who can recover from two torn quads that quickly? Young, well-conditioned athletes can sit out of action for more than six months recovering from tears like this. Even a six-month return would be a miracle.

It must have been humbling. Finally, Vinnie would be able to sympathize with his wrestlers. Maybe now instead of expecting more than a human being is able to physically accomplish, Vince would lighten up and just demand that his wrestlers have super-healing ability instead of the super-duper healing ability he always expected. I even wrote an article about how this experience might be good for Big Mac and allow him to see life through the eyes of his employees.

Boy, was I wrong.

Mr. McSuperman returned to the ring on April 18, 2005. It was a mere 12 days after *WrestleMania*. Jaws dropped. Women fainted. Babies cried. Vince McMahon walked again.

How did he celebrate? He auctioned off his leg braces on World Wrestling Entertainment's website. The proceeds went to the Make-A-Wish Foundation. Instead of the proceeds, maybe Vince should have donated his healing secrets to the Make-A-Wish Foundation. The guy recovered from two torn quadriceps in 76 days. I know people who can't get rid of a sore throat in 76 days. The auction listing looked like this:

> History has been made here on WWE Auction. For the very first time an item from **World Wrestling Entertainment Chairman Vince McMahon** has made its way to our collection! At this past January's Royal Rumble, Mr. McMahon suffered an unfortunate quadriceps injury during his appearance for the show's conclusion when restarting the Rumble Match between John Cena and Batista. Over the last three months, the man responsible for sports-entertainment's prosperity has dedicated himself to intense physical rehabilitation . . . and the results have showed! Mr. McMahon made a surprising return to *Monday Night* RAW on 4/18/05 at MSG to announce the latest WWE Draft Lottery. Amazingly the famous Mr. McMahon "power-walk" was as prominent as ever! Such a speedy recovery meant that Mr. McMahon had no further use for his **black leg braces** that supported the chairman's injury during his healing process. Recently, **Mr. McMahon personally autographed** both of his braces so that a lucky collector can own the auction find of their wrestling lifetime. Cement yourself as the new owner of this groundbreaking McMahon collectible and place your bids now!! **PROCEEDS FROM THE SALE OF THIS ITEM GO TO THE MAKE A WISH FOUNDATION.** Includes one leg brace. — WWE.com Auction

I love how it includes only one leg brace. If you buy the other one, you can connect them both together and protect Castle Grayskull.

So, did Vince now have a deeper understanding of the challenges his performers face? Did he learn something from this experience? Did he sympathize with those who had to recover from injuries? Give you three guesses.

On the May 16, 2005 edition of *Monday Night Raw*, Vince McMahon came to the ring and confronted a returning Randy Orton. Orton had been recovering from a shoulder injury and was out of action since *WrestleMania* on April 6th. Although unable to return to action just yet, Ort was here to address the crowd and get everyone re-acquainted with his character.

McMahon helped him out with that. He took the microphone and said:

What the hell has happened to you? Your clothes are hanging off of you. Your neck looks like a stack of dimes. What, are you on a special anorexic diet?

He might as well just said, "Ha ha. You're hurt. My legs are made from steel and UFO metal. You're a skinny little bitch!"

So much for understanding.

That was Vince being Vince. He has never come out and said "Hey guys, I'm now a Babyface." People cheer him because they respect him. He is still gonna be that arrogant, pompous, corporate asshole that people want to still hate. When he said that to Randy, that was Vince being Mr. McMahon and I think he does sympathize with people at various degrees at various times. But, he doesn't expect anything of anybody that he wouldn't ask of himself. The thing that you have to remember is, no, he didn't have to wrestle a full schedule, so it was a little bit easier for him to heal up. He was able to train a little bit longer and his body didn't take as much punishment as maybe Hunter's did or whatever. It's a whole different lifestyle and, at the same time, he works hard and does train in the gym . . . He is Vince, but he's also Mr. McMahon. He knows when to be Vince and he knows when to be Mr. McMahon. When he's on *Raw* or *Smackdown* and the cameras are on, he's performing and everything he says is to get a reaction. Randy knew it was coming. He's taken a shot at Randy and if people don't like it then good. He's Mr. McMahon. **— Tom Pritchard**

It's that type of go-get-'em attitude that has helped the Chairman wreak havoc on the world. You see, life isn't good unless it's lived at the expense of others. In other words, Mac's miracle healing meant more to him if it could be used to mock others in the same position. Randy wasn't healing at a McMahon-like level. So he was mocked. That's how Vince does things. He likes to make everything a competition in his head. He thrives on it. He eats it. It's his destiny.

CHAPTER 3

McMahonifest Destiny

No one will step up. WWE has this thing locked up. The others that tried only did it for a payday from some marks. Every person in this business with any reasonable intelligence knows WWE will be there as long as they want and WWE will let these marks blow millions and then just take whatever talent they want. — **The Honky Tonk Man**

Anyone who's ever been the head of an organization has dealt with a rabble-rouser. These people exist in any group. They fight those in charge. They rally those who are unhappy with the group's direction. They lead the angry minority into a revolt against whatever board or committee happens to be in charge.

What's the best way to deal with these bomb throwers? How do you squash their momentum without further inciting those who blindly follow the self-christened savior?

1. You can kick him out of your organization. You can find some loophole to bounce him from your books. That won't help though. His minions will rally to his side and have you overthrown for such abuse of power.

2. You can argue against him, but he'll argue right back. Any mistake you make will be maximized and analyzed to his followers and you'll be overthrown for being inept.

3. You can kill him, but then you'd probably get caught. In today's day and age of forensic science and DNA, you don't stand a chance of getting away with murder anymore. (Although, with today's system, having friends in high places might help.) Then you'd be in jail and you'd be overthrown for . . . well, being in jail.

It's so strange that doing these things could hurt you. By making this self-appointed messiah a target, you push his cause. You martyr him. Logically speaking, this shouldn't happen, right?

So what do you do?

4. You befriend him. You accept him into your circle. From that point on, he's neutered. Kill him with kindness and talk him up to those who think you were trying to oppress him.

There's no animosity here, people. He's my buddy!

The followers fall off. The angry man is now a regular ol' Joe. You don't get overthrown at all. Nice.

Why does this happen? Well, the reason is certain people feed on adversity. While some go out of their way to avoid conflict and clashing, some can't excel without it. They search for anyone to call an enemy, so they have something to fight against. For these people, success isn't a good thing unless it comes at someone else's expense. Take away that adversity and this once strong warrior loses his power.

So what does all that have to do with WWE, huh? Well, Vince McMahon is one of those people. I have never in my life seen a person who does so well when he feels victimized.

Now, this is not an insult or sarcasm. This is for real. When put under the gun and pushed against the wall, Vinnie Mac steps up and hits homeruns. He does more than invite conflict. He needs it.

Vince's enemies have always helped him excel. He fought and

beat the Federal Government in 1993. We've been reminded of this fact on a number of occasions. Tried for steroid distribution, Vince came out on top. Whatever side you fall into on the steroid debate, you have to admit that McMahon seemed to be beaming following the verdict. It wasn't so much the fact that he won that seemed to give him happiness. It was the fact that the federal government lost.

We would see this same attitude years later when Ted Turner's World Championship Wrestling came knocking at his door with some head-to-head competition. In the face of adversity, Mr. McMahon shines. He enjoys it. He thrives on it.

Don't get me wrong, when he's losing, he whines a lot too. The most comical could be the legal recourses Vince tried to take against wcw, citing "predatory practices." Yes. The man who destroyed all the regional wrestling territories of the 1980s by breaking his father's handshake agreements was crying about "predatory practices." Amazing.

That's not important, though. Whining or no whining, Vince has to rally against something in order to feel important. He's a rabble-rouser. That's what he does.

Go back and watch any wwe produced *History of WrestleMania* video package. They all include someone saying that people called Vince "crazy" before *WrestleMania 1*. The McHenchmen tell stories of how so and so didn't think that Mac could pull it off. They recount tales of being scoffed at by the angry, grizzled promoters of yesteryear. They speak about how if Vinnie failed at *Mania*, he'd be bankrupt and have to eat dirt until he died.

It's Vince's thing. It's what he does. It's what drives him to be the best. Actually, he's not driven to be the best, per se. I should clarify that. He's just driven to be better than the others he's competing against. If there's no one else, he's driven to be . . . well, nothing.

That's because Vincent Kennedy McMahon works best under pressure. He likes to be questioned. He revels in being misunderstood and vilified. This isn't a negative trait. It's a positive one. It's a personality quirk that should be emulated by anyone who wants to be successful in business. ceos of major companies have it. Founders of countless businesses boast this quality every day.

Here's the problem, though. Most of those companies have competition. While Coca-Cola has golden marketing campaigns now, how good would they be if Pepsi no longer existed? Would the Coke people get complacent? Would the freedom from the Pep squad threat leave them lazy and uninspired? Would they be saving all their good marketing ideas just in case someone new challenged them? Wow. That would suck.

I know it would suck, because it's happening right now in the wrestling industry. Vince McMahon, a promoter who all but gets physical pleasure from fighting other wrestling promotions, eventually ate all the other wrestling promotions. His one true inspiration for creativity was competition. So he got rid of competition. Uh . . . OK. I guess it made sense at the time.

Sure, it was cool at first. Big Mac showed up on Ted Turner's TNT station to announce his acquisition of WCW during its final episode of *Nitro*. He gloated. He smiled. He proclaimed, "I bought my competition." It was a magical night for the top dog of World Wrestling Entertainment.

Then something happened. Vince realized that without any competition around, he wasn't able to do certain things that need to be done in the wrestling world. It was a system developed since the dawn of the industry. It was the reason that small wrestling territories survived so long.

Old School Scenario: Wrestler A wrestles for the WWF. He feuds with everyone on the roster. He does all the spots that work. He's pushed until the fans get sick of him. At that point, he leaves and heads to another promotion. With a change of scenery and a fresh set of minds to recharge his gimmick, Wrestler A evolves. After a while, he returns to Vince's company and now battles the new names that have sprung up since his last appearance. Also, his gimmick isn't as stale, since it's been updated and/or changed.

Now, take away the other company and we'll redo that paragraph.

New School Scenario: Wrestler A wrestles for the WWE. He feuds with everyone on the roster. He does all the spots that work. He's pushed until the fans get sick of him. At that point, they keep pushing him. Fans get sicker. Then they let Triple H pin him. To combat his downward spiral, they have him wrestle for them on another night of the week. Eventually a 22-year-old kid with 50-inch biceps and the inability to perform a believable fake punch replaces Wrestler A.

That's sad, huh? As mentioned above, WWE has created a way to combat the staleness problem in wrestling. They divided their show into "brands." There's a *Smackdown* brand and a *Raw* brand. They're supposed to be mini-companies in and of themselves. They exist as if they were completely independent of one another. They each have their own wrestlers and staff members and were created to foster pretend competition with one another. So what separates them? Well, here are the differences:

Raw: Early in the week. Its colors are red and black.

Smackdown: Later in the week. Its colors are blue and silver.

That's it. It's like watching the same show. You can either watch sexual deviants have implied forced sex with announcers on *Smackdown* or you can watch sexual deviants have implied forced sex with announcers on *Raw*. Both shows have writers who answer to the same people. Both shows end up being about perverse and peculiar feuds, offensive and over-scripted characters, or simply illogical and flawed storylines. It all seems the same. Maybe that's because it *is* the same.

Alternatives exist, but none that come close to WWE's TV exposure or bankroll. World Wrestling Entertainment doesn't have much to steal from companies like NWA-TNA, a company still struggling but making small strides, and Ring of Honor, an exciting promotion with a cult following. The days of wrestlers leaving Vince McMahon one week and showing up on primetime television for another promotion the next week are over. Nowadays, if a wrestler leaves primetime WWE programming one week, he ends up watching primetime TV from his sofa the next. That's the wrestling landscape. While it must help Vince's ego to know he holds such power over people, it doesn't help his product advance or evolve creatively.

> I don't know how [the McMahons] do things, but it's not working. They need to change it. When I say "not working," they're making a lot of money, they always will make money. But they're losing money too. The fact that [Vince McMahon] is a businessman, I'm sure he sees it. If he's crushing companies like he says he did, or used to, or still does, then he needs to find out what TNA is doing and fix it. When I say, "fix it," I mean if he's gonna crush a company, crush it. If I were him, I wouldn't crush TNA, though. I'm not saying it because I work for TNA. I'm saying it because I'm a fan and I love to see competition. Competition to me is McDonald's versus Burger King. It's not this McDonald's on this block versus this McDonald's on that block. Because to me, that's the same company. — **Elix Skipper**

I love that McDonald's analogy. It explains the situation perfectly. That's not competition. There's no one else for the fans to choose but Vince McMahon. When the TV numbers start to go down, that doesn't mean fans are tuning to the competition. It means they're not fans anymore. That's not good. That's not good at all.

Not just that, but with no one left to draw from and no fresh ideas to present, the future of WWE's creative product is something a lot of people worry about. What's going to be the big thing of tomorrow? Who's going to be the next break-out star?

Things like that become a genuine concern. There was a time when the possibilities were endless. Now a lot of the guys who show up in WWE haven't had the opportunity to work on television before. Chances are they're "green" and need to wrestle for a few years. That's not good. That's not good at all.

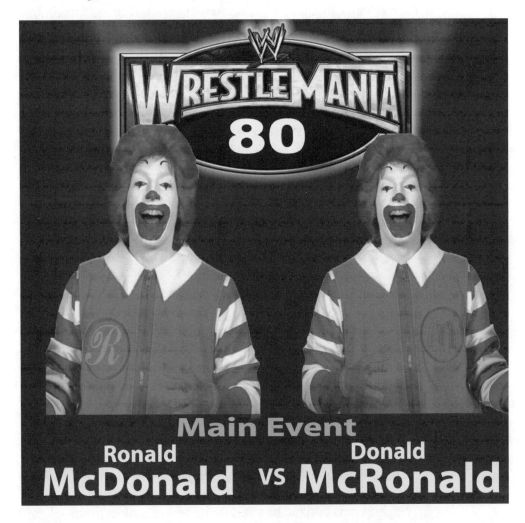

Back in the day, other promotions could do the building and you could steal their product come contract time. Now there are no other promotions that can truly create seasoned and world-renowned stars on a regular basis and trade off with the McMahons. That star building is squarely on WWE's shoulders. That's not good either. Who has the time for that?

It hurts World Wrestling Entertainment and it damages the industry as a whole. Professional wrestling isn't meant to be like this. To have one a virtual monopoly is to have no building blocks in place to create future stars. It's like cutting your own legs out from under you.

Even if Vince had taken WCW and truly given it to his son, Shane, it would have been *something*. Instead, McMahon bought the company and then presented it as an on-air gimmick group that his boy led into battle against the valiant WWE warriors. He also used the letters of the recently demolished promotion ECW on his program around that time too. Like WCW, it was an on-air gimmick group that was beaten up by the WWE wrestlers. His daughter Stephanie led

this group. The symbolism was enough to make you cry.

Now just to show you how much Vince McMahon likes competition yet doesn't realize his need for it, one only has to look at his behavior during 2005's WWE-sponsored ECW *One Night Stand* pay-per-view.

Realizing that the current product was beginning to become illogical and insane, Daddy Mac traveled back in time in his DeLorean and gave us a nostalgia show. It was the company he purchased four years earlier, Extreme Championship Wrestling, making a long-awaited return. This time they would be presented as a true wrestling promotion and not as an on-air gimmick group led by Steph. That's got to count for something, right?

The show was booked as a one-time reunion of Extreme Championship Wrestling's stars. Actually, it wasn't all of them. That would be impossible. Certain guys didn't make the cut, didn't accept or never showed up for the Dub Dub E show. Men like Terry Funk and Jerry Lynn, big parts of the company's history, weren't at *Vince's One Night Stand.* Don't worry, though. They had other plans that weekend anyway.

Another reunion show, *Hardcore Homecoming,* was booked for two nights prior. The main one organizing the event was Shane Douglas. Outspoken and cunning, Douglas always knew how to take advantage of a good situation. When World Wrestling Entertainment announced plans for their ECW show at the Hammerstein Ballroom, Shane's camp booked the old ECW Arena for a show two nights before it. He was going to present his own ECDub reunion, *Hardcore Homecoming . . .* right before McMahon did. Nice.

Even though these two events had been booked as Extreme reunions, it was hard to call either of them "ECW." For a wrestler like Terry Funk, who had a huge hand in helping ECW earn its hardcore following, those letters are just that — letters. Nothing more.

> You have to understand the truth about the situation is that it was not ECW. ECW was the name. E period. C period. W period. And that's it period. Because that cannot be ECW. Nor can Vince's show be ECW. It can be ECWish. But it can't be ECW because it's owned by Vince McMahon and it's just an offspring of his company right now and you have to understand that. Even though it has the same characters and stuff, they are not the characters that they were before. They are the controlled characters. — **Terry Funk**

The Douglas thing shouldn't have been a big deal, though. It was a small show that wasn't going to be on television. Released exclusively on DVD, *HH* wouldn't make much of a splash. Surely it was no match for WWE's version of Extreme.

Mac had more important things to worry about. He had a pay-per-view to promote and history to spin.

Prior to his *One Night Stand,* McMahon reminded us of how he owned the ECW "brand." On a sad, dark episode of *Monday Night Raw,* he told us how much he financially supported Paul Heyman's outlaw promotion. Basically, it was Vince, the man who represents everything "business" about wrestling, telling the wrestling world that he was the financial backer of the hardcore rebels. Ugh. Although it had always been implied on-air by the joint storylines between the companies, no one had ever openly said "Vince McMahon supports ECW" on television before. You know why it hasn't been said? Probably because it castrated the bad-asses of Extreme and made crazy outlaw owner Paul Heyman look like a hypocritical corporate suck-up.

You could say that it was huge mistake on McMahon's part to hurt the ECW brand name like this mere weeks before the pay show was scheduled to air, but the only problem is that it didn't seem like an actual mistake. While not conducive to generating new viewers, this revelation wasn't brought to light for that reason. In many ways it seemed as though Vince had dreamed about rubbing his ECDub involvement in the collective face of all the smart Internet wrestling fans for years. Screw making money. This was about a big ha-ha to all those whiny little ECDubbers.

> They thought they were being anti-WWF by supporting ECW! Ha! In your face, fans! The greenbacks went right back to me! The McMack, baby. Mo' Money! Mo' Money!

That's how it felt. Mickey Mac was intent on being the king and laughing his ass off. Who cares if it hurts the pay-per-view? In fact, let's do it one better. Let's make it the main reason for the pay-per-view. Instead of announcing matches and storylines, let's make it all about the WWE wrestlers invading.

OK, here comes the really funny part. Vince McMahon, the guy that bought all his competition, proceeds to start an on-air storyline prior to his ECW show. It was a conflict between "the WWE Superstars" and the "ECW Stars." He requested that *Raw* General Manager Eric Bischoff invade the show in the spirit of "competition." Why? Because competition creates excitement. No joking. This promoter who has no competition is delivering an on-air explanation about how competition creates excitement. Wow. (Vince should have come to the ring to Alanis Morrissette's "Ironic" before that speech. It's like 10,000 spoons, Vinnie Mac. It's like rai-ai-ainnnnnnn . . .)

No matter, though. He wasn't talking about real competition. No, that would be too real. This was pretend competition. That wasn't important. The most important thing to remember here is that Vincent K. McMahon had won the rasslin' wars. At the expense of ECW's name heading into a major show, Mac portrayed them as his pet project. Why? It's all for the sake of rewriting history. It's all for the sake of ego.

World Wrestling Entertainment has rewritten history ten times over. wcw, once Mac's number one competitor, has been presented as a group of cutthroat and frivolous yokels that never understood how the business works. They're portrayed as nothing more than a one-trick pony. wcw created the New World Order gimmick only after pillaging all of Vince's old stars. In the end, it was the genius of Vince McMahon that allowed him to overcome the evils of World Championship Wrestling.

We don't mention all the years that wcw presented a somewhat viable alternative to wwf's shows. We don't bring up the good times for the company, only the downward descent when *Raw* took over the cable ratings. That's just the way it is. Why shouldn't it be? He bought it. He can say whatever he wants. If I spent a couple of million dollars on something, I'd like to be able to say whatever the hell I want about it.

> Hey man, see that table? I paid five million bucks for it. It was made on Mars by Menudo.
> *That wasn't made on Mars by Menudo. You made that up.*
> Screw you, man! I paid five million dollars for it! I'll say whatever the hell I want to say! Now you shut your mouth!

So that happens. People with far less ego than Vince McMahon would do the same thing. It's his right and from this point on, he can go with that. Maybe one day another main company will truly challenge wwe's empire and be able to tell the fans a different side of history. Until then, we have Vinnie's vision. wcw was made on Mars by Menudo. So be it.

Anyway, let's get back to this ecw thing. Now, ECDub was a good show. However, even with the cozy position the company had been in since 2001, Mac still had that competitive bug in him. In what can best be described as one of the strangest things I heard all year, wwe required its entire production staff to attend the ecw pay-per-view. Why? Well, they were told, "We need to get our dvd out before Shane Douglas's."

No joke. That's what happened. Worried about the sales from *Hardcore Homecoming,* WWE sent its production staff to work over-time. After all, Vince McMahon only had TV time up the wazoo to promote his DVD. *Raw, Smackdown Velocity, Experience, Sunday Night Heat* and all the other shows in between had a chance to urge viewers to order his show. Shane Douglas and his band of rasslers had word of mouth and the Internet. Close call. Hmmm. Better get your production team there post haste.

So, the rush order was placed on the ECW *One Night Stand* DVD in order to squash the sales of a non-televised show with a much smaller budget. Think about it — WWE was trying to squash a com-petitor that was competing with the nostalgia show that they were putting on because people miss competition. Read that a few times. Let it sink in.

Fans "demanded" an ECW pay-per-view because the days of alter-natives were so much more enjoyable. WWE had no choice but to present it. However, they were out to beat someone else while doing it. You ever hear of the phrase, "He who does not learn from history is doomed to repeat it?" Yeah, me neither.

> He's worried about us? We're the paupers. He's worried about a piss-ing contest with the paupers? We can't piss straight. He can piss across a four-lane highway with people there to hold his dick for him. Yet, he's worried about us? — **Terry Funk**

Oh, one more thing. WWE hates ECW. They hate everything it stands for. Did I mention that? There's a big anti-wrestling contin-gency in WWE against any success of the cult promotion. For those who believe wrestling is nothing more than a male soap opera with an intrusive ring smack dab in the center, ECDub represents the gritty style that they wish would go away.

OK now that you got that, listen to this: WWE puts on the ECW show. They go out of their way to make it as real as possible. To quote Terry Funk, it was ECWish. They had the elements. They had the announcer. They had the aura.

They also had a lot of the fans. The small ballroom was jam-packed full of rowdy Extremists shouting things like "*Smackdown* sucks" and "Fuck John Cena." Now, while chants like that were always commonplace in ECW, WWE had never encouraged its fan base to tune in and see it. For years, chants of "WWF sucks" rang out through Philadelphia's ECW Arena. The only people who saw it were Extreme Championship Wrestling's fans though. Never before had WWE encouraged its own audience to tune in and witness an entire venue full of people chanting that their shows suck and that the WWE Champion should be fucked. Wow.

The screaming from the crowd was so intense that in a pre-show episode of Spike TV's *Sunday Night Heat*, chants of "Shut the fuck up" drowned out unenthusiastic WWE announcer Michael Cole on live television. The production truck tried to censor it but ultimately gave up when they realized they'd have to silence the audio every other second.

Now all of this is funny. It's insane to imagine that World Wrestling Entertainment would sell its fans on the idea of watching an anti-WWE audience applaud the anti-WWE sentiments of the performers. The night featured "unscripted promos" from Paul Heyman and Rob Van Dam. To give the night a true anti-WWE feel, we were treated to "real life" interviews. Basically, RVD and Heyman, the two WWE contracted employees, spoke from the heart and held nothing back.

Oh . . . oh, in case you were wondering, that last sentence was sarcasm. They were WWE *employees* for crying out loud! No matter how anti-WWE the promos were, they weren't unscripted. Vince McMahon didn't become a mazillionaire by allowing people to bash him on his own show without his knowledge.

It's like witnessing a speech at an employee dinner. The witty guy in sales lifts his glass and begins to roast the boss. Before he begins, he tells us all that no one knows what he's going to say. It's all straight-shooting insults.

The only problem is that no matter how "unscripted" it is, it's not the entire truth. It's not the same sentiment he would relate if he were employed elsewhere. For example:

An "unscripted speech" from a *current* employee would include things like:

I've been held back from showing this company my true potential. No one gave me a chance to shine. They held me down and didn't let me show what I could do. I could have made this company a ton of money, but wasn't given the shot. It's not fair!

An unscripted speech from a *former* employee would include things like:

I hate my old boss. I hate his crappy family. If I could, I'd kick him and his loved ones in the face . . . repeatedly. That sack of crap should rot in hell and then get a disease. I spit on him and all he's done. Up yours, jackass! I hope you get hepatitis.

See the difference? Me too.

You know how it sort of came off? Sad. You know what was sad about it? Seeing the wrestlers at *One Night Stand* do all the things they used to do as ECW, only under WWE's banner. The show seemed so authentic that it was as if Vince was trying to prove that it was fake all along. It was all his. It had always been his. Only now, it was official.

That's what you do when you own everything. You prove points, flaunt your victories and squash other rabble-rousers.

Take WWE Executive Vice-President Eric Bischoff for example. In the late 90s, Easy E nearly killed WWE. You remember all that New World Order stuff? That was his thing. After WCW went out of business, Vince hired Eric. To torment him. After all, this was Eric Bischoff. He used to give away the taped *Raw*'s results on the air during WCW *Nitro*. He challenged Vince McMahon to a fight. He left Mac nasty voicemails. He said things like this:

There's no need for spins or dirt-sheets. We can settle this like true men, Vince. Just you and me. You can do it . . . come on, Vince. Step into the ring. Do what so many other people would love to do. Get your hands around my skinny little neck. You can do it . . . if you've got the guts. Do you, Vince? Have you got the guts to REALLY show up? I do . . . do you? Just think of it. Just think how great you'll feel if you're able to step into the ring and break my jaw . . . knock me out . . . snap an arm or a leg! Whatever you'd like, Vince! It's no big thing. But it takes guts. That's

what it's gonna take, Vince. Have you got the guts, Vince? We'll find out
. . . we'll be waiting for you, Vinnie Mac. With open arms.

McMahon never arrived at the wcw pay-per-view to fight Bischoff. Instead, Bischoff arrived at wwe's pay-per-views years later . . . as an employee.

So now the Bisch works for Vince. Sucks to be him, huh? Since he's been in wwe, Bischoff has had an 80-year-old woman thrust her crotch into his face, his head shaved and is constantly reminded of his wcw failures. Any time a wrestling history lesson is given, wwe explains how Eric Bischoff was the sole villain in it all. The funny thing is that during these documentary dvds, they'll trash him and then cut to him talking about the bad things they just said. At times, he gets a glimmer in his eye and seems nostalgic for the days when he was free. While it's weird to hear them vilify him in a video package and then shoot to him talking about how evil he supposedly was, it's something we've gotten used to. They go out of their way to make him look bad. During these filming sessions, I think they use the same lighting on Bischoff that they did for Richard Nixon back at the Kennedy debates.

My favorite Eric Bischoff Embarrassment happened at *Taboo Tuesday*. EB had just lost to Eugene, his "mentally handicapped nephew." As per the pre-match stipulation, Bisch had to have his head shaved.

Vince was front and center like a coked-up four-year-old on Christmas morning. Jumping to and fro, he clapped and delighted in the fact that Easy E apparently died his hair. Although his pre-wwe stints included a phase of embracing gray hair, Eric's locks had been dyed black for his McMahon days. When the razor hit his scalp, we all saw the truth. Vince was laughing like a nutcase.

I have no idea why, considering that Vince's hair seems to change from gray to brown and back on a regular basis. Also, to the best of my knowledge, Eric Bischoff has never worn a rosy pink three-piece suit.

By the way, we should clarify something no one else has. When he was younger, McMahon played the on-air role of an announcer. Each week, he would wear brightly colored suits. Whether canary yellow or bright orange, these outfits were amazingly gaudy and strange.

We tend to forget that many of today's fans are too young to

remember the mid-80s. They hear about the suits and say, "That must have been the style then. The 1980s were cheesy."

Well, while the 80s were cheesy in some respects, the suits weren't part of the style. Even back then, people would look at the TV and say, "Why the fuck is that man's suit light pink?"

Just wanted to make that clear. I haven't seen it addressed anywhere else. That was a long time ago. McMahon isn't that quiet little announcer anymore. Oh no. He's a McMonster. How did that happen?

Well, there's something about the McMahons that people don't know about. It's a secret that involves a being you've never met. This being is taller than the Giant Gonzales and more powerful than Bill Kazmier. If you don't know who those people are, you're out of luck. There's no time to explain. One's tall and one's powerful. You should have been able to figure that out. Context, people. Context.

CHAPTER 4

Galoogore Comes

to Greenwich

At the stroke of midnight on December 31, 2000, a prophecy was fulfilled. While the world was celebrating the start of the New Year, few realized the true importance of the date.

New Year's Day 2001 marked the official start of the millennium. As the first year in the next thousand, many cosmic changes were predicted in the years preceding it. Numerous philosophers felt a final battle would occur between good and evil in 2001. Provided these seers were accurate, who would these chosen warriors be? Who would lead the final war for planet Earth?

That question was answered on New Year's Eve 2000. As the clock struck midnight, a home in Connecticut was visited by a strange being. That being was Galoogore, the Lord of the Eternal Army.

At first, Vince McMahon and his children were shocked by this intruder. Mom Linda had just stepped out to pick up some Bugles and A&W Root Beer, leaving her family behind as the only hosts to this otherworldly creature.

Galoogore was tall. His head scraped the ceiling as he approached, and every step he took caused the McMahons to tremble in fear. Their hearts were beating rapidly and their foreheads were beaded with sweat. Who was this monster and why had he chosen to harass their family?

"Whoa, whoa, whoa, Galy Gorey! What up? What up?" Shane inquired, his arms flailing wildly while he bounced around the room.

"Yeah," chimed Stephanie. "Whoooo are yoooooou to come into owwwwwwwweeeeerrrrr hooooooowwwwww-sssss?"

Galoogore fixed his eyes on the two children and began to speak. His voice was cold, yet sympathetic. It seemed to say "Hey, I'm the Lord of the Eternal Army, but I like to let my hair down now and then." His words had a powerful aura about them. They needed to be listened to closely. Their importance was unimaginable.

"McMahon Family. You have been chosen by those who rule the universe. Your task is to lead us to a new era of power. Lead the charge. Lead the revolution."

With that, Galoogore pointed his bony finger at Stephanie. She flew into the air, spun around and landed with a thud. Shane, distraught over his sister's apparent injury, spoke out: "Whoa! Whoa! Whoa! Yeah! That's it! That's it! Bring it on, Galoogore. Bring it on! No one does that to my sister! Then again, this means that I'm the only heir to the company after Dad dies . . . wait, no! No! I need to defend her honor. I need to . . . ahhhhhhhh!"

A second finger point lifted Shane-o Mac high in the sky. Just as his sister had done before him, Shane flew into the air, spun around and landed with a thud.

Irate, Mr. McMahon finally stood up. This was his house, dammit, and he was going to take control.

"This is my house, dammit, and I'm finally going to take control." Galoogore's face contorted into a grin and he extended both of his hands forward. Rather than give Daddy a sole finger of power, the Lord of the Eternal Army used ten fingers. The power was unfathomable. It was biblical.

Vince began to convulse. His body shook and his eyes rolled around in his head. The more he vibrated, the brighter his eyes glowed. When the prolonged jolting of power had ended, Vinnie Mac crumpled to the ground in a heap.

After five minutes unconscious, Big Mac awoke to find Galoogore gone and his children laughing. What was going on? What was the meaning of this?

"Look at me, Dad! Whoa! Whoa! Check this out! Yo, yo, yo, Vinnie Mac!"

Shane waved his arms until his father finally looked over. As soon as he did, Shane-o lifted the family's grand piano above his head. He twirled it on his finger like Curly in the old Harlem Globetrotters cartoons. He then placed it down, ran up the staircase and promptly jumped down to the hard wood floors thirty feet below. After landing, he jumped up and dusted off his WWF jersey.

Stunned, Vince began to sit up. He turned his attention to Stephanie, who looked quite different.

Her chest had grown to three times its original size. Her face, now twisted into an evil grin, seemed intent on finding something to destroy. Her first target was a phone book, which she grabbed and tore as if it was a memo pad.

That wasn't the amazing part. What followed was truly spectacular. Steph opened her mouth and let out a blood-curdling scream that shook the china cabinets and chandeliers. All over Greenwich, dogs barked, car alarms went off and glass eyes shattered.

This couldn't be true. When Vince finally stood up, he realized that his hips were looser than ever. He could swagger like a hula girl dashboard ornament. This was the strut! This was the stuff! He promptly strutted over to the refrigerator and lifted it above his head. He then ran to the garage, picked up his car and tossed it onto the roof.

The McMahons were granted the power to take over the world. They were unstoppable. As the new millennium began, a new era of intimidation was upon us.

Now, I know you have two big questions. The first one, of course, is "Hey, was Galoogore leader of the Good Eternal Army or the Bad Eternal Army?" Well, there's really no answer. We're not sure. You have to look inside yourself to know. The second question is obviously, "Is that true or did you make it all up?"

Well, I made it all up. Then again, it might be true. If it's not, then how the hell do you explain this:

Vince McMahon
April 13, 1998: *Raw*, Vince McMahon vs. Steve Austin

For years VKM had played the coy announcer on WWF television. He had a yellow suit and big hair. There was nothing bad-ass about him.

Before telling you about the *Raw* in '98, I want to take you back even further. The year was 1993 and Vinnie was still about four years away from unveiling the evil "Mr. McMahon" character on TV and . . . actually, I should clarify that. He was four years away from unveiling the character on WWF TV. The first glimpse of Mr. McMahon happened in Memphis.

In a mini-feud with USWA hero (and WWF villain), Jerry "The King" Lawler, Vince cut his teeth as an arrogant character and engaged in some rasslin' banter. The King invited Vincent onto his King's Court talk show to hype his upcoming appearance at a Memphis show. The interview segment, although never aired on World Wrestling Federation TV, illustrated just how ridiculous wrestling writing was back in the early 90s. Things may get corny nowadays, but no one could hold a candle to some of the goofy stuff they were scripting back then. Want an example? Well, this is how they closed out that rare King's Court appearance:

> **Vince:** Right in your own hometown of Memphis, you'll be exposed for the kind of King you truly are . . . a Burger King!

> **Lawler:** Well, let me just say this. Oh yeah, that's real cute. So you're saying you'll be there Monday night at the Mid-South Coliseum?

> **Vince:** You bet your joo-wels.

> **Lawler:** *(raising fist)* I'll tell you this Vince McMahon. Monday night, this Burger King is gonna give you a Whopper. Ha ha ha. What do you think of that?

> **Vince:** If that's the case, I assure you it won't be a Happy Meal.

Duh. I wonder why they couldn't fit a Chicken McNugget reference in there too. Hey. Forget that. Why not a Big Mac line? Seems like it would have been appropriate. Anyway, with lines like that to recite, it's no wonder VKM took a few more years before debuting his character on WWE Television.

It went down on the April 13, 1998 edition of *Raw*: In a stunning move, WWE owner Vince McMahon decided to take matters into his own hands when dealing with back-talking WWE superstar Steve Austin. Rather than wringing his hands and gulping in fear, McMahon finally agreed to fight the Texas Rattlesnake in a match on *Raw*.

Throughout the episode, Vinnie Mac's friends and family begged him to reconsider. After all, at the time Vince was 54 years old and facing someone half his age with more in-ring experience. VKM scoffed at them. This is something that had to be done. No matter how ridiculous Big Mac's chances against Austin were, he needed to stand up for himself. At match time, Vince recalled a comment Stone Cold had made earlier. He said that he could beat the WWF Chairman with one arm tied behind his back. Although viewed as an act of cowardice, this move is what made the announcers treat McMahon as a viable threat to Steve Austin. While Mac is strong in physical stature, he was still a 54-year-old man facing the WWF Champion.

The match was ruled a no contest and McMahon lived to wrestle another day. At least he stood up for himself this time around. He showed that no matter how old you are, you can still battle those who challenge you. You might not win, but dammit — you'll leave a mark.

November 16, 2003: *Survivor Series*, Vince McMahon vs. The Undertaker

The Undertaker is one of the most evil competitors to ever wrestle for World Wrestling Entertainment. He's played a demon, a biker and a demon biker. He's taken on everyone that the promotion has put in his way. Beating The Undertaker is a big deal. Not everyone does it.

The 2003 *Survivor Series* presented an interesting challenge for the Dead Man. His opponent was unlike any other. Undie would be facing a former WWE World Champion. He'd be facing a man that has battled Ric Flair in a street fight. He'd be facing a man who took on Hulk Hogan at a *WrestleMania*. He'd be facing a man who made out with Trish Stratus, Sable and Torrie Wilson on WWE TV. He'd be facing Vince McMahon. You remember Vince. He's the old guy from years ago. He sure accomplished a lot since then, huh?

Anyway, Big Mac had decided that the Taker was getting a bit spoiled in his old age and chose to stop him from winning any further Championships. In October, Vince interfered in Undie's World Title match against Brock Lesnar. It cost him the title and garnered a strong enemy for the aging promoter. Uh oh.

The two faced off the following month at the *Survivor Series.* It was more than just a match. It was a Buried Alive match. The winner would be whoever placed their opponent into a gimmicked grave site and dumped dirt on top. What would happen? Who would win?

It was Mr. McMahon, that's who. With help from Kane, Vince, the guy who was considered too old to face Steve Austin in 1998, beat a company legend in one of his own specialty matches. He didn't even have to make Undertaker tie one arm behind his back. Talk about progress.

> **Observation:** Hmmmm. I think someone liked doing the wrestling. What do you think? I also think that a certain someone decided he should be a tough guy if he's going to do the wrestling. No one likes to be a wussy character. If it's your company, you ain't got to play no stinking wussy . . . no matter how old you are. He who has the gold makes the rules. You know how it is.

Shane McMahon

February 15, 1999: *Raw,* Shane McMahon and Kane vs. X-Pac and Triple H

Shane McMahon, although appearing as an extra in many WWF skits throughout his lifetime, didn't really get a chance to be a character until *Sunday Night Heat* debuted. Much like his father before him, Shane-o Mac was placed into the slot of ringside announcer. He would call the action and help paint a picture of the wrestling action for those of us with broken picture tubes in our televisions. There was only one problem.

Shane was really annoying. I don't mean a little annoying. I mean annoying with a capital "AHHHHHHHHH!" He would blurt out "Whoa! Whoa!" He would interrupt his cohosts. He would freak out over the most common of moves. It was almost unbearable. I mean, Vince had some quirks himself when calling the action, but none so pronounced, out of place and irritating as those of his son. Maybe announcing wasn't the right thing for Shane to do. There had to be something else that he could do on-air for a wrestling federation.

Hmmmm. Diva? No, that's for girls. Referee? Bor-ing. Oh, I know. He could be a rassler!

That's what he did. On the February 15, 1999 edition of *Raw* (one night after Daddy Vince had taken on Steve Austin in a steel cage at *St. Valentine's Day Massacre*), Shane found himself in quite the quandary. Triple H, recently estranged from his on-air and then-off-air love interest Joanie "Chyna" Lauer, challenged her to a match. In fact, he wanted to make it a tag match. How about if Hunter teamed with Sean "X-Pac" Waltman and Chyna teams with Kane? That would be fair, right?

Before that match could be made, Shane showed up and told Joanie that she had the night off. This tag match wasn't happening. In light of the situation, Pac made a suggestion to Little Mac. How about taking Joan's place yourself, Junior Jr.? Let's make it Kane and Shane against Trips and . . . X-Pac. Blah. It would have sounded cool if his name rhymed with Trips, right? Kane and Shane versus Trips and Blips or something like that. Oh well. Life goes on.

McMahon didn't accept at first, but chose to give the DX Duo their match on one condition. Sean-Pac could put his European Title on the line. That way, if Shane-o Mac somehow defeated him in a fluke, he'd capture the title too. In other words, Shane figured that if he's gonna get his ass kicked, he might as well get it kicked trying to win something. The match was made and it was on like Teflon.

The contest started as you thought it would. Kane wrestled the opening moments and allowed the boss's son to watch from the corner. He pummeled both Hunter and X all by his lonesome until Pac found himself knocked from the ring.

At this point, Shane-o pounced and began striking Pac-Man with punches and kicks. Chyna arrived and lent a helping hand to Team KaneShane by clotheslining Waltman, the man who would eventually crash Joanie's *Surreal Life* reality stint and write Internet pleas to her from Kinkos.

The first time McMahon saw any real action was after The Big Red Machine and Hunter both found themselves on the ground in pain. Red tagged Shane in, but was horrified to see that Triple H was merely faking. He tagged in Paca, who proceeded to go buck on Vinnie Mac's baby boy. All looked dark when X-Pac set Shane up for his patented "Bronco Buster," a homoerotic move that sees Sean Waltman place his opponent's head on the bottom turnbuckle, run into him full force and then "ride" his face with his crotch. Yes, you read that right. He rides their faces. Now you understand why all looked dark.

Kane wasn't going to let anyone do that to his partner. He grabbed Waltman by the throat and the two scuffled. By the time Sean had made his way back to the ring, Chyna-Doll had handed the European Title to McMahon. He waffled the Face Rider with it and covered him for an easy one, two, three. Shane McMahon had become the new European Champion. He did it without ever having to see any real action.

Now came the problem. How does a promoter's son hang onto his Championship against a six-foot tall, 200-pound rassler? I mean, X-Pac isn't the biggest competitor, but he's still a big guy and Shane doesn't even know how to wrestle! By the time their rematches rolled around, McMahon had enlisted the services of his Mean Street Posse, a group of friends from Greenwich. You couldn't blame him. After all, he's not a wrestler. He's Vince McMahon's son. The intrigue of it all was wondering how and when he would lose that title to one of the real professionals.

November 16, 2003: *Survivor Series,* Shane McMahon vs. Kane

Some night *Survivor Series* was for the McMahons, right? While Daddy, with his Spidey senses, prepared to take out The Undertaker, Shane McMahon readied himself for the Monster Kane!

You see, it was The Big Red Machine who tombstoned Shane's

mama, Linda, on the metal entrance ramp. That was enough to cause anyone to show up and defend her honor. In this case, a true hero emerged. That hero was Shane-o Mac!

No longer a Mean Street Puss-ay, Little Mac now had the strength of 50 migrant workers and could leap tall buildings in a single bound. The feud was intense to say the least.

Shane tossed the Monster into a flaming dumpster. Kane survived and no explanation was given why.

The Big Red Demon hooked McMahon's testicles to a car battery in an act of perverse terror. Little Mac's testicles survived and no explanation was given why.

Shaney Mac insisted that Kane meet him at a restaurant. When the Monster arrived, he was treated to a stern talking to. Before he could retort, McMahon left. Kane didn't murder him with the dinner knife on the table and no explanation was given why.

On another occasion, The Machine was lured into a limo by Shane. When he got inside, McMahon drove it head-on into a truck. Kane went to the hospital. Despite being a villain, he had the sympathy of the announcers. They talked about how horrible it was to see this happen to someone. Why? Who knows? As you may have guessed, no explanation was given why.

When the two initially met at *Unforgiven,* it was Big Red coming out on top in a Last Man Standing Match. Despite jumping off the Titantron — a height of over 50 feet — Shane-o lost. He also lost at the *Survivor Series* ambulance match. That didn't change the facts, though. This Shane was a new Shane. The guy from 1999 would get killed by this high-flying, fearless version. Since the late 90s, Mac had jumped from numerous heights and held his own in feuds with Blackbelt Steve Blackman, his father Vince and Andrew "Test" Martin. Speaking of Andrew . . .

Just to prove how tough he was, Shane-o challenged Kane-o to the *Survivor Series* match by pummeling Test on a live edition of *Raw.* He brutalized this guy. With a bum foot, Martin couldn't defend himself and Shane tore him apart. After a decisive beat down, Mac called out for The Monster to accept his challenge.

There was only one problem with all this.

Test was genuinely injured because of an in-ring mess-up at a house show . . . that occurred at the hands of Shane. Yes. Little Mac not only injured this guy due to his recklessness in the ring, but he got to beat him up on television a few nights later. How's that rationalized? When Ahmed Johnson hurt people in the ring, everyone complained. When Shane did it, the writers scripted segments that allowed him to kick their ass on cable two days later.

When Vinnie's kid finally hooked up with the unburnt menace at the *Series*, he lost once again. However, the fight was close. It was so close, in fact, that it's hard to imagine that this was the same guy from that 1999 tag match.

Observations: Funny how Shane McMahon needed Kane to defeat a 200-pound mid-carder in 1999, yet was on the same level with him merely four years later. Galoogore must have loaded this kid up with some sort of woovy berserk powers. Normal people don't advance like that. Nothing could turn someone from a geek to God in such a short period of time. Forget taking steroids. He'd have to be taking asteroids.

Stephanie McMahon
March 30, 2000: *Smackdown,* Stephanie vs. Jacqueline

WrestleMania 2000 was right around the corner and World Champion Triple H was preparing for his four-way match against The Rock, Mick Foley and Big Show. The pay-per-view, billed with the tag line "A McMahon in Every Corner," was looming and The Game's then on-air wife, Stephanie McMahon, was standing by his side in eager anticipation. Yet something was missing.

The fact of the matter was that her TV husband was the World Champion. Shouldn't Stephanie have some gold of her own? After all, she had wrestled one match and everything! It was a tag encounter that saw her and Test defeat Jeff Jarrett and Debra. Why couldn't she get a shot at the women's title? She deserved it. (You have to remember that this is the girl who rationalizes her high position in WWE by saying she earned it by answering the phones at Titan Tower when she was 14. Tells you a lot, huh?)

The Women's Champion at the time was a wrestler named

Jacqueline. She was a tough stick o' dynamite from Texas and the announcers couldn't fathom the thought of Steph defeating the top-heavy Champion. None of us could. She was the silver-spoon princess. How would she possibly defeat an accomplished wrestler like Jackie?

She must have been wondering the same thing because Stephie Mac refused to enter the ring when the bell rang. She chose, instead, to run away as fast as the wind could take her. The Mac-ette appeared to be running scared because . . . well, she was. There was no way that she could defeat this rassler!

Then Triple H showed up with his DeGeneration X buddies. Sean "X-Pac" Waltman tripped Jacqueline. At this point, the referee's attention was diverted and fellow D-X Member Torri spiked the Women's Champion into the ground with a crushing DDT.

From there, it was all elementary. Mrs. McHelmsley made the cover, got the win and was rewarded the women's title. The entire gimmick of her title victory was that she wasn't a wrestler. Rather, she had friends. The woman who was too frightened to actually wrestle the Women's Champion, now had to defend it against all comers. Uh oh. How would she survive?

October 19, 2003: *Unforgiven*, Stephanie McMahon vs. Vince McMahon

I have a hard time keeping a straight face as I type this. Without a doubt, Stephanie McMahon's character transformation was the most over-the-top insane one of the bunch.

By October of '03, the Billion Dollar Princess had engaged in catfights with Sable and Trish. She had faced 300-pound hairball A-Train in singles competition. She teamed up with a one-legged 150-pound partner, Zach Gowan, to face the 7-foot-tall Big Show and *Smackdown* Champion Brock Lesnar. Yes, Steph had been busy since the days of being scared shitless of Jacqueline. She was once afraid of a 5'2" woman. Now she could hold her own in fights with 7'2" men. Why? You know why. It's because she's part of the writing team. Duh.

Anyway, this all led to the biggest feud of the Mackette's career. For the first time ever, it was a father versus daughter match! That's right. *Unforgiven 2003* featured an I Quit Match between WWE owner Vince McMahon and *Smackdown* GM Stephanie McMahon! WWE hyped the fact this would be the first time a father versus daughter match had ever taken place in wrestling. Wow. First ever? Really? Why didn't any other promoters think of booking a father versus daughter match? Oh, wait. I know why . . . because it's ridiculous.

If you find that absurd, you'd probably find the October 16th, 2003 edition of *Smackdown* pretty silly too. In a melodramatic moment of insanity, Big Van Stephanie ate up 20 minutes of airtime talking about her life as Vince's daughter. I can't describe how terrible this promo was. Watching it, you got the feeling that the McMahons have no earthly idea how little people care about them and their lives. Somewhere between 1999 and now, they lost sight of the fact that the wrestling business is about the wrestling — not whether Stephanie got what she wanted for Christmas when she was five . . . or whatever the hell she was bitching about during that interview.

In the end, the two locked up and it was pretty nuts. There was something unsettling about seeing Vinnie Mac choke out his daughter while she gasped for air. Even worse was the fact that she was allowed to be portrayed as a valid opponent to him. As if it wasn't bad enough that McMahon made wrestlers half his age play off like they were intimidated by him. Now he had to portray himself as almost equal to his daughter. Therefore, Steph was on the same level with the wrestlers on the show. Grand.

Insane, right? This is the girl who was scared of little Jackie. Now she's holding her own against the guy who defeated The Undertaker. Oh Galoogore, what have you done to this family?

> **Observation:** Un-fuckin'-believable. Also, notice that all three of the McMahon ego matches occurred around the same time. That should give you an idea of how utterly terrible that WWE time period was for the fans.

* * *

All in all, mind-blowing, right? I mean, come on. There's no other excuse for these monumental changes within the McMahons and their on-screen characters other than Galoogore the Powerful.

Well, either that or they just realized that it's their company and they can do whatever the fuck they want. That's always a possibility, don't you think?

Let's not pretend here. I said in the beginning of this book that I don't play Devil's Advocate and I won't play it now. These characters, as outlined above, are glaring examples of how McMahon family members care less about being realistic and more about feeding their own egos.

Let's be honest. If you turned on *The Simpsons* each week and started seeing shows devoted solely to how its creator, Matt Groening, was a God among men, we'd know that something was up. When the writers of a story involve themselves and their loved ones as characters in the fantasy they're constructing, it's damn near impossible to stay impartial no matter how hard you try to pretend otherwise.

I should rephrase that because Big Mac and the Bingers aren't even trying to pretend otherwise. The ego-driven vanity storylines they place themselves in couldn't be any more obvious. Their crazy evolution from their debuts to their 2003 matches proves this. Sadly, I'd like to write a ridiculous example of someone blatantly making themselves seem tougher because they're controlling the story, but I can't come up with any that are more ridiculous than the examples that the McMahons have already scripted.

That's why it always makes me laugh when I hear how the McMahons were once the company's most interesting characters. While the statement is true, it speaks of characters that no longer exist. The original family, with the exception of consistently robotic mom Linda, is dead and gone. The characters that replaced them aren't even from the same planet as the originals.

You see, the Stephanie, Vince and Shane of yesteryear did work. Why? They were based on reality. Vinnie really was an aging promoter with something to prove despite being outmatched. Shane-o actually lived the high society lifestyle and could get under the skin of the working class as an on-air wuss with backup. Stephie genuinely was a princess that turned her nose up to chipping a nail.

Now they're not based on reality whatsoever. They're based on ego. We're talking unfiltered, balls-to-the-wall ego. Vinnie is now a He-Man who can house anyone on his payroll. Shane-o still lives the high society lifestyle, but he can now soar through the air and intimidate monsters. Stephie is still a princess, but now she's an Amazon Warrior Princess who can stand-toe-to-toe with her daddy, the man who can house anyone on the roster. Talk about changing personalities.

How does that work? What made the McMahons go from a real life family to the Incredibles? Is it Galoogore or is it ego? The answer is clear when you consider these three things:

1) Vince and his family, like anyone else in the world, have a certain amount of ego.
2) I made Galoogore up. He doesn't exist.
3) There is no 3. It's ego.

All this considered, can you imagine how the McFamily would handle it if they somehow brought an actual wrestler into the mix? If the chairman can push his son and daughter as superheroes, despite their lack of size and ability, can you imagine what he would do with a family member who genuinely looks the part? Could you picture the heights that person would reach with the most powerful wrestling family in the world pulling the strings? If, as we saw in the cases of the Galoogore crew, nepotism takes priority over believability and logic, how many insane decisions would be made to keep this connected wrestler looking better than all who stand in his way?

I WANT YOU TO PUT OVER MY SON

What I'm really trying to say is forget hopscotch. Screw badminton. To hell with Hungry Hungry Hippos. There's only one Game that matters in this millennium.

His name is "The Game" Triple H. He's the biggest star in WWE. The whole company has centered on him for years. When it comes to this business, the McMahons set their clocks by Hunter Hearst Helmsley. They've spent tireless hours devoting storylines and angles to making him a star. He has it all. He has the look of a superstar. He has tremendous ring skills. He has superb conditioning. What more could you want?

How about a wedding ring? You see, he may have all those attributes, but most importantly, he has Vince's daughter as his wife. Does that make a difference when it comes to his successes and stories in WWE? Keep reading. I'll let you decide for yourself.

Game on.

CHAPTER 5

To the Hunter Goes the Spoils

If you're asking if I would ever date a wrestler, certainly I would. However it wouldn't be good business for me to get romantically involved with anyone in any aspect of our business.
— Stephanie McMahon, *Off the Record,* August 1999

For nearly a decade before he married Vince McMahon's daughter Stephanie, Triple H wrestled all over the world. He was Terra Ryzin and Jean Paul Levesque in WCW. He was Hunter Hearst Helmsley, the American Blueblood, in WWE. He did his job. He took his lumps. He earned his stripes.

You see, The Game isn't your typical "son-in-law" of the boss. He didn't start wrestling after exchanging nuptials with the McPrincess. He didn't show up on the first day of work with a silver spoon in his mouth. Hunter clawed his way to the top tier of the company and had all the ups and downs that most guys go through. Sometimes even worse.

At *WrestleMania 12*, he lost to The Ultimate Warrior in thirty seconds. The match planning involved Trips asking Warrior what the plan was and UW responding "I'm beating you in thirty seconds," before walking away. I'm not kidding. That's how it happened.

When Hunter and his good friend Shawn Michaels had to bid farewell to their buddies Scott Hall and Kevin Nash who were leaving for wcw, they broke character at a Madison Square Garden House Show and took a bow. Despite being on separate sides of the good guy/bad guy fence, the group bucked authority and did what they wanted. After the Michaels-Nash main event, they all embraced. Hall and Nash couldn't be punished by wwe, because they were leaving anyway. Shawn Michaels couldn't be punished because the entire company was centered around him. The only one left was Helmsley. Scheduled to win the upcoming King of the Ring, Hunt was stripped of the honor and saw it go to Steve Austin and the birth of Austin 3:16. Ouch.

So, make no mistake. Triple H is a wrestler. It's why people respect him. The controversy surrounding Hunter Hearst Helmsley isn't whether or not he became a main eventer because of his McMahon matrimony. On the contrary, H was in the mix long before he ever wed Stephanie, either on-screen or off. There's no debating that.

Here's the thing with Triple H and his marriage. As it relates to wwe, he's in the family. He'll always be around. He'll never leave. He's solid.

That's a selling point with the McMahons. One of the main reasons why Vince worked to get his evil character over with audiences during the *Monday Night Wars* is because he knew that he would never leave his own company.

It's like running a backyard wrestling federation. The kid who owns the camera or the belt is always the World Champion. Why? Because it's his backyard wrestling federation. The reasoning he gives is that he knows he'll always come to the backyard wrestling tapings because he has the camera and belt. Although his real reason is, "Because I can."

When confronted with this question on Canadian interview show *Off the Record*, Hunter defended his position and claimed he would never be allowed to overshadow the other wrestlers. As usual, it all had to do with Vince and his genius.

One of the things that people don't understand too is that it's a filter. Everything goes through Vince [McMahon]. And trust me, I don't care who you are, Vince is going to do what's right for business first. You know, we all make suggestions and it all filters through him. I'm readily accepting the fact that, you know, uh, I'm not going to be the top guy in a period of time. I'm accepting of the fact that I'm a big enough star in what I've accomplished in this business that I'll always be a big star in this industry. — **Triple H,** *Off the Record,* **July 2004**

Vince is the filter, huh? Mr. McFilter? Well, that's all well and good. The only problem, and anyone who's ever had a Brita water pitcher knows this, is that a filter should be changed every few months. After a while it fills up with carbon particles and other random crap that you don't want in your drinking water. For the past few years, wwe's sports entertainment version of H_2O has been so polluted that you have to wonder what the hell the Filter King has been letting leak through each week.

Is Vince McMahon the naked king that has no clothes? How do I know he has pimples on his butt? Because he's the naked king and doesn't realize he doesn't have any clothes on . . . Triple H is a hell of a performer. But again, he's the one that has to watch the maneuvering of the people within the company. He's the one that has to watch that he's not running around with his weenie hanging out. He has to make sure that he's not the one without any clothes on. He's become the king's son. He's gotta be careful, because he could be running around naked too. That's what's happening to him. They're running around pulling his strings and laughing at all his jokes, I'm sure they are. I know I would be. Hell, I'd be up there laughing like hell if he was saying anything even a little bit funny. I'd like to hear one of his jokes. — **Terry Funk**

Sadly The Game and his father-in-law don't care if they have any clothes on or not. It's not even a factor to them. Insane decisions are made without a second thought because, well, Vince can. However, the "I'll push my family first because we'll never leave wwe" reasoning seems to hold filtered water with Vince. He knows that he won't leave his own company, so his evil Mr. McMahon character needs to stay popular. By the same token, barring a major scandal, Hunter will never leave.

Even if a new WCW springs up next week and starts stealing WWE stars, Vinnie Mac knows that the H Man is here until death does him part. You really need to get a guy like that over with the crowds. He needs to be Mr. *Monday Night Raw*. Yeah! That's the ticket. Triple H can be Mr. *Monday Night Raw*!

The reasoning, when isolated, makes sense. There's only one problem. Wrestling is a delicate balance and the success of the product and story is contingent upon a number of things. Like any scripted serial, WWE needs to protect the credibility of its characters or else they hit snags. Big snags.

The reason it's not easy to get a character like Triple H over as a super monster wrestler is because you need to do so without sacrificing the credibility of too many other performers in the process. How do you get a wrestling superman to be seen as a superman by fans? You have him beat the hell out of everyone. One problem, though. Those wrestlers have to come back and wrestle again next week.

Yeah, it's fake. I know. They don't really win or lose. That's all good. The problem is that there's only so many times you can watch a guy fake lose before you start to think he's a fake wimp. In the fantasy world of pro wrestling, Hunter rules while everyone else bites the big one.

When this happens, your show's in trouble. Soon that one superstar will be left with no one else to conquer. Eerily similar to Vince McMahon's real life situation in a wrestling monopoly, Trips is left with no competition. While new stars should be built up and elevated, they're built up and knocked down. How do you make heroes that way? How do you create money-making characters?

Is there nepotism in World Wrestling Entertainment? Yes. Let's not pretend otherwise. Anyone who's watched WWE programming for more than two weeks can see it. *Monday Night Raw*, the company's cable monster, is built around Hunter. It's his baby. Long and tedious promos from The Game aren't occasional, they're weekly. No one sees more television time than the H Man.

The excuse Hunt gives for his overexposure is that he's the most intriguing character on the show. Fans know him and want to follow his feuds. Good point.

Then again, maybe he's the most intriguing performer on the show because he gets ten times more TV exposure and character development than other guys get. The whole show's about him. It's written that way. It's like saying "Webster gets the most TV time because he's the most interesting character. Not George or Ma'am." Well, of course he is. The show is called *Webster* and he's the central character. That's why he's most intriguing. Just like Triple H is the central character on *Raw*. The other performers don't help make up the ensemble. They're Hunter's supporting cast.

The difference between *Webster*, or any other form of TV entertainment, and wrestling is that wrestling needs to build up all of its characters in order to ensure future success. Whereas Batman can beat the Joker at the end of his first movie and move onto the Penguin in his next, wrestling doesn't work like that. It's as if Batman beat the Joker and moved on, but you still had to sell the Joker as a viable threat against someone else the following week. Unlike action films, wrestling's unsuccessful villains have to come back and fight another day. They still have to have enough credibility to sell tickets in their future conquests. The unsuccessful heroes have to be able to do this too. Lose to the Champ one week. Challenge someone else the next. It's a delicate balance that can make or break careers depending on how the aftermath is handled.

When you combine that dilemma with a politically charged case of nepotism, you have a recipe for stale wrestling programs. Triple H, the son-in-law of Vince McMahon, is the *Raw* World Champion. Wrestlers come to dethrone him. They fail. After that, they're promptly ignored while we figure out who the Champion should eat next.

If you've ever had a job or gone to school, you know what favoritism is. I learned about favoritism in third grade when my teacher was dating one of the student's dads. Guess who handed out all the ditto sheets. Guess who stood first in line. Guess who got to lead the pledge.

Is it right? Not really. Then again, she must have had a different relationship with this student than she had with any of us. She wasn't making *me* waffles in the morning right after sex with my dad. She obviously knew her boyfriend's kid better than she knew any of us. It's only natural that she trusted and liked him the most.

Now you know where Triple H stands in the mix. He's in the family. Vince McMahon likes him. He likes him a lot. He'll never leave. He'll never walk away. He's perfect. He's just completely and utterly perfect. He had Vince at "hello" and all that. So, what could go wrong?

Oh, plenty. As we mentioned earlier, Hunter's character has successfully undercut the well-being of *Monday Night Raw*. By not elevating new talent or making opponents come out of his feuds looking good, Helmsley has damaged the future of the industry he says he loves.

In his own defense, Triple H always points to the fact that he was a top star before marrying Stephanie McMahon. He claims that nepotism cries are unfair because he'd graced the main event long before tying the knot.

So noted. Then again, that's not the point. No one is saying that Hunter became a main eventer because he married Stephanie. That wouldn't be true. He was a main eventer long before that. He didn't become a top guy after marrying Stephanie.

No. He became the all-powerful, omniscient, god of time, space and dimensional travel. Merely being in his presence will burn your retinas and force your brain to implode. The aura of power that emanates from his *Raw* character can kill a small puppy and make old women cry. That's what he became after marrying Stephanie.

Triple H isn't a main eventer anymore. He's transcended that.

What he's become is a character that destroys any other character he touches. He'll devour you whole, spit you back out and watch your character fall apart the next week.

Is this done on purpose? I say yes. I've said so since the start.

People say that I don't respect Triple H because I say all these things. How can I claim that Hunter Hearst Helmsley has purposely thwarted the careers of many men all for the sake of boosting his own? I've been told he's misunderstood, vilified, prejudged and just trying to make things better.

The irony of all this is that I actually respect Triple H far more than anyone who defends him. I hold his insight, skills and intelligence to a higher degree than anyone who makes excuses for his actions does. I have the utmost respect for The Game.

How can I say this? It's simple actually. There are only two ways to view Stephanie McMahon's husband when it comes to his role in World Wrestling Entertainment. You either think he's an evil politician who's held back wrestlers he felt might threaten his personal power; doing so without any regard for the money it may cost his company, family or fan base. Or you think he's the most incompetent, inept buffoon to grace the professional wrestling industry since the dawn of man. You choose.

With a track record like Mr. H's, you have to wonder how anyone can feel he's done all this accidentally. He brags daily about his prowess for understanding the industry. He's more than a student of the game, he is The Game! He's admitted to eating, sleeping and sneezing this business. How can someone so steadfast in his insistence that he knows all make so many mistakes? What mistakes?

Let's take a look at all of Triple H's epic feuds. We'll start from the time he joined the McFamily and work our way to the day the World Title left *Monday Night Raw* and went to the *Thursday Night Smackdown* brand, freeing it from Hunter's deathgrip. Sound good? Good. Now take a look at all this and tell me it's accidental. . . .

October 2002: Kane

Triple H had barely washed the rice out of his beard before stepping forward to accept the challenge of Kane. A masked monster, Kane's gimmick involved him being locked away by his father, Paul Bearer, for most of his pre-adult life. After all, The Big Red Machine, as he was called, had been scarred by the burns of a house fire set by his brother, The Undertaker, during childhood. Red's survival had been kept a secret from everyone — including his own brother.

Wait . . . no one knew he was alive? That's right. No one. When Paul Bearer finally sprung the big news on the Taker in 1997, it was shocking. "Your brother Kane is alive!"

Undie couldn't believe it. What a secret. This whole time Paul had kept Red shielded from those who would persecute him. No one knew he had survived the fire. No one knew he was alive.

Then, in 2002, WWE decided they were tired of all that. Kane's character was based on being locked away. However, his feud with Trips was based on a background that he wasn't supposed to have.

Yeah, for some strange reason World Wrestling Entertainment decided to book Triple H in an altercation with Big Red and script the entire storyline to go against the very nature of Kane's character. Despite the fact that the Monster's entire gimmick was based on his burned and secretive history, they put him into a feud that undermined everything — and I do mean everything — that he was based on.

Helmsley claimed that Kano went to wrestling school, met a woman, killed her and raped her. That was the premise. Apparently,

Kane was, as Hunter said, "a murderah." He pined for a girl named Katie Vick. They met while the Monster was training for his career. When she didn't return his love, he killed her and then had his way with her. That's the story that we were told.

Huh? How did he go to wrestling school? What happened to Paul Bearer's stunning secret? It made no sense. We needed the Monster himself to set things straight. He had to tell Triple H that he had the wrong man. How could he know Katie Vick? How could he have been in wrestling school? He was in a basement eating field mice and licking the furnace at the time.

So, the dark and scary monster finally responded. He didn't grunt and groan like a true boogeyman, though. No. He spoke like a big normal guy in a leather mask. Aw gee.

With mic in hand, Big Red admitted, "Katie Vick was a friend of mine." Although he said he didn't kill her. They were merely driving to a party and she died in a car wreck. It was always a skeleton in his closet because . . . well, he was the driver of the car.

What? What? What? He knew her? But, but . . . that's insane. For the five years preceding this feud, WWE had presented Kane as an ostracized loner with no friends. His whole gimmick that he was hidden away was a burnt secret. Now he had friends?! He went to wrestling school?! He left the basement?! He went to parties?! Wait, wait, wait . . . he drives?! The Thing in the Basement drives?! Sounds like a normal life to me. Why is he so angry then?! Ahhhhh! My head!

The only real conflict in all this was voiced by Trips himself. The conflict wasn't whether or not Kane knew the woman. It wasn't about whether or not he liked her "in that way." No. It was about . . . ready? He wondered if The Big Red Machine raped her before or after she died.

Note to everyone on the planet: If your entire feud is about whether you rape living or dead bodies, I'd say that your chances of being popular with fans dwindles a bit.

To prove his point, Trips shot a video of himself parodying Kane raping a dead body in a coffin. He wore the Machine's mask and entered the funeral parlor. He then climbed into "Katie Vick's coffin," stripped and had simulated sex with a mannequin. It was one of the dumbest skits ever shot in the history of television. As the act came to a close, Helmsley reached into her "head" and proclaimed, "I really did it. I screwed your brains out!" With that, he tossed a handful of white jelly-like goo into the camera.

Shocking? Not really. Stupid? Yeah. It was stupid. It was really stupid. If stupid were peanut butter, this skit would have been . . . well, a lot of peanut butter. (Sorry. I don't know where I was going with that.) I couldn't grasp the logic of this feud on a number of levels.

Problems with Kane-Hunter storyline:

1) How did Triple H simulating sex with a corpse make Kane look bad?

2) He was locked in a basement!

3) Repeat #2 like 500 more times.

Sadly, this whole thing, skit and all, was meant to get a big response. WWE compared it to the TV show, *Six Feet Under*. For those who don't get HBO, *Six Feet* is the story of a family that runs a funeral home. No idea how WWE figured it was comparable. It's not a show about having sex with dead people. I don't know what show Vince McMahon is watching that he thinks is *Six Feet Under*, but it's not. I've been watching the show since it started and I don't remember any member of the Fisher family romancing one of their deceased clientele.

Forget *Six Feet Under*. That's not why WWE did it. They wanted people to be outraged by it. That's it. This was the same time as the highly publicized "gay union" between Billy and Chuck on *Smackdown*. Vince McMahon was doing anything for attention. Nothing shocked me about them at the time. I wouldn't have been surprised if he had Kurt Angle set fire to a sack of baby seals on *Sunday Night Heat*.

Oh . . . oh, not only was this feud about necrophilia. It was about total domination. You see, Triple H beat Kane for his Intercontinental title. Since Trips was World Champion, the IC belt was absorbed and vacated. A strong mid-card tool, the Intercontinental Title was designed to give the wrestlers who weren't ready for the main event a reason to come to work. It was something for the struggling newcomers to use in order to gain respectability. That was gone now. It was used to feed the monster that is Triple H's Championship.

Before long, WWE realized the folly of the Katie Vick storyline. It killed everything about Kane's character. It killed the aura of fantasy that surrounded wrestling. It killed everything.

You see, "murder" shouldn't really exist in wrestling. If you tell the fans that someone can be killed within the confines of a story-line, it begs the question, how can someone get hit in the head repeatedly with a sledgehammer and not die? How come a back-breaker doesn't break someone's back? How can a wrestler get punched dead-on in the face over and over and over and over again without getting bruised?

Well, that's because wrestling's fake. In the fake world of wrestling, no one dies. They all live to fight another day. If two wrestlers are feud-ing and one attacks the other with barbed wire, the one attacked will be back by the end of the show looking for revenge . . . with an over-sized bandage on his head. If someone can get killed in wrestling, it makes all the other feuds seem petty. If you can attack your opponent with a bat and not go to jail, why can't you just stab him in the chest with a screwdriver? They must not really hate each other all that much.

Katie Vick isn't mentioned anymore. Her name hasn't been memorialized and she's never brought up . . . by WWE. Wrestling fans and writers discuss it all the time. To many, it's synonymous with "stupid storyline." It killed Kane and ended with Triple H holding every singles title on *Raw*. The only one who looked even remotely good at the end of this distasteful stupidity was Hunter. Funny that this was also his first feud as a married man, huh?

Also, some time after all this ended, Hunt reared his head in Kane's life again. This time, he defeated Big Red and forced him to remove his mask. When his mask came off, he wasn't even burned. Wow. Four years down the drain. There you have it. A gimmick killed with the wave of a pen. When all was said and done, Hunter had taken Kane's mask, belt and pride. No word on why The Game didn't decide to castrate him live on pay-per-view too.

I've been in those meetings where certain writers have brought to Vince's attention that maybe this or that wasn't very good and they should do things a different way. Vince will agree with it and roll the dice there as well. It's 50/50. I'm sure there's some days where Vince listens and some where he had his mind made up. I don't know, for instance, who came up with the Katie Vick angle, but I understand that Vince loved it. If he loved it, it's his show. He can put on whatever he wants. But it's evident by how fast they dropped the angle that he came to his senses and said we better go somewhere else with this.

— Tom Pritchard

November/December 2002:
Shawn Michaels

The one guy who gets over The Game ends up being someone that didn't need to. Shawn Michaels, a respected wrestler with more achievements than most, was the one to step up and finally take the strap from Triple H for a while.

The Heartbreak Kid and Hunter are friends, so that's cool I suppose. Whatever. Triple H is allowed to be friends with people. The

problem with this was that it didn't elevate anyone or use the H-Man's past victories to build up a new star. Whereas a victory over The Game would have done wonders for a Rob Van Dam or Booker T, wwe opted to give that honor to Shawn, a guy who's been winning titles since Vince McMahon was in his forties.

That's not to say that The Gamer didn't use this position to better himself. He did. How? Well, he lost to Michaels in a newly conceived "Elimination Chamber" match at *Survivor Series*. The idea was that six men would each be locked inside chambers made of "bulletproof glass" constructed within the giant in-ring cage. At time intervals, each one would be released. Whoever survived the match by avoiding pinfalls and submissions would be the winner. The six men involved were Triple H, Shawn Michaels, Rob Van Dam, Kane, Booker T and Chris Jericho.

OK. First of all, the "bulletproof glass" was shattered in the first few minutes of the match. Announcer Jim Ross, who deserves a medal for the way he covers for some of this insanity, screamed, "It might be bulletproof, but it's not strong enough to withstand the force of Kane's power." (Well, I'll tell you this much. He may be a dead body rapist, but he's a powerful dead body rapist.) We didn't say "bulletproof glass" anymore after that. In video game releases following this match, WWE made it possible to shatter the glass while playing Chamber matches.

So what's the big deal? It sounds like WWE was adding more and more wrestlers to the mix. With all of those names involved in the match, it sounds like all of them would look better by association. Right? Right?

You'd think, right? It doesn't help them much if you make them look like second string rookies in said match, though. What do I mean? Check this out:

> The match went 39:14.
> Rob Van Dam was eliminated by Booker T at 13:31.
> Booker T was eliminated by Chris Jericho at 17:33.
> Kane was eliminated by Chris Jericho at 22:50.
> Chris Jericho was eliminated at 30:34.
> Triple H was eliminated at 39:12.

Those numbers say a lot. While it seemed like there would be six men in this match, it felt like a lot less. The early eliminations of Booker T and Rob Van Dam seemed illogical considering how both men had been floundering since facing Triple H months earlier. A strong showing by all involved would have done wonders for WWE's main event slot. Rather, they chose to eliminate two men before the match even reached its halfway mark. The reasoning? Who the hell knows. By the end of the 39 minutes, you barely remembered who else was in the match besides the final three. In fact, the final nine minutes featured only Triple H and Shawn Michaels. That's only four minutes less than the total amount of time that Van Dam stayed in the match.

Shawn won the strap and followed up with an amazing title match against Rob Van Dam on *Raw*. People salivated for this match. They prayed for this match. There were diehard wrestling fans sitting at home with candles lit, praying to for this match to happen. It did. Most fans thought it would forever be a dream match. Shawn had been on a career hiatus since dropping the World Title to Stone Cold Steve Austin eons ago. Many thought he'd never be back. RVD was wrestling for other companies during the Heartbreak Kid's initial WWE run. Their paths hadn't really crossed until now and considering their similar wrestling styles, this match looked like it was going to blow the roof off the place.

When it finally happened, it was great. The two of them showcased their skills and showed fans what the World Title picture might look like with a different champion leading the charge. Then, just as it came to a close, reality came running out to the ring. On this night, reality had long wet hair and spit water a lot.

In other words, Triple H ruined it. He came out at the end and went on the attack. There was no real winner. Did Rob get his revenge? Did he take out Trips? Did he finally beat HBK?

Who cares? Aren't you paying attention? This isn't about Rob! Who cares what he did? He teamed with Kane or something. Whatever. This is about The Game, people.

Hunter — he's the real star of our story here — went on to beat Shawn Michaels anyway in a three stages of hell match at *Armageddon*. This match consists of three separate matches. The winner takes two out of the three victories. It also insures that this one contest will eat up a good amount of pay-per-view time and showcase both the participants huge. This one went 38 minutes.

Strange that even in defeat, Helmsley receives more TV time than the rest of the performers. His loss is to someone that doesn't benefit from it. Having Shawn Michaels beat Triple was exciting, but didn't make anyone look at him any differently. He's Shawn. He's already a big star. Maybe someone who wasn't a big star already could have used a rub like this. Never mind me. I'm just thinking out loud. Making stars isn't what it's all about. Just like the song says, it's all about The Game.

January–February 2003: Scott Steiner

Holla . . . cause I'm about to drop you on your head!

Since WWE had successfully destroyed their crop of anti-Hunter heroes on *Raw*, they reached outside the box. They reached into a box that they should have reached into in 2001. They reached into that nasty little WCW box.

What am I talking about? Well, in 2001, World Wrestling Entertainment purchased World Championship Wrestling. The Turner-owned group had hit bottom and WWE swooped in to buy them out. It was a great way to get their hands on a wrestling video library that had always eluded them. It was also a chance to get the contracts from WCW's dilapidated and rapidly shrinking roster.

What followed was a half-assed *Invasion* by the WCW stars Vince McMahon had purchased. The sad thing was that Vinnie Mac neglected to purchase any of WCW's big name contracts. These guys were locked away in million dollar Ted Turner deals and could sit at home and collect for doing nothing. Unwilling to buy any of them out, Vince simply waited until the contracts ran out to get them.

One problem here. Although WCW was backwards in all their planning, they knew how to lock up their big names. By the time these contracts were set to expire, all these guys would be too far removed from the industry, rusty and unable to perform on a big level. Had the *Monday Night Wars* continued until 2003, there was no way these wrestlers would be in any position to negotiate.

So, McMahon waited until Scott Steiner's contract expired. Then he hired him.

Now, let me go on record as saying that Scott Steiner had a great gimmick. He was huge. Actually, he was beyond huge. If Scott had looked like this in 1993 when the WWF was indicted for steroid distribution, the prosecution would have simply had to hold up a picture of his arms. That would have been it.

> Ladies and gentlemen of the jury, look at this guy's fuckin' arms. Are you kidding me? That's all. The prosecution rests.

So he was humongous. Not only that, but Scotty was raunchy. He had a gimmick very different from that of most wrestlers. While some would cut promos about how they were going to beat their opponents, Steiner would detail how he would please a freaky woman. Just when you thought it was going too far, he would twist it and take it further.

"As they reach the Big O and hit Nirvana, they scream out . . . Big Poppa Pump, you are the Big Bad Booty Daddy!"

It was so over-the-top that it became funny. Not funny in a cheesy way, but funny in a real way. Big Poppa was the type of jacked up hornball you warn your girlfriend to stay away from in a club. "Sorry, honey, if he takes a liking to you, I can't stop him. So either stay away from him or deal with what happens. Have you seen his arms? If he comes after me, I'm gonna book."

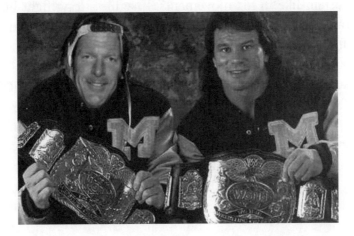

So what does WWE do? They take this natural bad guy and turn him good. Good? Yes. Good. I know what you're asking. What's his gimmick? It couldn't have stayed the same. Who wants to cheer for the jacked up horny guy? No one. That didn't stop the McEmpire. It turned the Big Bad Booty Daddy into a hero. He went on to challenge Triple H for his title. All hail your new hero — the Jacked Up Horny Guy! Yay!

How did it sell the match-up between Jack Horny and The Game? It had them compete against one another in bodybuilding posedowns in order to sell their Royal Rumble match. As stupid as that sounds, it's all good. The match was so horrible that nothing could have really sold it. WWE could send me candy and flowers and I still wouldn't pay for that match again.

Scotty was in no position to wrestle in the main event. A combination of being out of the ring for so long and battling many injuries caused Steiner to botch a number of moves. He seemed lost at times and pained at others. Rather than innovate, something he carried as his calling card early in his career, BPP just repeated the same tosses and suplexes over and over. The crowd turned on him quicker than anyone would have guessed and were damn near ravenous by the time the slips and falls started coming. He dropped the Champion a number of times and the crowd really let him have it.

It was surreal. Rarely had WWE found itself in a situation like this. It was reminiscent of the 1994 *SummerSlam* pay-per-view. One half of the main event featured The Undertaker facing off with a fake Undertaker. The problem was The Undertaker's character was Frankenstein-like in his movements. Imagine a long fight between two Frankensteins. Think about it. Hey . . . wake up! The fans were silent for most of that match. They weren't silent for the Steiner-Hunter one, though. They booed it out of the building.

It was obvious that Scott should have been swapped out of the feud after the Rumble. Instead — get this — WWE booked a rematch between them on the next pay-per-view. Wow.

Of course, Triple H won. After this, Scotty didn't see much main event time. Steiner's run against The Game did nothing for his WWE career. It also didn't add a new name to the top tier of *Raw*. That seems to be a running theme.

March 2003: Booker T

There's racism in wrestling. Let's not kid ourselves here. Saying that there's no racism in wrestling is like saying there's no racism anywhere. There's racism in the world and wrestling exists in our world. Therefore it's bound to be there.

It's not new either. 1980s' wrestler Kamala, known for his Ugandan headhunter gimmick, shared a story about how racism isn't only about what's said to you. Sometimes it's about what you're not meant to hear. Sometimes it's about what you have to figure out for yourself.

The only thing that I heard – well, I heard a lot of racist slurs, though – but the biggest one, and I hope you don't mind me saying this. No cursing or nothing, but I heard [then-WWF agent] Chief Jay Strongbow say something one time. [Hulk] Hogan, who was a super nice guy, told him "Look, we're drawing good. Let Kamala beat me. Not for the belt, but just let him beat me." I forgot where we were, but it was sold out. And Chief said "No, no, he don't need to beat you." So Hogan said, "Did Vince say he didn't want Kamala to beat me?" Chief said, "No he didn't." So Hulk said, "So let him beat me." And he said "No." So he took Hogan off and I just sort of eased around and eavesdropped on him, and he said "Look, Kamala's just a big black nigger with paint on his face." Yeah, that . . . I heard myself. "He's just a big black nigger with paint on his face. You the goose." So after I heard all that, back in the dressing room, he came back and Hogan had a look on his face. You know, he didn't want to tell me that. He didn't tell me. The only thing Hogan said was "I can't talk no sense into him." **– Kamala**

The feud between Hunter Hearst Helmsley (white guy) and Booker T (black guy) could have been based on a number of things. Instead it was based on tongue-in-cheek racism.

We're not even talking about good racism. This wasn't Col. DeBeers asking to paint Derek Dukes white in the 80s' AWA. Now that's in-your-face, no bullshit racism. This wasn't 1990 with McMahon dressing Tony Atlas up in a huge head thing, giving him a spear to toss and calling him Samba Simba. Now that's some ballsy racism. As much as you might despise things like this, you have to respect those that chose to air it. They knew what they were putting on TV. They owned their actions and embraced their outlook.

> Look, this is some racist shit. We're puttin' some racism on TV. Brace yourself. We're about to get all racist up in here.

This wasn't even close to that. This was ridiculous, non-committal stupid racism. It was as if WWE wanted to push the envelope, but they wanted to be able to yank it back as soon as they could if they needed to. After all, this was the same company that had dead body humpin' mere months earlier.

So Trips went nose to nose with Booker and told him that winning the World Title was not an option. Why? Well, Book's "people" don't win World Titles. Yup. His "people." Relax. Back down. It ain't me saying it. It's Triple H.

That was the hook to get us into their *WrestleMania* match. Booker's "people" can't do things like that. One thing, though. There was tap-dancing all around the word "black."

At no point did Trips ever say, "Booker, you can't beat me because I'm white. Muwahahahaha!" Nope. He used double talk to stuff the bull back into the horse when the complaints came in. Come on, people. Hunter didn't mean blacks. No. He meant those who aren't as rich as he is or something. Actually, the spin became that Hunter had meant "entertainers" and not "blacks."

Gotcha. I guess Hunter's mention of "nappy hair" was meant to poke fun at the stereotype that entertainers have nappy hair, right? Sure thing, Champ.

In case there was still any doubt over what this feud was about, Booker came out on the March 10, 2003 edition of *Raw* and announced he had been behind bars and once held a "gat" to someone's head. Hunter's manager Ric Flair then arrived and asked if T wanted to be his chauffeur. After beating Flair into oblivion, Booker went to the locker room area where he walked in on Triple H wetting his hair in the sink. That isn't slang for anything. He was genuinely wetting his hair in the sink for some unknown reason. When Booker approached, Hunter tossed a dollar at him.

So tell me, kind reader, is your nappy-headed, dollar-grubbing chauffeur in the entertainment field? Sounds funny, right? That's because it is funny. This was a racist angle that WWE didn't even have the "grapefruits" to admit to.

> James, get over it. What else could they have based this feud on? Booker was black. That's all there is to it. He was being told that he would never hold Triple H's title because "his people" don't win titles. It was meant to evoke a response.

That would work . . . except for the fact that Booker had already been a World Champion. He was the last WCW Champion on Ted Turner TV. In fact, the very same title that Triple H wore around his waist — the one he said Booker T's type of people couldn't win — was the exact same one that Booker had held at the time of WCW's demise.

The statement was factually flawed. WWE even admitted to Booker being a former WCW Champion. That's his thing. He looks at his hand and calls himself a "five time, five time, five time, five time, five time World Champion." When he debuted in World Wrestling Entertainment, he brought that title with him. To say he couldn't hold it for any reason was ridiculous — racist or not. He had just held the title the year before.

Oh . . . also, The Rock's considered black and he won a World Title. Ron Simmons, another black man, won one too. I guess with a hot button topic, it's not important to check validity. It's just important to make the shocking statement and see how people react.

Then again, maybe Hunter meant that entertainers don't hold the World Title. After all, that's how they spun it. Well, what the hell does that mean? They're all entertainers, aren't they? Hulk Hogan wasn't an entertainer? Ultimate Warrior wasn't an entertainer? Ric Flair wasn't an entertainer? Give me a break.

I know what you're thinking. Saying that an entertainer can't be

World Champion doesn't make too much sense. Well, you're god-damn right. That's because he never meant "entertainers." They were just too scared to say what they were all really thinking.

Triple H went on to defeat Booker T in a forgettable and ultimately meaningless *Mania* title defense. No need to be sad, though. Look on the bright side. At least there was racism, right?

April/May/June 2003: Kevin Nash

You may remember Kevin Nash as the wrestler who took the bow at MSG, then took off and left Hunter to take the punishment. Well, by mid 2003, he was back and better than ever.

Well, that's not entirely true. Big Kev was actually in worse shape than ever before. He had just returned from one of the strangest injuries in wrestling history. It was so bizarre that it was almost monumental. It's a moment that ranks right up there with "Shockmaster" Fred Ottoman tripping and losing his mask upon his wcw debut. It was truly crazy.

On the July 9, 2002 edition of wwe *Raw*, Nash returned from surgery on his bicep. After missing a few months of action, Big Daddy Cool was back in black and ready to address the wwe audience. This address led to a match — his return match — on the same show. Kev teamed with the Big Show, Chris Benoit, Eddie Guerrero and X-Pac to face Rob Van Dam, Spike Dudley, Bubba Ray Dudley, Booker T and Goldust. It would be the return of the seven-footer with a propensity for womanly hair and leather pants. That's right. Big Kev's back.

In 1994, Nash won his first World Title by defeating Bob Backlund in about nine seconds to capture the wwf Title. Eight years later, it would take Kevin nine seconds to injure himself upon his return. That sound you hear, my friends, is Father Time waiting for no man.

Kev was tagged in by Pac and rushed immediately after that nappy-haired entertaining chauffeur, Booker T. After an Irish whip and boot to the face, Nashy ran to the good guy corner to ambush Book's allies. Suddenly, he hit the mat clutching his leg and we had to wait until the following April to see The Man They Call Diesel do his thing again.

Welcome back! See you later!

Sad, though, when you think about it. Kevin was getting on in years and he needed to slow down. While still physically imposing, he simply couldn't perform on a level befitting a main eventer. Couple that with the strange injury on live tv featuring him returning to action for less than the amount of time it takes to count during a game of Hide and Seek and you have some real issues to deal with. Maybe it's time that Big Daddy settles into the mid-card and helps elevate young talent.

Nah. Let's feud him with Triple H . . . for three months.

Why? Well, it could be that wwe saw something special in Nash. Perhaps it knew a way to connect him with the audience. Maybe it had big plans that would make him a superstar. Whatever the reason, I'm sure that being Hunter's buddy didn't have anything to do with it.

Actually, it had a lot to do with it. At least, I hope it did. If this wasn't booked out of friendship, then as I mentioned earlier, these people have no idea what the hell they're doing. You have a show that is having difficulty creating new stars. So what do you do? You book your champion in a three-month feud with an older star who breaks down more than a 1987 Plymouth Duster with sugar in its gas tank? You just featured a main event conflict between Scott Steiner and Triple H and saw how quickly the audience will turn on a top hero who can't cut the mustard in the ring. So what do you do? You put Trips in a prolonged altercation with a guy who hurt himself walking across the ring. Amazing.

On a good note, WWE wasn't focused solely on this conflict at first. It was busy introducing Bill Goldberg to its audience. Bill's feud with The Rock was the top conflict for awhile. That was the main thing the pay shows were built around. Even though The Game was World Champion, he knew he could sit and allow the dream match of Bill-Rocky to truly sell the show. This left Hunt and Kev to stink up the place with a bad match and not have to be featured as the most prominent match on the card. I tell ya, if I was Hunter and wanted to do my friend Kevin Nash a favor by feuding with him even though he wasn't in the condition to be put in such a high spot, I'd do it during the time period when I'm not expected to sell the pay-per-views. Wouldn't you? It's almost as if he knew the matches were going to suck out loud and planned accordingly so he couldn't be blamed. That's just me talking, though. Pay no attention.

They wrestled each other in a six-man match at Backlash. They faced off in singles encounters on *Raw*. They tied it up at Judgment Day. They battled in a Hell in the Cell Match at Bad Blood. It was the feud that refused to die.

You know what the conflict was based on? Well, remember earlier when we talked about Hunter's being punished for the Madison Square Garden in-ring bow by his buddies? That was about seven years earlier. That bow in 1996 signaled the end of the "Klique." Now, in 2003, it was that kliquey friendship that this whole altercation was about. Yawn.

It was weird. Triple H hates Shawn Michaels, but likes Kevin Nash. Shawn Michaels hates Triple H, but likes Kevin Nash. So who would Nash choose to be friends with? Will it be Shawn or Hunter? Hmmmm. What a cliffhanger! Who will Kev choose to hang out with or play Legos with or whatever the hell he does with his friends? I can't wait to find out! I'm being sarcastic right here. What a dumb way to push a title match. Who's going to be friends with who? Who cares?

By the tail end of this feud, the fans were so down on Kevin Nash that you could hear the yawns during his matches. No one cared. Even the announcement that Nash and Helmsley would tie it up in a Hell in the Cell match, the company's top attraction, couldn't save it. As a last ditch, desperate attempt to get the crowd back into the Bad Blood pay-per-view, WWE introduced *New York Times* bestseller and Sock Puppet Stuntman Mick Foley to referee the event. With two weeks until the show, World Wrestling Entertainment pretty much stopped mentioning Kevin's name on-air unless they had to.

> Folks! Order *Backlash*! It'll be bestselling author and former multi-time WWE Champion Mick "Mankind, Cactus Jack" Foley refereeing the most hellacious match in WWE history, the Hell in a Cell, when the Cerebral Assassin — the World Champion, The Game, Triple H faces off against Kevin mumble, mumble . . . Call your local cable operator for availability!

In the end, it was the H Man once again coming out on top while Nashy galloped off into the sunset in search of other companies that he could act too cool for. That's not important, though. The important thing is that WWE managed to go another three months without the World Champion elevating someone in the eyes of fans. That's what's important. Who's next?!

July–December 2003: Bill Goldberg

Before explaining Bill's conquests in World Wrestling Entertainment, it's important to look at two quotes from him prior to signing with the company:

I personally believe that everything I've stood for when I got into the ring would be compromised and succumbed to the circus-like atmosphere that's out there, and that's putting it mildly — *Desert Sun* interview, January 17, 2002

Then there's Hunter Hearst Helmsley. I've heard he's said some derogatory things about me. Whether he has or not, when I met him, he was a cocky prick. I'd love to turn heel on his ass in the ring any day. — *I'm Next,* Crown Publishing, 2000

So . . . what do you think this guy's chances look like in World Wrestling Entertainment? Come on. Have you been reading this book so far?

Bill Goldberg owed his career to eating opponents. It's a style that creates stars while killing promotions. Bill ascended to the top of wcw by beating everyone on the payroll and doing it quickly. In the end, it helped to create a solid name but hurt the credibility of the rest of the roster. It also helped to introduce Goldberg to an unrealistic world of wrestling and a spoiled attitude. His rise to the top was unlike most wrestlers. There was little in the way of dues to pay. He was treated like a star from his debut. wcw's management loved him. He needed to learn reality. Luckily there's someone up north ready to teach it to him.

There was a scene in the movie *The Toy* where Jackie Gleason wants to prove to his son, Eric, that the business world is a cutthroat place. Thumbing his nose at liberal Jack Brown, played by Richard Pryor, Gleason orders his employee, Mr. Morehouse, to drop his pants. When Morehouse questions the order, he's told that his job rests on whether or not he obeys it. His pants fall and the Great One tells his boy, "that's reality." Strangely enough, the pants-dropper was played by Ned Beatty. You might know him as the camper who was forced to squeal in *Deliverance.* Weird, huh? Did he specifically look for high profile roles that involved flashing everyone his underpants? But, I digress. That's beside the point. We were talking about how Goldberg learned reality.

This time around it was Mr. McMahon playing the role of Jackie Gleason. Goldberg was Ned Beatty. Squeal! Squeal!

Bill debuted on World Wrestling Entertainment on March 31, 2003. No one could really figure out why he was being signed to begin with. Bill Goldberg wasn't a wrestler per se. He was a killing machine. He smashed people and car windows with ease. In the fantasy world of wrestling, that means you have to beat everyone. You have to be unbeatable and quick in your brutality. That's how Bill made his money. That's what made him a star.

One problem, though. WWE already had a guy like that. It had Triple H. He was the man who was dominating *Raw*. He was the man who held the World Title. And, as you read earlier, he was the man Goldberg called a cocky prick in his book. Now Billy Boy was a member of the one-ring circus . . . and the cocky prick was the ringmaster. Would WWE possibly use Billy in a way that would maximize the amount of money he could bring in?

So Bill debuted and two weeks later WWE used him the way it should. It took this behemoth barbarian who's known for being destructive and easily enraged and scripted him in a segment with Goldust. For those that don't know, Dust is an effeminate character who strays into homoeroticism while emulating dead 1950s Hollywood stars. Wow. That sounds horrible when you write it out like that. I guess we're just desensitized. Anyway, Goldust told Bill they're cousins. Get it? No? Come on. Goldust and Goldberg? Actually, I don't get it either. Anyway, the flamboyant Dustin then took his trademark Marilyn Monroe–esque wig and placed it squarely on Bill Goldberg's bald head.

That happened two weeks after they debuted him. Two weeks.

Remember that question from two paragraphs ago about making money? The answer to it is no. No it didn't. It's as if WWE watched Goldberg fighting in WCW during his career high. Vince sat there salivating and thinking of all the ways that he could use Ted Turner's golden goose to his advantage if he could only sign him. All he kept thinking was, "What a talent! What a specimen! If only I could get him into a fruity blonde wig, we'd be gold!"

Actually, he probably wasn't thinking that. During Goldberg's high point, McMahon was still competing with WCW. If he'd signed Bill back then, he probably would have used him correctly. This was 2003. WCW was dead. It wasn't about money. It wasn't about competition. It was about revenge.

So they get him into the wig and it's all downhill from there. It was time for Buffalo Bill to start his push to the World Title. That trip began in July and went straightforward to *SummerSlam*. Goldberg-Hunter 1 would be magic.

It would also be watered down and ridiculous. With the biggest name in World Championship Wrestling outside of Sting on their roster, WWE had a chance to book a dream match. Berg, although involved in dumb angles from time to time, was always portrayed as a dominant force in WCW. He beat Raven for the U.S. Title on his first try. He did the same with Hollywood Hulk Hogan's Heavyweight belt.

Yes, I know it's fake. However, it's part of his character. He's a crushing machine. Every scripted form of entertainment stays true to what works for its characters. For Bill, that's what worked. It's what set him apart and made him a cash cow. That's why people liked him. Without that dominance, he was nothing more than a Stone Cold Steve Austin rip-off.

Whoa. Hold up, Goldberg Fan. That's not me talking. That's Vince McMahon. In an August 1998 AOL chat, Vince was asked how he felt about the still unproven Berg and responded, "You mean the Stone Cold rip-off?"

That was pretty indicative of WWE's stance on Bill when he was in WCW. It was so bad, in fact, that the company took Duane Gill, a small older wrestler known for losing most of his matches, dressed him up like BG and called him "Gilberg." The entire character centered around mocking Goldberg from afar. When Duane came to the ring, he made ridiculous faces and would copy Bill's limited move set before being defeated. Wow. WWE actually devoted an entire gimmick to making fun of another wrestler outside their company. That should tell you how Vince and friends felt about Billy Boy.

So here we are. The guy they mocked, Bill Goldberg, now worked for them. It's his first shot at Triple H's title. Would Hunter suffer the same fate as Raven and Hogan? Would The Game help Berg's character by losing convincingly in their first encounter? You haven't figured out the way the game works yet? Are you drunk?

In case you haven't guessed by now, the answer is no. No, he didn't. Making matters worse, Bill's first title shot wasn't even in a one-on-one match. It was part of the Elimination Chamber. Remember that fun? The wrestlers involved in this one were Goldberg, Hunter, Chris Jericho, Shawn Michaels, Randy Orton and Kevin Nash. Yes — Kevin Nash. Yes, I know what I said before about his horrible main event run. I wasn't lying. I told you the truth. Yes, I know it's insane that he was still booked in main event slots. The book's called World Wrestling Insanity for a reason. If WWE did things that make sense, it would be called World Wrestling Making Sense. Then again, that wouldn't be as catchy. Thankfully, it doesn't make any sense. Thus, we keep the original title.

So Bill Goldberg loses to Triple H in the Elimination Chamber. Straight up, he loses. The guy whose entire persona was based on his spectacular winning streak had lost in his first WWE title shot. You remember Ken Jennings' spectacular winning streak on *Jeopardy*? OK. Now imagine he follows that up by appearing on *Wheel of Fortune* and misspells everything. While you still remember his amazing victories on *Jeopardy*, you can't forget the fact that he was trying to spell cat with a "k." Get what I mean? In other words, Triple H should have waited and allowed Goldberg the chance to steamroll through him on match #1 before eventually showing him his strong, wedding ring–wearing pimphand.

So The Game slaps him down and people can't believe it. The closing moments of that match couldn't have been any more perfect. It was the absolute best way to get the title on the newcomer. Fans were dying for it. Goldie was poised for it. The image of Bill preparing for victory in the Elimination Chamber was a great one. It was a magic moment. The crowd was on its feet and Trips looked all but finished. Suddenly, Ric Flair slid Triple's trusty sledgehammer into the ring and he used it to knock the Goldbergler out for the pin.

Talk about botching a huge opportunity. There's no denying that. Some people could argue that this was a "tainted win" for The Game considering his use of a weapon. They'd be making an invalid argument, though. This was an Elimination Chamber. The match had no rules. Sledgehammers weren't illegal. Triple H beat Goldberg. Had Goldberg procured a sledgehammer, he could have used it too. No tainted win here, folks. Berg lost. That's it. wwe missed a big opportunity. End of story.

So, how did they celebrate this botched booking decision? Guess. Go on. Guess.

They had a party in the ring after the match.

I'm not joking. *SummerSlam* was on Vince McMahon's birthday and following this horribly missed opportunity to properly use a performer they purchased, they had an in-ring party once the cameras stopped rolling. They should have unfurled a big banner that said "Happy Irony Day!"

So Trip and Goldie embarked on a rematch the following month. Hunter lost, but it just didn't have the same oomph. Bill had already lost once. Now he won. Blah. The first encounter took a lot of steam out of this one. The only way to really build up a babyface title rematch is when the original encounter ended in controversy or by cheating. As was said, if there's no rules, it's not cheating. Goldberg wasn't cheated out of a win in the first match, he just lost. Then he won. While it looked like he was on top of the world with his title, the fact of the matter was that he was simply 1–1 with Helmsley.

The real intrigue of this title change was Triple H's pending hiatus. The Game had signed on for a supporting role in *Blade 3* and had to take time off for filming. That's right. Hunter was gone! No more! For once, wrestling fans would have a chance to see what *Monday Night Raw* would be like without Stephanie's husband on everybody's mind. Monday nights without Triple H. Could you imagine?

Keep imagining. Two weeks later, Trips figured out a way to keep his name on everybody's lips. He appeared in a pre-taped skit and placed a bounty on Bill's head. Anyone who could take down Goldy while The Game was away would collect $100,000.

Yes. You read that right. Hunter was going to be off television, but the main storyline of the show still centered around him. It was still all about The Game. Keep in mind that when wrestlers take more than two weeks off from WWE, they're all but written off the programs. Funny how when Triple H leaves for awhile, it's written into the show. It's not only written into the show, it becomes the show's main storyline.

Just to make sure that Triple H's bounty stayed on everyone's mind, WWE gave Goldberg an opponent who definitely wouldn't outshine Hunter. They gave him Mark Henry.

A former powerlifting Olympian, Henry was famous for playing the role of "Sexual Chocolate" in the late 90s. The most memorable on-air moments for Chocolate included engaging in oral sex with a transvestite and watching his 80-year-old lover, Mae Young, give birth to a rubber hand. This actually happened many years ago and I still have no earthly idea why she gave birth to a rubber hand. No clue.

> Relax, James. So Mark Henry goes up against Bill. What's the big deal? Maybe this could be the storyline that gets him over as a main eventer. Maybe people will look to Mark Henry as a top guy. Maybe Goldberg can get him over.

Well, why is Goldberg being used to get people over when he's less than a year into his WWE stint? Why is a character that needs to dominate all foes feuding with someone who's been looked at as a mid-card wrestler for years? What crapfest lottery did he win in order to get put on elevating-the-mid-card duty?

It didn't matter anyway. It wasn't about Bill or Henry. It was about Hunter. The entire duration of Goldberg's championship reign was overshadowed by someone who wasn't even in the arena half the time. It was all about Helmsley. The announcers brought it up during Bill's matches.

> *Who's gonna collect Triple H's bounty, King?*

The interviewers brought it up during his promos.

What do you think about Triple H's bounty, Bill?

Everybody talked about it.

Would you like fries with that, sir? By the way, who's going to collect Triple H's bounty?

If this were an episode of *The Twilight Zone*, Goldberg would just be seeing swirling circles and people's faces flying by saying "Bounty . . . Bounty . . . Bounty . . ." This title reign wasn't about the Champion. It was about the challenger . . . who wasn't on television . . . who had happened to be married into the family. Basically, it was "The Story of Triple H's $100,000 — featuring Mark Henry and Bill Somethingorother."

Even funnier was the fact that H never specified that this bounty was for wrestlers only. In essence, he offered it to anyone. This led to rampant speculation that a desperate fan would try to really hurt Goldberg and then ask for the reward money. It also provoked me to buy a brand new crowbar in case I saw Bill at the supermarket or something.

Now, as I said at the start of this section, you can tell Bill Goldberg's entire story through quotes. What you read earlier was pre-WWE. The following are during WWE. In fact, it's right smack dab in the middle of all this. Trips was still hovering over Bill's character and he had just offered money to any person on earth who would hurt him. I wonder how Goldy felt about all this. Time to check in on the second installment of quotes from Bill. We call these two the "during quotes":

[Vince McMahon's] passion for the business is unmatched by anyone who I have ever seen and I think that shows through with the success that he's had. And I'm just very appreciative that he had the confidence in me to be an integral part of the program . . .

In the beginning it was a little standoffish. There's a very hesitant feeling out period, I think. In all honesty, I look at him not only as a boss but also as a friend. He's totally different than what I would have imagined. – *Byte This!*

Whatever you say, Champ.

Goldberg wasn't the only one making quotes, though. In her fourth quarter conference call, shortly after Bill's *Byte This!* appearance, WWE CEO Linda McMahon called Bill "a disappointment." That's gotta sting. Maybe just a little.

The $100,000 Grand Prize in "Who Wants to Beat up Bill" was collected by Dave Batista, a returning stablemate of Triple H. It didn't make a difference, though. This wasn't about Dave. You know the deal by now. It was about The Game . . . oh, and Goldberg. Almost forgot him.

Anyway, Trips and Goldy rematched yet again at the *Survivor Series*. With the bounty now gone, collected by Hunter's Evolution stablemate Batista, Berg was free from Hunter's gamy grip. He closed the contest by taking out all of Triple's henchmen with a sledgehammer and then tossed it aside in order to pin the former Champion on his own.

There you go. It looked like maybe Bill was on the right track after all. He finally beat Triple H conclusively and shut down all the nay sayers. Maybe the Goldberg push would be a success after all. Maybe all the critics were wrong. This whole thing was finally starting to make sense.

Less than a month later, Bill lost the strap back to Hunter. It was in a Triple Threat Match with Kane. So much for making sense. On that note, the slide down the ladder of success began.

Goldy bummed around for a little while longer. He appeared at the yearly Royal Rumble. The Rumble is an event where participants choose entry numbers from 1 to 30. Numbers 1 and 2 start off and every two minutes the next number runs to the ring and joins the fight. You have to be the last man not tossed over the top rope in order to win. The prize is nothing to sneeze at, either. In fact, the winner goes on to face the Champion at *WrestleMania*. Obviously you want the last number for the best chance at victory, right? Right.

Bill was #30.

He lost.

From there, he had a mini-feud with announcer John Coachman and mid-level tag team La Resistance. His final WWE appearance came at *WrestleMania 21*. He fought Brock Lesnar in a "dream match." It was a dream that became a nightmare when the fans, angry over both Goldberg and Lesnar leaving the company after the contest, chose to slam the two of them with a barrage of boos. It was a sad and fitting ending for his time with World Wrestling Entertainment.

It turned out to be the end of Billy's time in the rasslin' ring altogether. While it may appear that he had a short career, BG actually experienced more than some wrestlers could ever dream of. In WCW, he was overpushed and worshipped by management. In WWE, he was misused, ostracized and ridiculed by management. Sure, Goldberg brought some of that upon himself by going to WWE. That was his choice. However it also balanced out his time with Ted Turner's company tremendously. How many performers can go from one end to the spectrum to the other, in terms of their career and character, in such a short time frame? Some guys wrestle for 30 years and never experience that.

The saddest part may have been that Goldberg himself called it before even entering the promotion. Remember those quotes he made before his debut? Yeah? Remember the ones he made during his time there? OK. Well now, here's the closing chapter. Read the third and final installment as Bill's career came full circle:

> [Working for WWE] was one of the most agonizing, excruciating and miserable times of my entire life. I enjoyed the fact that you could get 10,000 to 40,000 people screaming and chanting your name, but having to listen to these morons backstage and live with them was not good.
>
> Being part of [WWE] was like being part of the Hindenburg going down. It just left a bad taste in my mouth.
> **— Goldberg, TBO.com, May 2005**
>
> I'm done. Vince McMahon can kiss my tuchhus.
> **— Goldberg, halftime interview at Lakers/Spurs game, June 2004**

The Crippler Chris Benoit's story is a strange one. It's unusual because it all started off so well. It looked damn near perfect. It was going so well, in fact, that Triple H actually took time away from the World Title picture to focus on other pursuits after he lost to Chris at *WrestleMania*.

We're getting ahead of ourselves. Benoit was on *Smackdown* and won the Royal Rumble that Goldberg didn't. His prize included a shot at the World Championship. Rather than challenge the top title-holder of his own brand, Brock Lesnar, he chose to turn his attention to Helmsley's *Raw* strap. It was finally going to be Chris Benoit's time.

The Crippler's time was always just about to happen. For years, he was just about to be champion. wcw handed him a World Title win, but he chose to vacate the strap and leave the company over differences with management. Instead, he decided to join wwe. Once he got there, he was considered an unofficial World Champion, so to speak. He'd never lost the Ted Turner title and now he was in McMahonland. What do you think happened? What do you think might happen if Vinnie Mac was able to sign away the kinda sorta World Champion from his chief competition? Guess. Come on.

Oh, alright. Triple H, the World Champion at the time, beat him in his first match. Chris debuted and Trips pinned him. The following week on *Raw*, Benoit and his friends actually joined up with The Game and became his henchmen. This was back in the year 2000. Hopefully this gives you an idea of how long all of this stuff has been going on.

While in World Championship Wrestling, Crips had been saddled with a nickname. Christened "Vanilla Midgets" by Kevin Nash, both he and Dean Malenko faced what would be a continued criticism throughout their careers. Nash joked that they were bland. He laughed at their size. He explained his inspiration for this nickname in an interview with the *Pro Wrestling Torch* newsletter in 2005:

> It was one of those deals where I loved what they did, but at the same time, it's like watching a porno with a guy with a four inch c–k. It doesn't matter how he moves. I'm a big guy, I want to watch big guys wrestle. That's just me. I didn't appreciate what they did, but at the same time when I took over the book and Eric told me, "I'm paying these guys 500, 600 thousand dollars a year, you have to get them over," I said, "F–, because you did bad deals with people, don't expect me to get people over. F–, it's going to be hard. When a guy looks like your neighborhood gardener on the gas, it's tough. If a five-foot-seven guy walks through the airport, it's not gonna be . . . I'm very surprised Vince [McMahon] did that [signed and pushed them]. Vince was never that guy. Vince was always, like, "When he walks through the airport, he's got to turn heads." He wanted that bigger than life guy.

Nice, huh? You may remember Kevin Nash from earlier in this chapter. He's Hunter's friend with the bad knees. Now Triple was feuding with one of the vanilla midgets. It was a four-incher against The Game. Come now, I'm sure Helmsley had nothing but the best intentions towards the Vanilla Crippler . . . er uh, the Canadian Midget. Uh . . . something like that . . .

So Benoit challenged Hunter and the two of them suddenly found Shawn Michaels wrapped up in their issues as well. Somehow the Heartbreak Kid got himself into the thick of things and *WrestleMania* became more than Benoit-Helmsley. It became Benoit-Helmsley-Michaels for the World Title.

In a stunning and celebrated victory, Chris forced Hunter to tap out to his Crippler Crossface submission and captured the World Title. It was an amazing contest that saw all three men use innovative situations and believable interaction to tell a story within the ring. No matter what's said about Triple H, or Benoit and Michaels for that matter, in this book, you can't take this match away from them. I could write 2000 pages about why Hunter Hearst Helmsley's character is hurting the WWE product, but it wouldn't stop me from commending him for his performance in this particular main event. In fact, his wrestling skills are rarely questioned. His promo and speaking skill are a different story, though. In a big match situation, however, Trips always comes through.

Let's make that clear. This seems like the best time to mention it. Provided his opponent can have a competent match, Triple H will always deliver in a big match situation. He takes pride in what he does from bell to bell. He's an amazing in-ring performer who realizes his legacy will one day boil down to videotapes of pay-per-views. You don't want to present anything less than your best when you know that generations of people will see it through the magic of videotape.

One month after *WrestleMania*, the three squared off again in a rematch at *Backlash*, WWE's post-*Mania* pay show. It was another great performance and this time Chris got the submission win over Shawn Michaels. Crips was really coming into his own.

Then it happened. Triple H moved on from the World Title and embarked on his own magical adventures. Sure, he still chased the World title, but there were bigger fish to fry. Because of this, Benoit's involvement on the show seemed almost like an afterthought. His title reign was nondescript and his storylines followed suit. They never gave him anything tangible to work with. His feuds were about nothing. His character was about nothing. He was a great wrestler with a World Title. He wrestled well. That was his thing. Who needs a wrestling promotion to do that? It's the wrestler's job to wrestle well. It's the company's job to then sell that wrestler to the audience. In this case, only one of the two parties involved fully held up their end of the bargain.

Also, Benoit's involvement in Triple H's upcoming feud with

Eugene took a toll on his credibility too. We'll get to that in a second, but in a nutshell, WWE had the World Champion play a supporting role in Hunter's feud with a gimmick wrestler. As I said before though, we'll get to that in a bit. First let me tell you about Shelton . . .

March 2004 Mini-Feud: Shelton Benjamin

Ready for this one?

World Wrestling Entertainment held its Draft Lottery in March of 2004. It was a randomly selected trade-off between the two WWE brands. Created to generate fake competition between shows in order to make up for the lack of genuine competition after Mac bought WCW, the Lottery helps to freshen up the programs. *Smackdown*'s roster and *Raw*'s roster are both fair game. If your number gets called, you're up. That's how it works.

Well, that year *Raw* chose Shelton Benjamin. Shelton had been a long-running member of the "World's Greatest Tag Team." When he was sent packing for the other show, his partner, Charlie Haas, was left to fend for himself on *Smackdown* . . . until he and his wife, Tough Enough 2 winner Jackie Gayda, were fired less than a month after their wedding in 2005. Those were their problems, though. WWE had Benjamin poised to achieve bigger things.

Bigger things indeed. On the March 29 edition of *Raw*, Benjamin pinned Triple H. It was shocking. It was amazing. Here was a virtual unknown in the world of singles wrestling scoring a pinfall over the indestructible Hunter Hearst Helmsley.

The two had a rematch the following week. Guess what? Helmsley lost by countout.

In fact, Triple H never scored a real win over Benji for the remainder of the year. The closest he came was getting a victory in a "Beat the Clock Match." However, despite winning, the H Man didn't "beat the clock." Therefore he lost. Once again, it's shocking.

Now ask yourself something. How could this happen? After all, considering how all of his feuds have worked up until now, it's pretty out of character for Trips to participate in a storyline that doesn't end with him as King God of Everything. Weird, right? So what's up?

If you smell a rat and call shenanigans, then you win a shiny new carrot. Why did this angle play out the way it did? Why was someone so obsessed with keeping himself two notches above the rest willing to play the beatdown boy in a feud with a rookie? I'll tell you why.

Remember that Draft Lottery? You know, the one that sent Shelton Benjamin over to *Raw*? OK. Well, that same Lottery also sent Triple H to *Smackdown*. That's right. The Game was a blue shirt–wearing *Thursday Night Smackdown*er for all of one week. One week? Actually, less than one week.

Get this. Following his Draft, *Raw* General Manager Eric Bischoff threw a fit. Why? Because he couldn't run *Raw* without Hunter! No kidding. That was the premise of all this. The idea was that Hunter Hearst Helmsley was so valuable to *Raw*, it couldn't run properly without him. Amazing. So how did Eric get back his self-appointed golden goose from *Smackdown*? He made a trade.

He traded former WCW Champion and Hunter's *WrestleMania* challenger from the year before, Booker T . . . and Bubba Ray Dudley . . . and D-Von Dudley.

Yes. In exchange for Triple H, Bisch traded Booker T and both Dudley Boys. One of the most decorated tag teams in wrestling was sent over in a group package with Booker for one man. It was all for Hunter.

Talk about stroking one's own ego. It took these three men to equal one McSon-in-law? We weren't talking about three weekly losers here, either. They all had skills. They all were respected by fans. Now they were punks who needed to be paired up with each other in order to get the Magical H Man back on *Raw*.

Think about it, though. What does that truly say about Triple H? After all, the idea is to have the champion feud with someone and have that someone go on to stardom, right? You want to elevate different stars. You do that by feuding them with your top name.

Well, Booker T feuded with the top name. He feuded with Hunter. Hell, he even challenged Triple H for his World Title at a *WrestleMania*. He was the top challenger and the #1 contender at the biggest show of 2003.

Now, a year later, he needed to have two other guys by his side in order to equal one Helmsley. What the hell is that about? If anything, it sounds like Book ended up in far worse shape than he was before facing the Champion. Not only that, but the Dudleys looked like garbage in all this too. Hey, at least Triple looked good in the end, right? Actually he came out of it looking really good. He was better than three of *Raw*'s top guys put together. How's that? It must have been like Christmas for Triple. He should have been on cloud nine. After all, in one foul swoop, he was able to reinforce his star power, cut down the potential of three others and ensure his character was stronger than ever.

Right after that, he did this little program with Shelton Benjamin. Strange that the first time that the Cerebral Assassin truly "put someone over," it was right after an angle that helped to bury three other men. Read into it any way you want. I'm just saying that the timing is strange. Don't you think?

June-August 2004 Mini-Feud: Eugene

Vince McMahon likes to push the envelope. In fact, he likes to destroy the envelope. Vinnie Mac hates that envelope. He pushes it, pummels it, pulverizes it and sometimes even pees on it.

That how we got Eugene Dinsmore, the mentally handicapped nephew of *Raw* General Manager Eric Bischoff. Played by Nick Dinsmore, the character was something that both Nick and the company agreed on. According to World Wrestling Entertainment, this particular hot button character would be presented in a tasteful manner. Many people were skeptical because . . . uh, well, nothing WWE does is in a tasteful manner.

So on April 5, 2004, they debuted Eugene. He played up his character to the hilt. Paired alongside the stuffy William Regal, who grew fond of him over time, Dinsmore embarked on a rise that most newcomers dream about. Within weeks, he was a top name on *Raw*. On a program constantly condemned for having a glass ceiling, Gene was proving the critics wrong. He was on a one-way trip to the top of the card. Glass ceiling, shmass shmeiling. Watch this inspiring character rise to new heights.

He did . . . until he ran into the Ceiling Master.

By June, the seeds were being sown for a Triple H–Eugene program. To help boost Dinsmore's star power prior to his feud with The Game, WWE utilized both The Rock and World Champion Chris Benoit to generate fan interest in him. Often times, Benoit seemed to be all but forgotten when it came to *Raw's* storylines because of the attention paid to Dinsmore's character. Fans started wondering how a company that spent so much time centering everything on Triple H, under the rationale that he was World Champion, could change its stance so drastically when someone else had the strap. Funny how it always seemed to work out that way.

So Benoit did back-up for Eugene. The Rock embraced him as a friend. How did Dinsy repay them? Well, when asked who his favorite wrestler is, he said, "Triple H." Although many wrestling fans were up in arms over this, they figured that considering his gimmick, it made sense that he would like Hunter.

This had to be a dream for The Game. Finally, a feud with an opponent that kisses his butt during promos. How does it get any better? During his squabbles with Scott Steiner and Goldberg, he had to listen to them berate him. Now he had someone who would call him "the best." Then Eugene would suck on his own fingers and wave.

It got even better than that. Trips was not only able to have his ego fed through Dinsmore's promos, but he also got to outsmart him! He convinced Eugo that they were best friends. Triple, alongside his apprehensive Evolution partners, reached out his hand in friendship to Din and did everything he could in order to rip him from his friends, Chris Benoit and William Regal.

It also allowed him the opportunity to say things like this:

> I'm bigger than The Rock. I'm bigger than Chris Benoit. I'm bigger than anybody, Eugene. I'm the biggest friend that you have.
> — **Triple H**, *Raw* July, 2004.

Lovely.

After claiming to be on the up and up as it related to his feelings, Hunt offered Dinsmore a chance at a dream. He would get to fight Triple H in a match!

Look, I'm going to be honest with you here. Eugene's feud with Triple H was actually booked correctly. I don't want to review each and every segment because they all served some sort of purpose for Dinsmore's character. In the end, he turned out to be a pretty marketable character, put over big time by Hunter Hearst Helmsley.

Sure, Chris Benoit took a major hit in all this. He looked like a punk for playing less than a starring role in a storyline despite being the World Champion. He took a bigger hit when Eugene eventually chose to leave him and Regal behind to join Evolution's friendship circle briefly. (Come on, you didn't think WWE would have Eugene choose them over Hunter at first, did you?) In essence, this program kicked Chris Benoit's ass. With so much concern over poor widdle Gene Dinsmore, no one cared about the Rabid Whatshisname.

This wasn't about that, though. This was about Eugene. It was about getting his character over with the fans. People now had a new name to applaud on *Raw* and we shouldn't begrudge them of that. Not everyone that Triple H feuds with goes on to look bad in the end. That's just us being cynical.

Oh wait, hang on. This story has a twist at the end.

Dinsmore looked good at the end of this feud . . . for about two weeks. Then, in what can best be described as the September *Raw Amnesia Special*, he met Triple H for a final time. Inside of a steel cage.

Now keep in mind that WWE spent endless weeks building Nick's character. He wasn't just "handicapped," he was a rassler! He deserved respect. The fans finally got that. They respected him. The announcers respected him. The wrestlers respected him. He was a powerhouse and wanted nothing more than to prove he could do anything he set his mind to.

By September 6th, Gene was a month removed from losing to Helmsley at *SummerSlam*. Although unsuccessful, Dinsmore was still treated as a genuine wrestler by the commentators. He was treated with even more respect two weeks later when he embraced interference from Randy Orton and scored a pinfall on The Game.

Respect was gone by September. Those who once held Eugene in high regard from the announce table, now feared for his well being. Why? Well, this young man was stepping into the ring with — wait for it — Triple H. Yes, the same Triple H he beat a week earlier. The same Triple H that he wrestled at *SummerSlam*. Same guy. Same bouncy hair.

Only now, we were all worried about him. Jim Ross was reacting as if someone smothered his dog. The whole thing reeked of a burial. Now that the Cerebral Assassin had transitioned to his next victim, er, uh, opponent, Randy Orton, Dinsmore seemed more and more like a sacrifice for Trips. This wasn't a match. It was an execution.

Eugene was demolished. It was insane. Months and months of work were put into building this guy and WWE undid it all in one night. Not only did Hunter beat him, he also bloodied him. After the match was over and the Gamy One was victorious, he returned to the ring and demolished him with a sledgehammer.

There wasn't too much Eugene for WWE fans after that. He wrestled Eric Bischoff that October at *Taboo Tuesday*. He did a tag title run with William Regal. You know, nothing special. A year later, he was all but forgotten by WWE's writers.

You can't say that Triple H discriminates. Handicapped or not, he'll bury your ass all the same.

August 2004–January 2005: Randy Orton

What I'm going to say may seem like a big statement considering all that you've read so far. It's true, though. Ready? No one got screwed like Randy Orton did. No one. There's not one person on this list that has a right to be as upset as Orton does. No one. Goldberg's close, but no dice. The Legend Killer should get the Golden Screw statue to symbolize this honor.

No one could have survived in the position that Randy was put in. Never before in the history of wrestling, maybe even television, has a hero been presented so poorly. The sheer number of missteps, blunders and backward logic that was put into his segments, feuds and predicaments would make anyone shake their head in amazement. Even if you've never watched wrestling a day in your life, you'd take one look at this and know it's nonsensical. You don't need to be a wrestling promoter genius to see that the handling of Randy Orton was ridiculously booked. You just need to be awake.

It was so bad that it made you wonder if other forces were at work here. After all, Trip . . . well, before going off on a tangent, let me tell you about the whole thing.

It started at *SummerSlam 2004*. Randy Orton, the 24-year-old Evolution member, was set to face World Champion Chris Ben . . . uh, something. It doesn't matter. People were ignoring him at the time anyway.

So Orton was on the road to stardom. He prefaced this title shot by doing an in-ring promo on an August *Raw*. In this segment, he called out all the 24-year-olds in the audience:

> Pop quiz. What did you do when you were 24 years old? What did you do? What did you do? Up there. Fat girl in the front row, what did you do when you were 24 years old? Did you pay off that student loan? Did you finally get that brand new set of wheels? Did you finally move out of your parents' basement? Well, I'll tell you what I got my mind set on. It's on becoming the youngest Heavyweight Champion . . . ever! The youngest World Heavyweight Champion in history. And this Sunday at *SummerSlam,* nothing – nobody – nobody – is gonna stop me from having my date with destiny!

Sounds like a hell of a heel, huh? What a bad guy! The fans thought so. Six days later, Randall pinned Chris Benoit on pay-per-view and made good on his threats. He became the youngest World Champion in wwe history. Boo! Boo, bad guy!

This was it. Finally, fans could see what life would be like with another bad guy holding the title. No more Triple H. It was time for Randy Orton.

This raised all sorts of questions, though. For starters, Hunter had to be jealous, right? (I mean on-air Hunter. We know that the off-air one was.) His gimmick was that he was obsessed with the title. He wanted nothing more than to squash all those who attempted to take it from him. Now, his partner had it. What's up with that?

It's an interesting predicament. Could Trips actually turn good? Could Orton call for a mutiny in Evolution and grab the reigns of the group from under The Game's nose? After all, he was the new heel on the block. This was the future. Hell, the kid was 24.

That's an achievement, no matter how you slice it. Randy had performed so well as a bad guy that he ascended up the ladder and captured the top title. He had all the mannerisms of a heel. He was cocky and aggressive. There was nothing likable about him. People tuned in to watch him get beat up. He always seemed to win, though. It made you tune in again just to see if someone could shut him up for good.

Ort had played the good guy early on in his career. It tanked. He had funny hair and no character whatsoever. It wasn't until he started popping up during important *Raw* segments with an "RNN Special Report" updating his arm injury that people started to react. Mr. RKO was born heel. What would Triple H do?

Oh, that's simple. The night after Randy won the World Title, Triple H and Evolution turned on him.

So what does that mean? It means that Randy Orton was now a hero. That's right. A hero.

All of his mannerisms are heel mannerisms. Any success he's ever had in his career has been as a bad guy. Fans were eagerly awaiting title defenses by an evil Orton. Everything about everything as it relates to Randy Orton was about being bad.

Not only that, but Randy Orton was catching heat from people before even taking the title from Benoit. Was he too young? Was he too inexperienced? Could he carry the strap in a way befitting a Champion or would he just be another name on our totem pole of failures? So that was going on too. Now let's put all the facts together.

Randy Orton had to prove he was worthy of carrying the World Title. He was only a good character as a rule breaker. The night after winning the World Title, they turned him into a good guy.

Are you kidding me? This was insanity times ten. He's a bad guy. That's how it works. He won the title because he was a believable bad guy. Now, at the critical point in his proving stages, you turn him good? Why not make him wrestle with one arm tied behind his back? While you're at it, you can have small ferrets bite his knees during interviews.

This was blatant sabotage. To not see that this was a mistake, you'd have to be completely inept when it comes to wrestling and storytelling. As I already mentioned, I respect Hunter Hearst

Helmsley too much to call him inept. That's why I call it sabotage. Which would you call it?

> So, James, he turned good. That's a bad move, but it could be salvageable. What made Randy turn good? Did he finally tell Triple H to shut up and then attack him? Oh wait, maybe he stopped Hunter from cheating in a match with Eugene or something. No, no, no, I got it! He saved a Diva from the evil clutches of Evolution.

Wrong. Wrong. Wrong. He turned good because his friends beat him up.

That's it. That's what made him see the light or whatever. We were supposed to cheer for him just because Triple H attacked him. There was no other reason given. I'm not kidding. There was nothing. Until the moment that The Game turned his thumb upside down and ordered Batista to drop him to the ground, Orty was firmly planted by the side of Hunter and his buddies. In essence, the babyface turn of the new World Champion was all about the fact that he'd been rejected. World Champion Reject. It has a funny ring to it.

OK, OK. Here's the best part. Ready? Less than a month after becoming the youngest World Champ in WWE history, Randy Orton lost the title back to Triple H at the pay-per-view *Unforgiven.* The rationale people cite for the title change? You're gonna love this.

Randy Orton wasn't clicking too well as a good guy. It's always better for the hero to be chasing the villain World Champion. That's why it made sense that Trips should hold the title and Ort should chase it.

Wow. The rationale about a hero chasing the villain is usually true. The only problem with this scenario is that there was no reason for Randy Orton to be a good guy! They created this backwards scenario and then flipped the title back to Triple H based on it. If Randy had never been turned babyface for no reason, he wouldn't have to be chasing a villain. He'd be the villain! He'd be the champion! It's amazing.

Even more insane is that WWE took three steps to do one. Here's what they did:

Scenario # 1

1. Randy Orton wins the World Title from Chris Benoit.
2. Randy Orton turns good.
3. Triple H wins the World Title from Randy Orton.
4. Randy Orton chases Triple H's title.

Instead, they could have just done this:

Scenario # 2

1. Triple H wins the World Title from Chris Benoit.
2. Randy Orton turns good.
3. Randy Orton chases Triple H's title.

Notice that under scenario two, Randy Orton doesn't have to lose to Triple H? Also, notice that scenario one makes it seem like Hunter is winning the strap to bail out Orton. That wouldn't be necessary if we just did scenario #3.

Scenario #3

1. Randy Orton wins the World Title from Chris Benoit.
2. Triple H does something else for a while. Maybe he takes a vacation to the Poconos or something. Let everyone else play, Hunter. You had your turn.

That didn't happen, though. We did scenario # 1. I know what you're thinking. You're thinking that it can't get much worse, right? Oh man. You are very wrong.

Right around the start of Randy's time as a hero, WWE decided that the best bet would be to keep his persona as is. You see, Randall may be a good guy now, but he's going to be an arrogant good guy. Yes, you read that right. Arrogant good guy.

How the hell do you swing that? An arrogant good guy? You could say this was sabotage, except this is the same company that routinely presents good guy rapists. So, it may be part sabotage, but incompetent writers also have a lot to do with it.

Many people like to point to The Rock in this situation. After all, Rocky Maivia is one of the, if not *the*, most recognized name in wrestling. The Great One played an arrogant good guy. Look at how well that worked out.

Well, they're right in the sense that Rocky was an arrogant hero. But they're comparing apples and oranges. There's one fundamental difference between The Rock's character and that of Orton.

When Rocky Maivia played a villain, he was a cool villain. He was a cool villain because he used certain mannerisms and catchphrases to taunt his opponents. He would ask if we smelled what he was cooking. He'd raise his eyebrow. He'd gallop back and forth across the ring and drop a quirky elbow on his battered foe. People dug that. It was funny in a way. Many wrestling fans wished that the Great One was a good guy so that they could see him do all of his gimmicks to bad guys. They were just salivating for a chance to cheer on his eyebrow, elbow and cooking.

Randy didn't have any of that. Randy had nothing. He was a bad guy. That's it. There was no catchphrase. There was no elbow. The only things he had were the RKO, a finishing move used constantly by stars of the late 90s, and spitting in his opponents' faces. That was it. Fans were supposed to rally behind a finisher they were burnt out on and phlegm on someone's nose. Oooo. Where do I sign up for the "Randy Orton Played Out Finisher and Loogie Face Fan Club?"

So it wasn't the same. Ort had nothing. WWE tried to rectify that by having him drop to one knee before hitting his opponents with the RKO. Big whoop. No one cared. The arrogant hero would have to march forward, even without mannerisms that the people could get behind. Sounds like pretty poor planning for an eventual hero, huh?

I mean, if the plan was to turn Randy into a good guy, why not start planning early? Why not create these personality traits prior to his turn? Make the fans want to cheer for him. Then when the turn comes, people would be excited to finally support him. Instead, WWE had Randy come out the week before his turn and insult all the 24-year-olds in the audience. Hell, he insulted everyone. Sounds like true preparation for the future star of *Raw*, huh? Then again, it's pretty obvious that was never the plan.

So it gets better. Now the problem was that WWE needed to keep Randy and Triple H apart. Since Hunter had maneuvered himself into the position of heel champion, Ort had to play the role of title chaser. He needed to keep himself occupied while the company tried to stretch his title match until *WrestleMania* the following April.

Yup. They wanted to wait until April to really give Mr. RKO a boost. You read that right. After a quick rise to the top, capturing the title at a record age, Randy's entire career was put into slow motion. Following such strong momentum, the company now had to slow him down. Again, no one saw a problem with that?

So they had to hold off on giving him a title. How? Well, again it gets worse.

The night after Hunter won the Championship from Orton, he came to *Raw* and wanted to have a big in-ring celebration. In the center of the ring was a giant cake. Trips and Evolution all did their little promos and then turned to the humungous dessert in the middle of the ring. They realized that none of them had ordered such a big treat for the celebration. What was in there? Hmmmm.

Randy Orton was in there! Oh hee hee hee! What fun! Duh.

For starters, it was obviously Orton in the cake. If you didn't realize it was Randy hiding inside the second you saw it, you should go outside and slam your head into the pavement. Who else could it be? Rip Taylor?

What I really hated was that it made Randy Orton look like a tool. Why did he go through all this just to jump Evolution? Even worse, how long had he been planning this attack? You'd think that it's pretty self-defeating to go into a title match and plan your revenge around your opponent's victory party, right? I know. I know. It's fake . . . but come on!

Let's get back to the no-rematch for a long time situation. How could WWE keep Randy preoccupied? Who could he fight? Well . . . When he was a baddie, Orton was a member of Triple H's stable, Evolution. Besides Randy and The Game, the Evolvers included 55-year-old Ric Flair and powerhouse Dave Batista. See where this is going?

He could feud with them! That's right. Let Randy mess around with old Man Flair and the Animal for a while. That would keep him busy till his Gameship was ready for him.

Right off the bat, things were done backwards. Orton confronted

Ric Flair on an episode of *Raw* and delivered the often-repeated "You're Ric Flair Speech." It's basically a younger wrestler telling Ric that he's a legend. The Nature Boy is reminded of his past achievements and all but begged to leave Hunter's side.

The funny thing about this is that Ric Flair always ends up choosing Triple H. He's done it plenty of times before. When the angle ends, Naitch ends up attacking his "new ally" and then rejoining his Evolutionary buddies. Stupid Randy should have seen it coming considering that . . . you know, he was partners with them for so long. You'd imagine he'd know their tricks by now.

No dice. That night, Randy squared off against Evolution's Dave Batista in the main event of *Raw*. Guess what happened. Go on. You can guess. You know it. Flair turned on the young arrogant hero and sided with Triple H's gang. Making matters worse, the Nature Boy's interference led to Batista actually scoring a pin on Orton for the finish.

A month earlier, he was the hottest heel on *Raw*. He was the youngest World Champion ever and people were eager to see the show with a new top villain.

Now, he was a lame hero that no one wanted to cheer for. The only reason given for his good guy act is that his friends threw him away. He'd been duped by Ric Flair twice and lost the World Title to Triple H already. Now, he'd been pinned by Batista too. It keeps getting better and better.

Randy went on to face Ric at *Taboo Tuesday*. This feud led to the famous "I make virgins bleed" speech from Flair on an episode of *Monday Night Raw*. When the match finally happened at *Taboo Tuesday*, Randall was successful in his bid to defeat the 55-year-old inside of a steel cage. It was the closing moment of the night and many thought it was a good sign for the Legend Killer. He defeated a true legend inside of a hellacious steel cage. How could that do any damage to Randy Orton?

Well, afterwards he shook Ric's hand. At the time, it was looked at as a historic moment. Here's this gracious kid shaking hands with a true legend, someone who gave him a chance to prove his worth. Ort must really respect The Nature Boy.

That's what we thought at the time. In hindsight, taking the big picture into account, Randy Orton just shook hands with a guy who stabbed him in the back twice within a month and a half. It's some-one who blatantly chose Triple H over him on two occasions and thought nothing of putting the boots to him when the order came down. Storyline-wise, Orton shaking Ric Flair's hand really made him look like a wuss. Would you shake the hand of someone who did that to you? I wouldn't . . . and I'm not even trying to be a hero.

So now you have an arrogant, friendless, wussy good guy with no mannerisms losing to two of the three former allies in his stable. You're just dying to buy that T-shirt, right?

Again, I know what you're thinking.

> Two out of three, James? That's not soooo bad. He didn't lose to all the members of Evolution, right? After all, he still was too good to be stopped by the 55-year-old manager-type in the group. There was still something to this kid. If he lost to all three of them, I could understand being upset.

On October 25, 2004, Randy Orton officially lost to all three of them. In the main event of *Raw*, Ric Flair, at 55, pinned Randy Orton. The prematch stipulation specified that Orton would never again receive a title shot.

Going into this match, WWE chose to ignore the handshake that these two shared less than six days earlier. WWE didn't even push this showing of respect, which at the time seemed to help Randy's cause. Instead, it was presented as a rematch. It was a rematch that Cowboy Bob Orton's son lost. He lost it to a guy that was about the same age as Cowboy Bob.

Again, the rationale was that World Wrestling Entertainment was trying to build up suspense for the eventual Hunter-Orton show-down. To do that, it needed to have a reason why Randy was shut out of title shots. That was the rationale.

So the way it does it is by having him get beat by every member of Evolution. He tries to be friends with them, but they keep turn-ing on him and attacking. Makes perfect sense to me. Why not just strip him naked, dip him in tar and let him attach feathers to his ass before he wrestles too? That would probably get him over as a super-star quicker than what they're doing.

When the going gets rough, you know WWE's solution . . .

I don't get it. We can't seem to get this constantly jobbing, arrogant, gimmickless, gullible hero over with our audience. What are we doing wrong?

We need an Elimination Chamber match. We need to have Triple H beat five guys at once.

By Jove, I think you got it!

That's right. Once again, World Wrestling Entertainment rolled out the Elimination Chamber. This time it was for a debuting pay-per-view entitled *New Year's Revolution*. It was held in Puerto Rico and the event's name made no sense.

I should point out that Orton, while losing to the members of Evolution, regained his losses. He had both defeated and lost to Ric Flair. Same thing with Dave Batista. One victory eluded him. On January 25, 2005, one week before NYR, Randy Orton defeated Triple H.

Hooray! He won! He won! New Champ, right? Nope. The title wasn't on the line. How did he win? Every other participant in the Chamber interfered. All of them. I'm talking Chris Benoit, Dave Batista, Edge and Chris Jericho. It was far from a convincing win and really strange that WWE would put it on free television.

After all, wasn't this the dream match? Wasn't this *WrestleMania*? Why would it give away a match that it's spent forever and a day trying to avoid in order to present at *Mania*? It seemed sketchy. It seemed like maybe some people were having second thoughts about last summer's sure thing.

The Elimination Chamber came and Hunter won. He beat all of them. Once again, Orton lost and that's all that anyone cared about. His hot streak was officially dead. He was a wandering character with no real personality as a hero who lost to everyone. Ugh.

The thing that must have sent the young Ortonion to the hotel bar that night was that the focus on Triple H's eventual challenges wasn't put on Randy. Announcers and writers zeroed in on Dave Batista, one of The Game's last allies. When he was pinned by Orton, Trips appeared to watch and do nothing. It was meant to plant seeds in the fan's minds in the hopes they'd eventually cheer for Dave. It was also designed to transition Triple away from the Legend Killer. His time was over. Experiment done.

It was so done, in fact, that the next night on *Raw*, Randy interrupted Evolution's in-ring celebration. When he arrived, Helmsley laughed in his face and referred to him as a loser. Orton replied that he wasn't a loser and could prove it.

You know what his proof was? It was videotape of Triple H not helping Batista. Huh? Yeah. Makes no sense right? I guess he wanted to breed some dissention in Evolution, but why preface the video as proof that you're not a loser? It's not proof. It's proof that Hunter doesn't like his friends. It's not proof that you're not a loser.

It's like saying, "I'm not afraid of spiders. Here I'll show you. Look look. I'm eating a tuna fish sandwich. See? I told you I wasn't afraid of spiders." Silly example, I know, but sadly, it's fitting.

So at this point, WWE embarked on a storyline that would give Randy his title shot two months prior to the prestigious *WrestleMania*. It would be at the pseudo-prestigious Royal Rumble pay-per-view. Angered by his Chamber loss, he demanded a one-on-one rematch for the belt. *Raw* General Manger Eric Bischoff agreed on one condition. Ort had to defeat Batista in a singles match later that night.

This match had nothing to do with Randy Orton. He was an afterthought. He could have been Gerald Rosenbaum from Staten Island for all they cared. The match was about continuing Triple H's storyline with Dave Batista. How so? Well, it ended with The Game trying to interfere. He was stopped by Dave, who was then pushed into the steel chair Hunter was holding and pinned. After the win, people were talking about the eventual babyface turn by Tista, instead of the title rematch for the forgotten Orton boy.

The two met at the Rumble and Orton lost . . . again. He appeared to suffer a "concussion" during the match and found himself defeated. At first, many thought that his fake concussion might lead to a new character. Instead it was mentioned on TV for a week and then forgotten, just like he had been by those who said he would be the star of *WrestleMania*.

There's no denying it here. Even if you think that everything else in this chapter wasn't done deliberately by Triple H, you have to admit that this is downright insane. No one — absolutely no one — has been so blatantly squashed as Randy Orton was. There's no way that anyone who knows anything about wrestling could have constructed this feud the way WWE did and expect positive results. In fact, anyone who hasn't had a full frontal lobotomy within the last ten minutes couldn't have put this feud together this way and expected positive results. If this wasn't sabotage, then Triple H knows nothing about the wrestling industry whatsoever. If it was, then . . . oh, who are we kidding?

It was.

> You know, I've watched wrestling my whole life and I've been around it. I went and watched the cards every week for pretty much my whole life and when I got into it, I didn't want to believe it was about politics. I didn't want to believe anything that heavy could make that much of a difference. But as I go on and as I look, especially as I get older and look at other businesses and other people who have jobs and tell me about the politics at their jobs, I'm thinking "You ain't really seen nothing." Because the manipulation and the games that are played [in wrestling] are very real and they're played by people who, some are very good. Some are masters. Some aren't so good. But you really have to have a stomach for it. You really have to have a mindset for it because the political and conspiracy theories that go on, more times than not, where there's smoke there's fire. How could you let something that simple be that crappy by changing a heel into a babyface like that? Don't know. Was it intentional? Don't know. Do you think somebody's trying to hold on to something? Don't know. Do you think somebody's trying to bury somebody? Don't know. But just the fact that you're thinking that kind of tells me, hmmmm, if you look deep enough and you really got to the heart of the matter, you could almost imagine the conversation. That's kind of what I've done and when I watch *Raw* and *Smackdown* now, I'm imagining some of the conversations that have gone that led to things getting on the air, things that changed, or why someone is no longer on the show. — **Tom Pritchard**

February–July 2005: Dave Batista

Well, this is it. We've come to the end of the road. Batista became the man to finally put a genuine wedge between Triple H and his World Heavyweight Title (or "Precious" as he calls it lovingly in his head).

That's right. With countless challengers coming at him for years, Helmsley's fatal blow was dealt by the man who was by his side for most of it. It was the guy who collected that spotlight-stealing bounty on Bill Goldberg's head. It was the wrestler who helped to punk out Randy Orton like a . . . uh, well, punk. It was Batista, the former Deacon for Reverend D-Von, who stepped up and finally broke the chain of misery. He finally ended the obsession.

How'd he do it? Well, it was tough. Every attempt was made to stop him, but he journeyed forward. His storylines went from well-planned to insane. However, it all seemed to balance out in the end.

It started at *New Year's Revolution*, as we mentioned in the Randy Orton section. Symbolic of Orton's fade-out, Tista's fade-in occurred during the Elimination Chamber. It was there that we learned of Hunter's true selfishness. He was a glory hog. He didn't care about anyone else . . . fantasy wrestling-world speaking, of course.

The night after the Chamber match, Randy Orton arrived to show the footage to Batista and Hunter. He wanted to be the catalyst in Evolution's explosion. I guess he was. Some consolation prize, eh Legend Killer?

Up until now, the rifts between Tista and Triple were small. They involved Hunt calling him "stupid" (a recurring theme in the H-Batista war). They were nothing. It wasn't until the hugely shocking and unexpected videotape was revealed that everything got hairy.

Here's the funny part about this amazing video revelation. When Orton showed Tista the footage, he was surprised. That's right. He was shocked. Now, I know what you're thinking. You're thinking that Randy showed video from something that didn't air during the pay-per-view. This footage must have been top secret stuff that no one had seen. It must have been another camera angle or locked in Al Capone's vault or something.

Nope. The footage Randy Orton showed Dave was from the *New Year's Revolution* pay-per-view. The damning videotape was something that aired the previous night on PPV. That was the big friggin' shocker.

So, what you're saying is that within 24 hours of a grueling main event match, Dave Batista still hadn't seen the video tape of his loss . . . or run into anyone else that had either. No one mentioned it to him at the hotel? The airport? Denny's? The funky suit store?

No one. No one watched the pay-per-view, I guess. For a group like Evolution, people who pride themselves on studying the sport, not watching tape from a big match is ridiculous. That's supposed to be a given in the scripted world of wrestling. The loser of the match gets paid less. Hitting the referee is an automatic disqualification. Top wrestlers watch tapes from their matches. It's how it is.

It wasn't that way for Batista, I guess. Hopefully, he found time to get his hands on a copy of the 2005 Royal Rumble. Tista won that thing. You might remember the Rumble as the thing that catapulted Chris Benoit up the ladder (before he slid back down quickly) the year before. This time it was Dave winning a shot at the top title in World Wrestling Entertainment. He was still allied with The Game despite some spats here and there, but ultimately they were friends till the end. Hi-de-ho. Ha ha ha.

So now comes the big question. Who did Deacon Dave go after? Was it Hunter Hearst Helmsley, the *Raw* World Champion, or John Bradshaw Layfield, the *Smackdown* World Champion? Decisions, decisions.

Everyone on planet earth knew Tista would eventually choose Triple H. After all, everything was leading to this. It was all about the disintegration of the Boys Club. The group was no more and the writing was on the wall. It was just a matter of playing the waiting game.

The night after the Royal Rumble, DB came to the ring and thought about what to do with his chance. Trips said he would be honored to defend his title against Davey Boy. However, before he could really get into it, an interview with the *Smackdown* Champion appeared on the big screen.

JBL, the *Smackdown* Title holder, was often vilified by those who follow the wrestling. A good ol' boy who seems to be the inspiration for a Denis Leary song or two, Bradshaw's sudden success was just that — sudden. No one saw his title reign coming and when it finally did, no one could believe it.

After years of being nothing more than a mid-card bully, John saw his name changed and gimmick overhauled to embrace his real life propensity for stock trades and radical right-wing views. He got a cowboy hat and a limo and was christened "JBL." He was like J.R. Ewing from *Dallas*. Well, except that the guy who played J.R., Larry Hagman, wasn't into hazing rookies and never got fired from MSNBC for goose-stepping across a wrestling ring in Germany. Those two honors belong to John Layfield and John Layfield alone. God bless you, John. Heil you.

Anyway, Bradshaw was now pushed upon Dave as the main antagonist he should stop. Triple H did everything to push this horribly transparent plan upon the Royal Rumble winner. For some reason, Tista bought it all at face value. The announcers did too. It was obvious that the Helmsley character was trying to misdirect Dumb Old Dave. Anyone could see it. A five-year-old could see through the trickery. However, Deacon Dave and everyone on *Raw*'s payroll couldn't.

No one knew about all this until Hunter himself decided to make it known. On the February 21, 2005 edition of *Raw*, Helmsley explained the whole thing to Ric Flair. He told him the tale of how he ordered the JBL interview to play during Dave's decision-making promo. He explained that he had created a limousine identical to Bradshaw's in order to push Batista towards choosing Layfield. He gave it all up in one big confession.

Flair, who's either an idiot or an idiot, responded that he had no idea. It was a total surprise. After hearing it, he danced around and did his trademark "Whooo."

Wow. Seriously, he had no idea. He had been Hunter's butler or whatever for about two and a half years, yet couldn't see through these plans by now? People who didn't speak English could read between the lines in this one. If Helmsley had sprayed my TV screen with Windex, it wouldn't have been any clearer.

Here's the hokiest part of the whole thing. After weeks of this blatantly obvious secret plan being kept quiet, Triple H finally revealed it . . . but spoke so loudly that Batista, who was listening at the door, heard him.

Someone should learn to whisper. I mean, come on. This is the same guy who glued the horns from a bull onto his limo in order to trick Batista, but he doesn't know to keep his voice down while he's at work? Where does he think Dave works? Geico? He works for WWE, Champ. Chances are, he's backstage. Shut up. Anyone knows that. If you work at McDonald's and you hate the guy on the fry machine, you know to whisper when talking smack about him at work, because chances are he's around. After all, he works there. Duh.

So Dave Batista heard this ridiculously transparent ploy and headed to the ring to deliver his decision. Trippie joined him and reminded him of why he should go to *Smackdown* and fight the goose-stepper in a cowboy hat. According to Hunter Hearst Husband, if Tista were to head to the other brand and win the World Title, Evolution would rule the world! Trips on *Raw*. Dave on *Smackdown*. It's a magical conjunction.

No go, Gameboy. David informed his soon-to-be-former friend that he was aware of all the trickery. He'd heard it with his own widdle ears. It didn't matter, though. He knew his choice this whole time. A fight broke out and ended with Hunt laying on the ground. An angered former Deacon stood above him as the show came to an end and said:

> Hunter, I'm staying right here on *Raw*. *WrestleMania*, I'm taking the World Championship . . . from you!

Well, that's just fabulous. Here it was. Finally, the feud that fans wanted to see. Dave Batista would be facing Triple H at *WrestleMania*. This was what we were all banking on. There's no way that bad writing and Hunter's ego could get in the way of this. That's not to say that they didn't try, though.

The following week, World Champion Hunter delivered one of his most ridiculous in-ring tirades in recent memory. Although he was presented with a sure-thing opponent in a red-hot feud, Sideburns McGameface still had to put his own spin on it. We couldn't just have a match. We needed some sort of nonsensical bizarre reason to care about the match. That's the WWE way.

Check out this quote. It came out of Triple H's mouth the following Monday on *Raw*:

> I am Triple H! I am The Game! I am the best in this business! And that is not a damn catchphrase! That is not something made up to sell T-shirts or put asses in seats! That, my friends, is a fact — plain and simple. Fact! Don't believe it? Look around! Check it out for yourselves. Look high. Look low. There is not a person on God's green earth that can do what I do in this ring better than me! And now . . . and now, because he sat under the learning tree for two years, Batista is the guy? Let me tell you something about Batista. Batista is a child. He is a 300-pound child. In this ring, I am his father. — **Darth Hunter,** *Raw,* **February 2005.**

Who's your daddy? Triple H is. You know the irony of this? With the way WWE politics work, Batista would have a better chance at success if he actually was Hunter's son.

Here's the best part. During this feud, which was going well for the most part, Hunter actually found a way to bury someone who's already in the ground. He turned his attention to Randy Orton and reminded the fans of why he'd fallen off the charts.

The Game pointed out that Batista would go the same route as Randall. According to Helmsley, Randy was on top of the world when he was in Evolution. He had the World Title. He had it all. Now, without them, he sucked. Trips even pointed Ort's approaching *WrestleMania* match with The Undertaker and referred to it as Randy "begging for the scraps of *WrestleMania*." Holy God.

Why did he do this? Was Triple H going to fight Orton again? No. Was Randy siding with Batista in this war? Not at all. Was Randy Orton involved in this feud at all? Absolutely not.

There was no reason to mention Randall's hard times, other than to toss one last shovel of dirt on his grave. That's it. Barring intentional character assassination, nothing justified Triple's biting comments about the Legend Killer.

> But James, Hunter's a bad guy! He doesn't tell the truth. Fans know that. They'd see through his words and it wouldn't affect Orton at all!

Sorry, Charlie. Nope. You see, bad guys tell lies when they tell lies. If Triple H said that Randy Orton was scared of pea soup, then that would be lying. He didn't say that. He said that Randy was nothing without Evolution. That statement was true. People knew that. It was obvious. What Helmsley said was what everyone else was already thinking. For some reason, he felt the need to verbalize it on television. Had he not, some people might not have noticed. After all, that's WWE's job. It's supposed to present wrestlers in a positive way and downplay any hard times they hit. Luckily, we had Triple H to shine a flashlight on those hard times.

It's like a guy who breaks up with his girlfriend and says, "She was better off when she had me." If the girl is now dating the quarterback of the football team, then the ex-boyfriend is obviously lying to make himself look cool. If the girl is now dating a leper who smells like manure, then the ex-boyfriend is telling the truth. Well, Randy Orton wasn't just dating lepers, he was doing the whole colony. Trips made sure we knew that. Why? No reason. Just because.

Later that night, during the in-ring contract signing between Batista and Helmsley, an argument ensued. Trips went off on a long, drawn-out tangent. Tista simply called him an "asshole." This led to a brawl, which led to *WrestleMania*'s main event.

When *Mania 21* finally rolled around, Triple H defended the World Title against Batista. In the closing match of the evening, Davey B pinned the Champion and sent fans home with the image of himself standing tall with the title in his grasp.

All done, right? Not quite yet. You see, even though Batista had downed the Gamy One in a convincing manner, there was still the issue of rematches. These two had a few future battles still raging in their bellies.

What was the theme of the first rematch? It was Dave Batista's fear. Now, it's never a good idea to paint your newly crowned hero champion as fearful but WWE did so anyway. What was that fear, you ask? Was it his fear of success? Was it his fear of killing someone else? Was it his fear of becoming arrogant now that he was the top star on *Raw*?

No. Darth Hunter with his funny facial hair told the viewing audience that Dave was afraid of . . . the Pedigree. For those that don't know, the Pedigree is Triple H's finishing maneuver.

Helmsley prefaced this point by defeating both Hurricane and Rosey, a duo who would go on to capture the tag team titles about a week later, and then delivering a speech. Hunter likes speeches:

> Batista! You see this? One second . . . one second is all it takes! One Pedigree and that is you. You don't believe me? I vow to you that by the end of the night, this will be Batista. I will Pedigree his ass in this ring! It doesn't matter to me how big he is.

Yeah. Hmmm. Afraid of the Pedigree, eh? Funny how this didn't come up prior to their original match, right? You'd think that the fear of Hunter's finisher would have come into play the first time they fought. It didn't. Tista beat him. Unless this phobia sprung up following his victory (which would be illogical considering he'd already fought Helmsley and beat him), it made no sense.

Backlash rolled around and Batista beat him again. We needed another rematch though. What could we do? It had to have a stipulation. Also, it had to be about something even more ridiculous than Tista being afraid of Triple H's finisher. How would WWE swing that?

Easy. It put them in the Hell in a Cell Match and had them give promos like melodramatic nine-year-olds playing Wizards and Warriors.

No kidding, kids. The match stipulation was a good one. Gameface had always done well in the Cell matches and delivered the goods. Tista was still a virgin in the HIAC environment, but Trips would break him in. He'd be the tour guide of hell.

I say that because apparently the two of them were actually journeying to hell. If you listened to them speak, you'd know it. It was a never-ending trek of ridiculous statements and grandiose preposterousness that helped sell this Cell.

They were going to hell. They were going to kill each other. They were going to take one another's souls and encompass that in the never-ending abyss of darkness that can only be found in the Cell. You know — the usual.

Here's a sampling of the dialogue taken from their Hellish Contract Signing:

> **Stephanie's Husband:** You just signed your own death warrant.

> **Deacon Dave:** Good. Cause you're gonna have to kill me to get this.

> **SH:** Really? You're gonna have to kill me to stop me. You know something, Dave. You and I, we've been through a lot, huh. I know one thing, no matter what happens in Hell in a Cell, when Vengeance is done, this thing between you and me is gonna be over for good.

> **DD:** You said we were going to hell and I was gonna meet the devil. At Vengeance, I'm gonna kick the devil's ass!

If you're not rolling your eyes right now, then you watch too many fourth-grade plays. This was stupidity for the sake of stupidity. I wonder if the other Masters of the Universe were planning on joining this match.

Oh, I almost forgot the best part of all this. Remember earlier when I told you about how "Nature Boy" Ric Flair convinced Randy Orton that he was going to turn good and join him? Remember how stupid it made Orton seem when Flair sneak-attacked him? After all, Mr. RKO was a member of Evolution forever. He's seen these games before. He should have known better.

You do remember? Good, 'cause the same thing happened to Batista on the May 23, 2005 edition of *Raw*. Flair befriended him. Flair attacked him. Gullible Tista never saw it coming. Why? Because he's a big dummy. I can't really think of any other reason.

I mean, he was a member of Evolution when Naitch did the same thing to Orton a few months earlier. He knew the deal. He's seen this story play out before. To not see it coming, even though everyone else on the planet could, was ridiculous. It made Dummy Dave with his Miami gigolo suit look like quite the fool.

When Vengeance rolled around, Tista won once again. Trips went down to the Champ in an excellent match. As per Triple H's cryptic comments weeks earlier, this feud was officially over.

The next night, Dave was drafted to *Smackdown* in the 2005 edition of the Draft Lottery. He brought his World Title with him while Trips stayed on *Raw*. Finally something had come between Helmsley and his shiny belt. Triple's obsession with it would have to wait. He was no longer on the roster that challenged for it. He wasn't on *Smackdown*.

That was that. Dave Batista broke the curse. He ended the tyranny. He stopped the insanity . . . at least as it relates to Triple H and the World Title. If this were a movie, we would get a still photo of Batista and some sappy music while the credits rolled. All was over.

⁂

So where was I? Oh yes. Sabotage versus stupidity. If you read everything listed, you can see that Triple H has made numerous missteps in his feuds. Opponents were portrayed poorly, overshadowed or downright squashed.

From the time between his wedding to Stephanie and the day the World Title left *Raw*, Triple H had 11 feuds. Out of those 11, only two opponents actually ended up looking better because of their program with him. Two out of 11? One, Shelton Benjamin, got his leg up just following Trippie's trade from *Smackdown* for three men. The other, Batista, seemed to persevere no matter how poorly the writing team presented him.

A year after feuding with Hunter, Booker T needed two men to equal one of him in a trade. Also within a year, Chris Benoit went from main eventing *Mania* with Hunt to wrestling an undercard WM ladder match with five other people.

Scott Steiner, Kevin Nash and Bill Goldberg were all gone shortly after their failed feuds with him. Their stints against the Champion did nothing to make fans interested in them. That says a lot. While they may have lacked some sort of charisma or determination or whatever WWE spins it to be, they still feuded with the top name on the show and ended up being worth nothing storyline-wise after it was over.

Speaking of which, Kane's feud with Hunter left him in a tailspin that ended up plaguing him for years. His character, once a monster and a monster only, now had strange sexual undertones. After the Katie Vick debacle, a storyline so bad that WWE purposely avoids mentioning it, no one knew what to make of The Big Red Machine. It was all thanks to his big program with Mr. H.

Eugene was doing fine until The Game ate him in a cage.

Then there was Randy Orton. The biggest sabotage of all. He was berated, burned, botched and buried. After a horrendous storyline that did more damage to him than any scandal could have ever done, Orton's stock sunk to new levels. Even after the feud was over and Randy was trying to regain what was left of his marketability, Hunt felt the need to drive one last nail in the coffin by reminding fans of Randall's descent. No one got screwed like Randy Orton. Not Goldberg. Not Bret Hart. Not Debbie in Dallas. Orton trumps them all.

So what do you call it? Stupidity? Is Hunter stupid? Is he just so piss poor at picking opponents and working with them that none of his feuds seem to benefit anyone but himself? How is it that a company's Champion, the flag bearer of the roster, can't find ways to make others look good? Isn't that one of the main jobs of a Champion? Feud with a foe and watch them rise in popularity by association? That's sort of how this business works.

Funny thing about Triple H, though. He's able to help out wrestlers who have nothing to do with him. I've spoken to many performers who've never feuded with Trips or appeared on the same show with him and they all had positive things to say. Some even spoke of ideas that he gave them to boost their characters:

> I got the chance to talk to [Triple H] right before my debut, with my gear and stuff. I had the full-on giant zoot suit with the hat, the feather, the cane, the coat and everything. He pretty much dissected it and took the hat away. Took the feather away. Took the cane away. Took the coat away. And it really did a lot for my costume. He made a good point. He said "Later on, the more you're on TV, we can always add stuff. But if you start off with it, then we really can't get rid of it." You know, so it made me look tougher. It made me look more like a body-guard. It made me look more like from the street by just going with the wife beater, suspenders and the pants. So he's the one that really got my gear squared away right before my debut with my segment with Josh Matthews. That was the only time I really got to work with him, but he was always way cool with me. — **Aaron "Jesus" Aguilera**

Let me understand this. Triple H is able to help wrestlers, appearing on the brand he's not on, maximize their gimmick potential through slight changes in wardrobe but can't seem to realize that Randy Orton was being buried weekly? He understands the subtle nuances of the business when it comes to other performers that he isn't facing, but can't even understand the basics when it comes to the ones he is?

Some people say it's not all on purpose, though. Well, if he was genuinely trying to help raise the stock of wrestlers in the eyes of fans, what went wrong? This was all an accident? He must be the most incompetent, inept, bumbling fool ever placed in a position of power.

Either that or he's a manipulative, political saboteur, intent on destroying anyone who might be a challenge to his position of power.

Which do you think it is? Did he do it all on purpose or is he a moron? I think it's on purpose. I think he's a manipulator. Why? As I said earlier, I respect him too much not to.

CHAPTER 6

Reality Bites

Don't buy into that crap. Are you nuts? How do I feel about the reality of it? How do I feel about the reality of the reality shows that are unreality? None of them are reality shows in the first place. They're all controlled and manipulated. So Vince McMahon is controlling and manipulating that. That's what you have to understand. It's his product. He has his fingers on it. That's why we can't allow ourselves to be only his product. Because if we are, that means the Americana has gone out of the world of professional wrestling . . . and it's very close to being gone. — **Terry Funk**

Lots of people watch the show *Desperate Housewives*. It's a torrid tale of women who live on Wisteria Lane. Each has her own quirks. Each engages in some sort of conflict and drama. Each represents a cross section of the audience. Oh . . . and each one follows a set script depicting what her situation will be every week. It's a scripted TV show and the characters live in a world that exists on-air.

Wisteria Lane doesn't exist in the "real world." It exists in ABC's world. The lives of the women who live there are not real. They're fantasy. Reality doesn't belong in fantasy.

Could you imagine an episode of *Desperate Housewives* progressing over the course of the hour, trying hard to hook you into their fantasy world, and then suddenly cutting to a reality contest to determine the new cast member? Seriously, picture it.

> I'm sorry, Carlos. I'm in love with John, our gardener, and there's nothing you can do it about it.
>
> Gabrielle! I'm so mad, I could kill you both right now! However, before I do that, let's bring out this week's Housewife Search contestants. Wahoo! Puppies! Remember folks, log on to ABC.com to cast your vote. Now, for no reason at all, these girls are going to have a jumping jack competition for ten minutes! Wheeee! Come, Gabby. Jump with me.

Sounds dumb, I know. It's not so dumb when you take into account World Wrestling Entertainment's tackle of reality TV.

Always eager to prove he's more than a rasslin' promoter, Vincent Kennedy McMahon has searched long and hard for other avenues to excel at. There was bodybuilding. There was football. There were movies. There were ice cream bars. None ever grabbed the world by their tail like wrestling though. Yeah, but reality TV is popular with the young people, right? Well, WWE could do that.

WWE did have a genuine reality show for a while actually. MTV aired McMahon's weekly wrestling version of *Real World* with a show called *Tough Enough*, back when it still thought Vince was considered cool. The program was bland at times and didn't produce any World Champions. Lucky winners went on to great things like losing their job, being fired and shitcanned. Out of the six winners chosen from the program's run on MTV, only one went on to a title run with the company. By August 2005, the co-winners of *Tough Enough* Season 1 and Season 2 had been fired.

Then again, they won a contest for a contract and a contract alone. That was all they were really given. Nothing else was needed. The allure of wrestling for the then-WWF was enough to bring in any fan of the industry. Back in the late 90s, everyone wanted to be a wrestler. In 2004, that number had dropped significantly since its high of . . . uh, "everyone."

That's the issue right there. What good is a contest if your prize stinks? I mean, a WWE contract seemed like an awesome prize back in 1998 when the world still watched wrestling and everyone on your block had an Austin 3:16 shirt. Nowadays, it's not.

> Ooooo, lucky me. I win the wrestling contract. Now I can make just enough money to feed myself for two years until you fire me. Thanks, WWE! I love Triple H! Honk! Honk!

No way, Jose. The world was onto this scam. A WWE contract didn't mean WWE stardom. Just because you win the TE Challenge, it doesn't mean you'll be the next Ultimate Warrior. You could wind up on the company's B shows, late on Saturday night, losing to guys who don't even have entrance music. That's reality, kid.

So, what does WWE do? Well, it decides that most likely it'll end up jobbing out every *Tough Enough* winner it has. It knows it. There's no way around it. So it needs to give fans a reason to care about this competition. It needs to get potential contestants to realize that this is for real. How do they do this?

Does it make the announcement early on that the winner of *Tough Enough* will get a World Title match at the first pay-per-view after the contest concludes? No. That would actually generate interest in the wrestling product, while giving the winner instant credibility. Why do that?

No. It made it ever better. It gave away a million dollars. Yup. WWE decided that since the contract prize, once a hot commodity, now stunk up the room, it should give away some money with it. It would be a good way to make sure that whoever wins gets treated like crap by everyone in the locker room the day he walks in. How'd you like to be the million dollar 19-year-old, walk into the dressing rooms for the first time, and come face to face with some guy who's been wrestling since the Ford administration and eats mayonnaise sandwiches because that's all he can afford? Sounds great. Maybe WWE should have given him a big bucket of red paint so he could draw a bulls-eye on his ass, too.

A funny story sprung up around the time that the contest was announced to the wrestlers by head producer Kevin Dunn.

According to people who were there, after hearing about the $1,000,000 prize, the outspoken and somewhat disgruntled WWE star Rob Van Dam raised his hand and asked if he or the other wrestlers were allowed to try out for the million dollar *Tough Enough*. He briefly stopped to look around, then turned to Dunn and said that he was asking because none of the wrestlers in the room were making money like that.

Amidst all the laughter, Kevin rolled his eyes and told Rob that he could not try out for *Tough Enough*.

Anyway, WWE put on the all-new *Tough Enough*. This time it's for a million dollars! Yeah! Hell's yeah! Oh, oh, oh . . . one more thing. MTV wasn't airing it.

Well, that sucks. Then again, it was expected. As we mentioned, almost no one is watching anymore. Whatever. It doesn't matter. What channel was airing it? I bet it's better than MTV. After all, with a huge amount of coin on the line, there's no way WWE would present this in any way except top notch.

Well, it was UPN. It was the lucky channel. Not bad. Now the next question is what time, right? It was on Thursdays, around 8:00 p.m.

Time sound familiar? If you're a wrestling fan, you know it's when *Smackdown* had aired on the station for years. (If you're not a wrestling fan, you're probably thinking that's when *Seinfeld*, *Friends*, or *The Cosby Show* aired, depending on your age.) Yes, you read it right. *Tough Enough* actually aired *during Smackdown*. Its competitions were ten minutes long and they were wedged into the fantasy TV world of WWE wrestling.

Like Carlos jumping up and down with the Wisteria Lane hopefuls, *Smackdown* jumped from fantasy to reality and back again all in the same show. It was mind blowing in many ways, but you gotta do what you gotta do, right? I know that makes no sense, but it's hard to think of a rational reason for this decision. Rather than hurt your head by thinking too hard, just repeat, "gotta do what you gotta do." After a while, you'll feel better and stop requesting logic from these people.

Let's get back to the Tough Enoughers. You're probably wondering how these young men were trained? Quite tough, actually. Stories circulated of daily sprints in Titan Tower that would culminate in vomiting. The road to WWE Superstardom is a tough one and these youngsters had to prove they were "tough enough" in order to make the grade. So they were worked to the bone, pushed to the breaking point and forced to endure tiring struggles in order to keep their position in the contest.

Sounds like a good deal, right? After all, once fans saw this grueling workout on television, they'd surely respect the effort and strength that goes into being a conditioned WWE wrestler. Just wait until they see it.

We're still waiting. World Wrestling Entertainment didn't air that footage. In fact, I don't even know if there was footage. If there was, it didn't go out weekly on *Smackdown*. No. When it came to presenting the contestants to the voting public, something different was in the works:

Week one was simply video clips of tryouts. Nothing really stood out and the only highlight was a man, Marty Wright, screaming into the microphone during his promo. When asked how old he was, he said 30. After being asked again over and over by the judges, he admitted to being 40. Uh oh. That's a no-no. WWE judges cut him because they "don't like liars." Less than a year later, WWE decided that they do, in fact, like liars and signed Marty to a developmental deal. I still don't get that one. No other company would do that. If you got caught lying in your initial McDonald's interview, something tells me that you won't be grilling any Big Macs

So that's that. We moved on and things started getting wacky. The competitions, while strenuous behind the scenes, played out differently on television. By the second week of TE, fans started getting a better idea of why reality and wrestling blend together about as well as a tuna and crayon sandwich.

No one gets voted out on week 2 because one of the final eight, John Mayer, quits. He's not the same John Mayer as the singer "John Mayer," although I'm not 100% sure because, as I just mentioned, he quit the first week.

The competition on week one began with the seven-footer Big Show hazing the newbies in the locker room area. Show, that wild and crazy guy, really took it to these guys with shoves and pushes. Somehow they all ended up in the ring and each contestant was instructed to insult the Giant. After hearing the trash talk, he came out and each hopeful was ordered to take a bodyslam. While they all took the slamming, some didn't "sell" it. Rather than stay down and writhe in pain, a number of them — the most prominent of them being girly haired Dan Rodimer with his freaky smile — chose to stand back up and grin. Show helped him learn his place by delivering one more bodyslam . . . followed by a knee to the chest.

Immediate issues sprung up at Titan Tower regarding the broadcast of the footage. Some felt that the tape should be edited to make it look as though everyone had been decimated by Show without any sort of defense. Others wanted the tape to air as is. Both sides went back and forth with producers and editors being told different things for days. In the end, the tape aired mostly as is, with only some small edits. Seems like a lot of work just to broadcast a ten-minute segment of reality contestants getting fake bodyslammed for no apparent reason.

I mean, there was honestly no reason for this. As we mentioned, John Mayer had already quit the competition. There was no voting by fans that week anyway. Even if there was, I have no idea what seeing Big Show bodyslam them would do to help me make up my mind. "Hey, I like how that guy fell. He'll get my vote!"

I'm being unfair here. Why? Well, because the Big Show bodyslam stupidity turned out to be one of the most normal competitions they aired during the contest. If you can believe it, they actually found themed activities that were even less relevant to becoming a pro wrestler than that. Fans were asked to choose their winners based on such amazing feats of athleticism as:

- Dressing in drag and hitting on famous locker room hazer Bob Holly
- Making out with an 80-something-year-old woman
- Capture the flag

Lame, right? Then again, the prize for winning these events was pretty cool. After all, that's what reality shows are all about. On *Survivor*, Jeff Probst offers contestants blankets, cookies and all that good stuff in return for winning "reward challenges." For contests that don't involve winning rewards, there's immunity at stake.

Essentially, whoever comes out on top can't be voted out at the next tribal council. The prizes are what makes viewing these events fun for the audience. Without them, you're just watching nine starving people try to walk across a balance beam for ten minutes and then solve a puzzle for no reason. Who cares? That ain't fun.

So what were the prizes for these lame little events? Was it a chance to receive a private wrestling lesson from some of the top WWE stars? Nope, although that might have generated some sort of respect for the abilities of your established performers. Was it an opportunity to have their own match on one of WWE's late night B-shows? Nope, although that could have gathered more viewers for programs that are all but ignored. Was it immunity from being eliminated during the next vote? Nope, although that would have been . . . well, something.

Nope. WWE gave them nothing. These contests, lasting at least ten minutes each week, served no purpose. The announce team of Michael Cole and Tazz had to become creative and say that winning the event might "sway the vote," but that didn't mean much. The vote wasn't based on anything anyway. No one was wrestling. It was like *American Idol* without singing. What the hell?!

Not only that, but we also were treated to some impromptu "situations" during these rewardless challenges. For example, there was the night that Olympic Wrestling Gold Medallist and WWE's Credibility Kid Kurt Angle challenged shoot-fighting TE hopeful Daniel Puder to a "legit match" in the *Smackdown* ring. Puder obliged and damn near beat him by applying a known fighting hold to Angle's arm. The referee, aware of the predicament, counted a pinfall on Dan and gave the win to Kurt. Wrestling journalists went nuts. Many fans didn't even notice.

Why didn't they notice? Because WWE never mentioned it. Instead of acknowledging the closeness of the match, WWE spun it as if Kurt had easily pinned him in 30 seconds. Now, I want to make something clear. World Wrestling Entertainment was right to not acknowledge it. I'm not saying that they should have done full disclosure on this. Actually, I understand why they didn't.

You can't tell your audience that a virtual pre-rookie almost forced one of your golden children to submit. You also can't really reward his showing either. Otherwise, every young opponent who faces Angle for the rest of his life would try to take him down legitimately. I get that. Wrestling's fake. That's the way it should remain. You can't be encouraging every newcomer on the roster to take a shot at crippling your top stars when the opportunity arises. That's understandable.

What's not understandable is why they'd put themselves in that type of position. That's what happens when you introduce reality, no matter how controlled or manipulated, into wrestling. Wrestling's fake. That's the way it should remain. For years, people have said it to WWE fans. Now it's fans that should be saying it to WWE.

Reality? Come on, Vince. Don't you know that all this stuff is phony baloney?

OK, cold cuts aside, *Tough Enough* played itself out until only two men remained. It was Mike "The Miz" Mizanin, famous for his stint on MTV's *Real World,* going up against Daniel Puder, famous for hurting Kurt Angle's arm. The two would square off in one final battle as fans decided who was truly *Tough Enough.*

What was their last competition? Are you guessing "wrestling match"? After all, that's the job they're competing for. Why wouldn't they go out there and show what they're capable of? If you're going to expect the fans to pick World Wrestling Entertainment's newest in-ring performer, shouldn't they . . . you know, perform in the ring at some point?

Well, if you guess that they rassled, then — ding dong — you're wrong. Sorry. No wrestling match. Instead, they had a boxing match while wearing — wait for it — big boxing gloves. Yup. Big boxing gloves. It didn't have anything to do with wrestling. To be honest, it didn't even have anything to do with boxing. It was just stupid. Who cares though? They wore big boxing gloves! Hahaha! How funny! Look at those gloves! Those are too big for you! Hahahaha! How wacky it all is! Wacky, I tell ya!

Whatever. They boxed with big gloves on. WWE called it a Dixie Dog Fight. Other people called it other things. It was big glove boxing. It wasn't wrestling.

In essence, the entire thing boiled down to a popularity contest. Whichever contestant the fans liked most won. It was just like elections for a Junior High Class President, only there were no campaign buttons or flyers. There were just big gloves.

> I've asked myself over and over if the business has passed me by. If this is what the business is today, then it has definitely passed me by. That's not the business I grew up loving and watching. The problem is that I realize you have to change with the times and update things. But what made this business unique was unique personalities, unique characters and unique individuals that came into it. They wanted to perform and wrestle. They really had a passion for it. Some of those contests looked to me like they were made up to entertain somebody backstage watching. Like making out with Mae Young, which took balls, but didn't take a lot to learn how to perform in the ring. Again, evolution is part of the business. You have to accept change. But the bottom line is that it's still done in a four-sided ring, at least on WWE's side, and that should be your main stage. More and more, I see them getting away from that and I wonder if maybe the business has passed me by and I should just accept that. In some ways I do.
> — **Tom Pritchard**

So Daniel Puder won it. It's hard to pinpoint the reason why, although one would have to look at his showing in the Capture the Flag contest. In the closest to actual wrestling-related competition, Danny had to break through tag team wrestlers the Bashams and capture a flag on an opposing turnbuckle. When you factor in that no on-air mention was ever made of Puder's close call against Kurt Angle, the flag capturing was the closest thing you have to a tangible reason for his win.

That wasn't really why he won, though. He won because people liked him. He had a big smile and seemed like a good kid. Whether he really was or wasn't is immaterial. Fans had nothing else to go on. No one ever saw him truly wrestle, in the WWE sense of the word. Their votes were based on nothing other than who looked like a good person and which contestant everyone liked.

At the end of the day, that's what's important anyway, guys. Let's

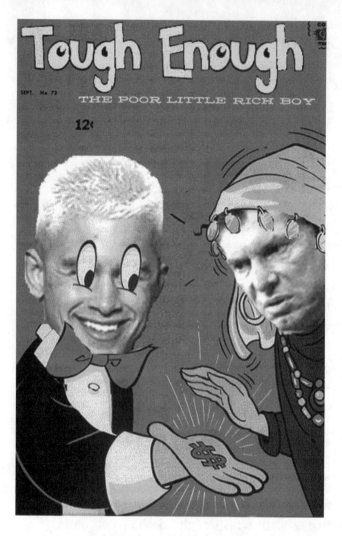

Tough Enough

SEPT. No. 73

THE POOR LITTLE RICH BOY

12¢

face facts. A lot of World Wrestling Entertainment's heroes from days gone by couldn't wrestle a lick. You don't need to be able to go 60 minutes 300 nights a year in order to sell some posters. You need to smile and say nice things to do that. Sadly, the way the industry is today and has been for a while, you don't need in-ring ability as much as you need to have charm. There's plenty of per-formers who've charmed fans with the same seven moves for decades. There's plenty of brilliant scientific wrestlers that bore casual fans to death. It's how it is.

In that lies the good thing about *Tough Enough*. It allowed the audience to pick their own hero. Instead of shoving some predetermined prima donna down the collective throat of planet earth, the McMahons finally gave the power of choosing the newest superstar to its audi-ence. Forget the wrestling. Choose the guy you like the best. Afterwards, make sure you buy all the crap we put his face on.

After all, that's what a popularity contest is. People pick who they like more and then that person goes on to become their leader or hero. The jury may have been out on his wrestling skills, but WWE knew one thing. They knew that people liked Daniel Puder.

All's well that ends well, right? Oh wait . . . there's just a few more things.

Within weeks *Smackdown* had a new performer. He'd won a million dollars, thanks to the love and support of wwe fans. While he may have be green in the ring, the audience would be patient with their newest good guy. After all, they liked him enough to give him a million samolians. That says a lot about how your fans feel about a person. So how did wwe use this sure-thing who was loved by fans because of nothing more than his charm?

They turned him bad.

What? Oh, I'm sorry. I'm sorry. What I meant to say was: *They turned him bad!*

I can't even begin to explain this. Why? Because every time I start writing out a reason why this was a bad idea, I feel like it's such common sense reasoning that it would be an insult to you, the reader, to do so. They turned him bad! The fans voted him the winner of a popularity contest and wwe turned him bad! Either this was sabotage, incompetence or just the introduction to the opposite sketches. Whatever it was didn't matter. They turned him bad!

Pude spent just a few weeks acting arrogant on *Smackdown* to no reaction before wwe officials decided to remove him from the main roster. In his weekly production meeting, Kevin Dunn informed his staff of this and made sure to call Daniel "a disappointment."

A disappointment? Come on, Kev. That's surprising. After a rigid selection process of dressing in drag and making out with old women, I can't imagine that he wouldn't shine. When you factor in that the popularity contest winner was turned into a super villain within two weeks, it makes for a real head scratcher. You have to wonder who in the Puder-wwe relationship was the real disappointment.

Oh, by the way, in September 2005 Dunn's "disappointment" was fired. After everything, the Million Dollar Kid didn't even last a year. In fact, wwe didn't keep him employed for the full length of his contract. Let's hear it for loopholes and months of wasted tv time. Hooray!

It's par for the course, though. Not counting Daniel's "season," *Tough Enough* had three installments. Out of those three installments, there were six winners. By the summer of 2005, out of those six, only one wrestler, John "Nitro" Hennigan went on to capture a title and achieve some success. One other, his co-winner Matt, was MIA. The other four, as mentioned earlier, were all fired. What a great contest! Where do I sign up? Humiliate me on TV and then give me my walking papers! Yay!

Now *Tough Enough* was rancid, but it paled in comparison to the *Raw Diva Search*, which occurred mere months before it. Oh man, I gotta tell you about this one . . .

Earlier in the year, WWE came to a realization. Business was in a slump. Numbers were waning. Something had to be done. Nothing was clicking correctly. Something needed to be corrected in order to get all the fans to tune in again.

Was that something Triple H's unchallenged dominance over the company? Nope. Was it the influx of nonsensical storylines with logic holes so large you could fit a country in them? Not at all. The biggest problem that needed to be corrected was simpler than all that.

WWE needed to hire a slew of untrained models to do nothing, give them better contracts than the men who have been wrestling for years and then expect them to fit in just fine backstage.

It's so simple. Why didn't anyone think of that sooner? We need women on screen! That's it! More of that! Oh . . . oh . . . here's the best part . . . ready? They don't even get naked on screen because it's Spike TV and not HBO or something like that! Yes! We'll pay these women to do things like have lingerie striptease nightgown pillow fights and they can't show any of their naughty parts. What more can a young adolescent boy want?

> I feel pretty bad for the girls because no one is training them correctly and it looks dangerous. I have always said women should not try to wrestle like guys. Fans, male or female, want to see women fight how they really would. I know for a fact that real catfights draw a house when it is done in an angle and storyline. But a women's wrestling match won't and neither will a Bra and Panties Battle Royal. If it's done in a storyline, a word that is now lost in the biz, then it can be done. Check out the attendance for the Jackson, Mississippi Coliseum back in 1986–1987. It was promoted as the first time that Missy Hyatt would face Dark Journey in a five-minute match, but only if John Tatum

were to lose to the Missing Link in one of the two parts of the double main-event. F.Y.I., back then you got paid on the house (attendance) and what match you were. The house was up over three times than all the previous ones for three to four months. My pay was $2250 and I am sure we both got ripped cuz it was Bill Watts [promoting]. So yep, the fans came to see the "bitches" fight! Women draw money and belong in this business. There is just not anyone that wants to go back and look at the formula to see how to do it. This is not Nuclear Space Technology. It is simple. It's soap opera, baby! Instead of giving the fans all you got in 10 minutes and seeing who can out do or do more than the other guy, it is easier to take your time, do a lot less and it will mean a lot more if done right! — **Missy Hyatt**

The weird thing about WWE's formula is that unlike Missy Hyatt's catfight with Dark Journey, today's conflicts aren't based on conflicts. While Missy's brawls with Journey were billed as a deep-rooted rivalry, the women today are all jolly and giggly. They don't get into fights per se. They recreate scenes from low rent dirty movies in the ring, only they don't have sex or take off their clothes. I'm not kidding about this.

Wait, wait, wait . . . we're getting ahead of ourselves here. Let's start at the beginning. Let's start with WWE's realization that they needed fewer muscle heads and more bubble heads crowding up the roster.

The announcement came on an episode of *Monday Night Raw*. Vince McMahon, surrounded by a bevy of babes, sat in front of a briefcase full of money. Who would be the one to win WWE's newest talent show? Who would be the next *Raw* Diva?

Sound exciting? Sound fun? Well, then obviously you didn't see it. The *Raw Diva Search* was a weekly contest that made *Tough Enough* and its cross-dressing funny boxing seem like *Masterpiece Theatre*. The best way to describe it would be to liken it to getting punched in the face over and over again by a monster that gets stronger each time while it screams at you in a foreign language. In other words, it was increasingly painful and made no sense.

Let's journey back and look at the insanity. Week by week, World Wrestling Entertainment found new ways to do what most red-blooded males thought was impossible. They made half naked women with implants seem boring.

Segments began airing to hype the contest in June 2004. They were long and tedious, but were there for a reason. The idea was to showcase the ladies who would be fighting for the quarter million dollar prize. Although many people would complain, a few drawn-out video packages on *Raw* never killed anyone. In fact, they give the staff and crew a chance to prepare the arena for the next match or skit. It's all good.

On the July 12th, 2004 edition of *Raw*, WWE's answer to a creepy uncle, Jerry Lawler, began to bombard us with innuendo. I guess someone in Titan Tower who enjoys seeing creepy guys wet themselves with glee in the presence of young women paired The King up with the contestants. Great. So, what did the girls have to say?

Nothing really. In fact, the point of the interviews wasn't to learn anything about these girls at all, but to see their "talents." We were tuning in to a professional wrestling show so we could watch a 55-year-old man in a king costume coax a girl into touching her nose with her tongue. I kid you not.

It gets worse though. While Candice Michelle's talent may have been licking her nostrils, the next contestant's talent was worse. Her name was Carmella DeCesare. She walked out and said, "I was the 2004 Playmate of the Year." That's it. Jerry Lawler replied that no one can question her talent now.

What? She got naked in a magazine? What's the talent? Even if she were a porn star, that would be more talent than this. At least then she'd be doing some sort of physical activity. Sure, being the 2004 Playmate of the Year is an *achievement*, but it's not a *talent*. No wonder WWE has a hard time "finding talent" . . . they don't even know what the word means.

OK. So far things are dumb, but not yet bizarre. It wasn't until the July 26th edition of *Raw* that things went beyond peculiar. They were off-the-charts nuts.

The finalists were informed that they'd be taking turns seducing a former WWE wrestler. Of course, that wrestler's identity was kept a secret at first, so your ears perked up a bit with wonder. Who would it be? What would have to be done? Oh man.

The wrestler was Kamala. Famous throughout the 80s as the face-painted Ugandan Giant who ate live chickens and howled, he was the last person you'd expect to see "seduced." Each girl was given 20 seconds to woo the Headhunter. How would a winner be decided? Who cares? Like *Tough Enough* to follow, these competitions had no prize. Making it worse, they had no winners. Fans were simply expected to vote for the woman who impressed them the most with their Kamala tickling skills.

I'm not joking. That was the point. World Wrestling Entertainment was asking its fans to choose the newest and highest paid woman on the roster simply by seeing how she forced the "Ugandan Giant" to giggle. Ugh. What's worse is that at twenty seconds each, the skits got long. As if hearing Jim Harris, the man who plays Kamala, make the "Ahhhh! Oeeeahhhhhh!" after being tickled once isn't strange enough, you had to go through it about 10 more times. It was enough to drive you insane.

I didn't see the point of it. Many other fans didn't either. Guess what? We're not alone. Guess who else didn't really get it.

> I was surprised and it was an honor to be called to do the thing with the Divas. And I don't watch wrestling or nothing like that, so I didn't know what it was going to be. I didn't know who the Divas were or what it meant or nothing until after I got there. . . . It was a little confusing at first, but then after Stephanie and Vince told me what they wanted done, I knew I could do what they wanted. But I still didn't know the meaning of it. It was only after I had done it that I caught on to what was happening. — **Kamala**

The next week World Wrestling Entertainment gave up on having any sort of competition. Get this — they made the girls beg for votes. That was the contest. Hey, why pay Kamala when we can just make these women grovel? Their sentiments went like this:

> joy, the bubbly one, said that there's nothing like being in front of a crowd of screaming WWE fans. WWE fans are the best fans in the world. She got a lukewarm reaction, which is sad when you consider that she just kissed the collective ass of the audience.

AMY, the movie/TV cameo one, said that she was real deal. She was in this for the long haul. The irony of that statement will spring up later. Oh, oh, also, she wanted to spank Evolution, the Triple H lead stable. Honestly, she said that.

CHANDRA, who didn't realize that she was supposed to be kissing up to the audience and not telling the truth, said that she promised her sister a car if she won. Amazing.

CARMELLA, the WWE appointed villain of the contest and Playmate of the Year, said that she had enjoyed her experience. She basically kissed up to company, wrestlers and fans. With her robotic delivery and dead eyes, the sentiments came off fake and creepy.

TRACIE said that she represented – and this is a direct quote – "the average single-woman in America . . . and half-naked, I might say!" You know, somehow I just never felt that the half-naked average single woman demographic was fully represented in the media. Thank God for this Tracie chick. At least she didn't promise anyone a car.

MARIA, the eventual on-air mockery, thought WWE was an amazing place to work. She also loved troops and WWE loved troops, so therefore she really loved WWE. Uh, how many people work for companies that don't love troops? Has your boss ever walked around handing out black ribbons and telling you to wear it in support of misery for our brave men and women overseas? A show of hands, please. No one? That's surprising.

CHRISTY, the nutty one, just did a cheer and then an awkward spin. It appeared to be a seizure at first.

MICHELLE, the one with the marketable last name, said that she was confident, charismatic, classy and athletic. The problem is that usually when people tell you they're charismatic, they're not.

That's the list of begging. That's how they broke it down for you. Now can you tell them apart? No? Well, let's try a bit harder. In fact, let's get some foreshadowing going on here.

Randy Orton, the man that Triple H ate for Christmas, was a name that many amateur Divas came to know. Orton, a young performer who achieved a great amount at a young age, has a habit of being a bit . . . shall we say, aggressive in his dealings with female employees. If you've ever seen the program *Malcolm in the Middle*, he's sort of like Reese only with 240-pounds of muscle. Don't watch *Malcolm in the Middle?* Then tough luck. How many pop culture references are you expecting here? He's a wild party animal that isn't afraid to let it be known. How's that? Good? Good.

So we can call it foreshadowing when Randall was chosen as the one to deliver the news on the latest elimination. It ended with the girl in tears. Classic stuff here, folks.

The August 9th, 2004 *Raw* started off with Randy Orton in a suit taking the result card from Diva Search Host John Coachman. He proudly pronounced that the "loser" was Chandra. Mockingly, he followed up with "I guess you're not buying your sister that car, are you?" Yeah, this was the girl who said that she would buy her sister a car if she won the week before. You know, in hindsight, I can't imagine why people wouldn't trip over themselves to grab the phone. After all, who doesn't want her sister to have a new car?

It gets worse, though. Ort went on to call her a loser and talk about the sting of failure. As she left, she started to tear, causing further taunts from the Legend Killer. It was mind blowing. Without a doubt, this was the most horrific lesson that any Diva hopeful was forced to learn. While the whole thing wasn't real in the sense that Randy Orton wasn't genuinely really speaking from the heart, it was real in the sense that this girl got eliminated from a contest she hoped to win. After weeks of hoping, you not only got sent home, but also mocked relentlessly on the way out. It was uncomfortable and you got a glimpse into how WWE and its performers really looked at these women as people. While many condemned these untrained girls for showing up at *Raw*, you had to remember that they simply answered the ad for a contest. It was the company that reached out and asked them to join — not the other way around.

The women rebounded well from this terrible scene, though. You know what? After tears and sadness, the best way to unwind is with an ice cream cone. That's right. The next week the women were each given 20 seconds to make an ice cream cone. Meanwhile, the fans were expected to pick the best ice cream cone creator. Why? Well, as you all know, any WWE employee worth their weight in salt knows how to make a sundae. Why do you think Hulk Hogan became such a big star? Because he had charisma or talent? Ha! It's because the

Big Hulkster in the Sky blessed him with the ability to make a cone head sundae that would blow Friendly's out of the water.

I'm being sarcastic. I wish I wasn't, though. At least then this segment would have a point. Again, there was no prize. There was no point. There was simply this:

JOY was the first one up. She decided to rub the ice cream and toppings all over herself. Now, I don't mean a little bit. I mean, like all over herself. It looked like the end of the movie *Carrie*. Only that was pig's blood and a movie. This was a woman actually rubbing herself down with ice cream and sprinkles. Crazy.

AMY decided to just eat the ice cream. After that, she gobbled some whip cream and finished with a spoonful of sprinkles. Her goal was to entice all the male viewers with food fetishes. Either that or she was hungry. Regardless, I had just sat on my couch and watched a woman eat ice cream for no reason. I was also about to sit through a bunch of others doing the same thing.

CARMELLA simply made an ice sundae but talked in a seductive voice while doing it. "Mmmm. Look at all these . . . ahhh . . . sprinkles." Weird, but at least she seemed to get the concept.

TRACIE picked up the ice cream and asked if I'm in the mood for something "sweet and spicy." Then, after realizing that she's holding an ice cream, she said, "Oh, not that spicy." I tune her out after that. I guess she could have done worse. She could have called it salty or crispy or a Cadillac or something.

MARIA just sort of mumbled to herself and ended up licking the ice cream. Mmmm . . . spicy.

CHRISTY decided to make this event the night that the world saw how completely insane she really was. She began cackling like Joan Crawford in the garden and said that ice cream was her favorite food . . . to play in. On that note, she began to slap her hands into it while screaming "Nyung! Nyah! Nyah!" I can't adequately describe how strange and disturbing this was. Imagine a young girl in a bikini standing in front of ice cream and then losing her mind. It's scarier than you'd think.

MICHELLE simply made an ice cream cone. It was educational. I always wondered how they got the chocolate syrup on the ice cream. Thanks, Michelle. I wish she would have taught me how to eat it too.

All these years I keep trying to stick it in my ear and something tells me that I'm just not doing it right.

The following week's *Raw* Diva game was a bit different. Rather than letting the hopefuls make fools of themselves on television, they were encouraged to sell each other out on television. Who would you vote off if you could? The wanna-divas were posed the question and voted via pretaped video. *Everyone*, with the exception of Carmella, voted for Carmella. One girl even said that her friends called Carmella a "dishrag." Wow.

The funny thing was that when they got up to Carmella's vote, she said it's hard to talk negative about anyone. Talk about getting blindsided, huh? Since she had to criticize someone, she chose to call out Joy for having a husband and family, citing "family values" as a liability. The next-to-last fake Diva, Amy, had her speech prepared like a *Reading Rainbow* book report. Loaded for battle, she said that Carmella made fun of wrestlers and didn't care about proving herself to the audience. Basically, the consensus was that everyone hated Carmella. That didn't matter though, all that mattered was the random votes of people online, and Michelle was sent home. Michelle, we hardly knew you. Actually, we didn't know you at all. Don't worry, though. She wasn't really gone yet. More on that later . . .

At this point, we're closing in on the final six participants. The following *Raw* started off with the *Raw* Divas coming to the ring with John Coachman front and center. He eliminated Tracie and then told each woman that she would get five minutes to say how much she loved him. Before that could happen, a surprise arrived.

If ya smellll-la-la-la-la what The Rock is cookin . . .

The Rock showed up and it was funny to see World Wrestling Entertainment bring in the People's Trump Card for this one show. You see, since heading to Hollyweird, as Hulk Hogan used to oh-so-wittily call it, the Great One was only appearing on *Monday Night Raw* occasionally. His sporadic appearances had to be used to their maximum potential. That's a given. So, did they use him to make a wrestler look good? No. They used him to make women in bikinis look good. That'll make some money for the company. I'm not sure how, but I'm sure WWE had its reasons. I'm also sure that those reasons made no sense.

Anyway, maybe it was a match made in heaven because the Scorpion King was in rare form that night. The thing with Rocky is that while funny at times, he can veer into sophomoric humor suddenly and without warning. For every People's Eyebrow or Elbow, there's a "lick a llama's anus" order or "monkey's nipple" reference. Yeah. Rock has issues.

So the Brahma Bull was raging and chased the Coach from the ring. Once left alone with the *Raw* Divas he broke into his standup routine. First and foremost, he imagined that all the women were "wet." Everyone ooo'ed and ahhed and he clarified his statement by adding on "with perspiration." Yeah. You get it? Ha ha! He also laughed about how ring announcer Lillian Garcia found herself fired from a sperm bank for "drinking on the job." Ah ha ha! Lillian laughed and clapped over the fact that she had just been called a sperm drinker on television. Different strokes for different folks, I guess.

After getting funny words like "wet" and "sperm" out of his system, Rocko tried to connect with the audience. He mocked the Divas and their ice cream cone making contests. According to the People's Comedian, wrestling fans don't want to see them eat "ice cream." No. The millions of fans want to see them eat "pie."

For those that don't know, "pie" is The Rock's code word for "vagina." He says "pie" because it flows better I guess. It's a little juvenile, but it's his thing. He also refers to his penis as "strudel." Take that for what you will. I think the People's Champion may have been sexually molested in a bakery when he was a kid.

> No! No! Not the cruller! What are you going to do to me with the cruller? Help!

Anyway, he promised pie eating and the crowd cheered because some of them might have been delusional enough to think they were about to watch hardcore porn during a professional wrestling broadcast. Rocky Maivia called for someone to bring some of these treats out. Who's gots da pies?

On that order, Japanese wrestler Yoshihiro Tajiri came out with a pile of pies for the women to do with what they will. Rocky laughed at Yoshi's appearance and agreed with an audience member who guessed that Tajiri must like "sushi pie." You know . . . because he's Japanese. Just one question, though. What the hell is sushi pie? Nothing like making a racist joke that isn't even funny, Rock. It's not offensive, per se. It's just not even a joke. It's as if he had Chavo Guerrero come out with the pies and he said, "Chavo, you probably like burrito pie."

Then again, this is the People's Champ. He's the guy who walked out of an interview with Opie and Anthony over something like that. An in-studio guest ran a wrestling message board. One of the people on it wrote a message that was considered racist by Rocky. It became a big scene. Why shouldn't it be? He shouldn't stand for people mocking his ethnicity. That's ridiculous! How dare they?! The Great One really cares deeply about things like that! Anyway, where was I? Oh yeah — sushi pie.

Strangely enough, people were still cheering even after realizing that it was real pie and not the naughty parts they thought it would be. Again, different strokes for different folks. If I wanted to watch women eat, I'd spend my afternoons at the Yogurt Barn.

So it was pie-eating time. Once again, let's put 20 seconds on the clock. Eat that pie, ladies . . .

JOY picked at the pie, but gave a speech about wanting Carmella "to eat crow." The crowd booed her loudly. Why? Well, for starters she was given the task to simply eat a pie and couldn't even do it right. Instead, she gave a speech. Her job wasn't to give a speech. It was to eat a pie and she managed to mess that up. That should have been a sign to WWE right there.

AMY, who Rock referred to as "lemon-fresh panties," understood the concept. She seemed to get the idea and dove her face straight into the pie, licking the cream off of it. Apparently she grasped the symbolism of the whole thing.

CARMELLA was up next. The crowd began to boo and Rocky asked them to stop. He told them that she "might come through." Huh? I don't think people were booing her because they didn't think she'd eat the whole pie, Rock. Let's be straight here, man. No one cared about the damn pie. So what did Carm do with the pie? She scooped it up, licked it, rubbed it on her chest and then on her arm. Yes, *Raw*'s viewing audience was tuned in to see a grown woman rubbing pie on her arm. If I wanted to watch women rub pie on their arms, I'd spend my afternoons at the Yogurt Barn . . . in Crazyville.

MARIA did a bit of everything. There was some licking. She got some on her nose. Whatever. By this time, the whole segment was getting boring anyway. Someone was going to have to do something completely bat shit insane in order to save it.

CHRISTY to the rescue! Remember her? She was the bat shit insane one. It was almost like karma that her turn came when it did, because she didn't let anyone down, especially those of us already questioning her sanity. In essence, she took a contest that's completely ridiculous and made it even more peculiar. I don't care what you say. That's talent.

So what did she do? Well, the crazy redhead had The Rock hold out the microphone for her and she let the audience in on a little secret:

> As you can see, my butt's hungry. It's been munching my panties all night, so I have to feed it.

With that, she placed the pie on the ground and sat on it. No one knew what the hell to make of it. I still don't know what to make of it. Christy Hemme's got issues. No joke. She's the type of girl that you could just picture attacking someone with a sharpened pencil. Her butt was hungry. She said that her butt was hungry. Amazing. Speaking of butt . . .

Afterwards, John Coachman returned to the ring with La Résistance by his side. He came back to take The Rock to task for running him out of the ring. Rocky called him "mama" and then dismissed the fake Divas from the ring.

From there, Rocky quoted Chinese "out of respect for Tajiri." What was the quote?

> Ching chong ding dow!

For starters, Tajiri isn't Chinese, but hey, what's it matter, right? It also ensured that if Rocky goes into any Chinese restaurant that employs wrestling fans, he'll get spit in his sesame chicken. It's segments like this that make his Opie and Anthony radio tantrum seem more and more ridiculous each day.

A big fight broke out and Rhyno came to the aid of Taj and the People's Champ. Woo-hoo. Whatever. This whole thing lasted 25 minutes and, to this day, I have no idea what it was supposed to accomplish. It was a rare chance to use The Rock as a part of *Raw* and WWE chose to have him host a pie eating contest. No point, folks. None. It seemed like a lot of time, effort and cameos just to introduce women eating dessert.

The next week, WWE invited trouble to its front door. It actually gave the contestants live microphones and encouraged them to talk trash about one another. That was the contest. The show was live. The mics were live. You gotta know what was coming.

In no time at all, streams of words starting with "C" began to fly from these women's mouths. It was as if they had all been possessed by ghosts of drunken sailors. If it was a curse word with a "C" in it, they said it. The "C" words were used in many different ways, too. For instance, Carmella was told that having one in her mouth doesn't make her a diva. She was also accused of gargling with something besides Listerine.

Even Stacy Kiebler, the host of this debacle, was embarrassed. Keep in mind, this is a woman whose job description includes bending fully over when entering the ring just so oversexed men can ogle her butt. If Stacy's embarrassed by your overly explicit behavior, then you're on another level.

Now keep in mind, during all this stuff going on during *Raw*, Vince McMahon was wondering why he couldn't get classy advertisers. I'm not kidding.

The next week, we're down to four girls. It's Amy Weber, Christy Hemme, Joy Giovanni and Carmella DeCesare. Now you gotta figure that this was going to be something normal, right? After all, we're down to the final four. No messing around here, kid. It was go time.

The girls squared off in an . . . arm wrestling match! Yup! Arm wrestling! It was finally something real that they could do in order to show us their strength. It was respectable. It was normal. There was nothing sleazy or insane about this. That's it. They would simply arm wrestle. Finally! Phew. Something that doesn't come off as trashy or embarrassing.

Oh, and the winner of the arm wrestling, got to throw Texas chili at the other three.

Dammit!! So close! We were so close!

The next week, Joy was ousted from the competition. The three remaining contestants are ordered to beat up John Coachman for thirty seconds each. Making a special cameo, Vince McMahon told Coach that if he moved, he'd be fired. If you didn't see this, you didn't miss anything. Don't worry.

When the grand finale finally took place, WWE sent Trish Stratus down to the ring. She berated the final two, Carmella and Christy. Showing that World Wrestling Entertainment's writers don't realize how to avoid blatant foreshadowing, Trish asked Christy if she'd use the prize money to buy decaf coffee. Then she asked Carmella if she'd use it to buy a personality. Obvious much?

I don't care how backward this company is. There was no chance that WWE would let their top female wrestler go to the ring and tell the girl who's about to win her $250,000 contract that she has no personality.

Surprise, surprise. Christy wins! Christy wins! Eh.

In her post-win interview, Hemme showed some real emotion, though. People were happy in a way. After all, nothing in this contest had meaning until now. The competitions had no prizes. The segments didn't showcase any genuine skill. The only thing that this time killer had going for it was that it would find one woman to work for WWE. Only one could win. Only one would get hired. It was Christy. People were happy. Finally the whole thing had some meaning.

Oh, oh, I almost forgot. Within about three months, WWE hired almost all of the girls who competed in the competition anyway.

So much for having meaning.

Amazing. Purely amazing. Here is World Wrestling Entertainment basing a whole contest around the fact that the sole winner would be hired and then suddenly, they're all on the payroll? No joke. Check this out:

> **Christy Hemme (Raw)** – Winner.
>
> **Carmella DeCesare (Raw)** – Hired less than two weeks later to face Christy in a match.
>
> **Maria Kanellis (Raw)** – Hired as a backstage interviewer who eventually adopted the illustrious gimmick of "idiot."
>
> **Candice Michelle (Raw)** – Hired as the on-air make-up artist.
>
> **Amy Weber (Smackdown)** – Hired the following month as John Bradshaw Layfield's on-air image consultant.
>
> **Michelle McCool (Smackdown)** – Debuted the same day as Amy and was featured as Rob Van Dam's on-air fitness trainer.
>
> **Joy Giovanni (Smackdown)** – Debuted the same day as Amy and Michelle as Big Show's massage therapist.

That was some crazy-ass *Smackdown* episode, I'll tell you that much. Before we go into these women invading the locker room like hungry ants, let's talk about some separate issues.

First, there was no reason to have these women on TV. Actually, I should rephrase that. I'm not saying that there was no reason to put them on television. They're pretty. That's the reason. I meant that WWE didn't give their characters any reason to be on TV.

How lazy can you get? Massage therapist? Yoga instructor? Now you're just grasping at straws. It was meaningless. Sadly, the silly vocational gimmicks they were given were just the tip of the iceberg.

Three different women debuted on *Smackdown* in one night. Three. Why? What was the rush to get them on the air all at once? Rather than debut one, introduce her character and then debut the next, WWE did it all in one shot. It made them seem generic. It took away any potential they had to truly connect one with the audience. Instead they were just a bunch of new *Diva Search* losers. What's the point of hiring them if you're not going to make them mean something?

> But James, they had to debut quickly. After all, the *Raw Diva Search* was still fresh in the minds of fans.

That would make sense . . . if WWE had actually used the *Raw Diva Search* as part of its gimmick. The contest wasn't really mentioned. We just had new women for no reason filling jobs that didn't need filling,

It's almost like a parody. You know those movies where they show some sort of sport selling out for money? The stadium is all souped up. The uniforms are new. Then, in the middle of the game, a girl in a bikini comes out and says "Hi. Look at my breasts for no reason." Everyone laughs. The point is made.

That's what *Smackdown* had become. Except there was no stadium or uniforms and it wasn't a parody. Sad, right?

Well, here's my favorite part of all this. WWE had just hired a $250,000 *Raw* Diva. They paid her a huge amount of money. Something so magnanimous and significant should make headlines all over the place. She must be a household name. With the amount of TV time, money and publicity given to her, Christy must be on top of the world.

Well, while compiling quotes for this book I asked many of the performers for their opinions on different people. My favorite response was from Missy Hyatt. It was after I asked her how she felt about Christy Hemme:

> I don't know who this is. — **Missy Hyatt**

Granted, Missy doesn't watch *Raw* weekly. But wasn't something of this magnitude supposed to reach out to people that don't watch

Raw weekly? Why would they give $250,000 away, if not to generate a buzz? I've got news for you. Missy Hyatt may not watch *Raw* every week, but neither do the other people WWE is trying to suck in with grandiose prizes for contests like this. They want the non-viewer to know the name Christy Hemme. If a non-viewer who has actually worked in the wrestling industry doesn't know her name, why would a non-viewer who hasn't know it? Seems like a waste of money, if you ask me.

By the way, in order to accommodate all these new women, WWE canned almost all of the women they had on their roster. Established women like Molly Holly, Jazz and Gail Kim were all sent packing. Huh?

These women, already recognized names in the company, could have helped to shape the skills of all the new Divas. How could they get this huge new group of girls over as wrestlers if they didn't have the established women around to put them over? Oh wait. I forgot. We didn't need them. Christy Hemme wasn't going to be a wrestler. Athletic ability wasn't one of the prerequisites to this contest.

Yeah. Screw that. Hemme wrestled Women's Champion Trish Stratus six months later at *WrestleMania 21*. The girl who applied for a reality contest and had no wrestling training prior to June was appearing on the biggest show of the year. Jazz, an established female wrestler that WWE spent a long time making recognizable, sat at home with her husband, Rodney Mack, who was fired from WWE the same day she was. It needed to be done though. Old performers have to go to make room for new ones. Hemme went on to a productive and varied WWE career that lasted a year and a half.

Yup. Christy was canned in December of 2005. You didn't need to be Nostradamus to see that one coming.

Wow. What a downer. Sorry. I didn't want to end this section on a downer. Didn't mean to bum you out.

OK, I'll lift your spirits. I'll bring you out of that funk. Amy Weber, one of the *Raw* Diva girls that went on to work for *Smackdown*, left the company in February 2005. After the "boys" decided to play a number of "ribs" on her, she gave notice to WWE and went home. Don't know what a "rib" is? Well, it's a wrestling term. Amy wasn't too familiar with it, either. Why? Because it's a wrestling term. Amy's not a wrestler.

Makes you wonder why no one in World Wrestling Entertainment realized that the gritty and hidden backstage boys club world of rasslin' wouldn't be any place for a prim and proper outsider. Even better, no one figured that the pretty non-wrestling girl with the big money perk-filled contract might catch a few nasty pranks now and then? (By the way, that's what rib means. It's a prank.) Amy caught it.

She raised the ire of others for stretching out in an airplane row, a big no-no that the "boys" know about but others might not. She got harassed when a Japanese Gentleman's Club flier was found with her picture on it. Despite the photo being one that had appeared on another magazine, the wrestlers still ripped into her for it. Many models know that this kind of photo swapping happens all the time. Then again, wrestlers don't.

This just brings us back to the question, "Why is a model in a wrestling locker room?" Could you imagine the things that go on there? No? Well, we'll get to that in a second.

Before we do, I promised you a happy closing note. Here it is:

> It is hard for me to comment because for the most part my involvement with the WWE was a very positive one. Vince was great and the crew was so hardworking. Most of the wrestlers were very sweet as well. Unfortunately, there are bad apples in every line of work, people who take themselves a little too seriously. If it wasn't for these people, I would still be working for the WWE. I just don't feel as though I should allow people to treat me like a piece of ****. You shouldn't be treated badly in any line of work. I don't need to go through an initiation or whatever excuse people want to come up with. I treated everyone with respect and kindness and I only expected the same. On a whole, the WWE is a great place to be and I was privileged to be a part of it for the short time I was there. — **Amy Weber**

CHAPTER 7

How to Beat Up the New Guy

I think it's camaraderie. We see each other more than we see our own family. You notice that if you get two wrestlers together, they call each other "brother." You actually treat this guy like your brother because you see him – I've seen some guys more than I've seen my own wife. When you're in a car with someone for 300 days out of the year splitting hotels with them or training with them or on the same planes with them, you need camaraderie. You need everyone to literally work together like a family. If not, if one brother doesn't like another brother then it just makes for a bad time. **– D-Lo Brown**

Good old wrestling hazing. It's as American as apple pie and . . . uh, American flags. You can't escape those war stories about crazy no-names popping the eyes of out of an eager hopeful's head under the guise of training.

Back in my day, the trainers were all crazy. They'd pop out your eye and shoot your mother if you messed up a headlock! We were motherless Cyclopses with wrestling licenses and we liked it!

Nowadays, it's not so bad. It can still be brutal at times, though. There's hazing, no different than a college fraternity or football team. Rasslers razz one another and ultimately forge a family-like sense of good-natured ribbing mixed with insane over-the-top scariness. I've heard stories that range from forcing a young wrestler to drink a six pack of beer to forcing a production assistant to lick a prominent wrestler's testicles. Ugh. Those fans salivating for a chance to travel on the road feeling a bit more apprehensive now? You picture the fame. You picture the fun. You don't picture the balls. They never picture the balls.

What is it about the wrestling business that sets it apart from other businesses? You don't see this type of inter-employee mischief in other companies, do you?

> Hello there, aren't you the new sales assistant?
>
> Yes. My name is Joe. Nice to meet you.
>
> Well, Joe, my name is Bob. I've been working here for nine years. Nine years, Joe. You know how long nine years is? It's a long time. It's almost like ten years. Anyway, you didn't come over and shake my hand before going to your desk. That's a mistake, rookie. I've taken the liberty of defecating in your lunchbox. If it happens again, I'm afraid you'll have to go in front of the "Salesman Court."

Now that's all cute and funny, but it's not a fair comparison. While it's good for a ha-ha to imagine Bob the Salesman pummeling the new assistant because he didn't shake his hand, it doesn't work as an analogy. Why? Because wrestler interaction isn't the same thing as office interaction.

> Oh! Because they're entertainers, right? Entertainers haze each other, right?

Well, not really. For some reason I can't picture Bob Saget whaling on Dave Coulier backstage at *Full House*. I'm pretty sure that Gordon on *Sesame Street* didn't hide Mr. Hooper's hearing aid. I doubt that Joe Jackson spent band practice beating up Michael. Well, maybe that last one was a bad example, but you get my point.

So what the hell is it? Why do wrestlers do these wild things? It's not professional in a business sense. It's not professional in an entertainment sense. What is it?

It's sports. In the realm of sports, wrestling's backstage hazing policy fits in perfectly. There's nothing out of the ordinary for it. It's something they do to forge camaraderie. Some wrestlers need the assurance that future opponents are tough enough to keep their head in the game when a match is on. The last thing you need is to be injured by a guy preoccupied with his wife's indiscretions or past due bills at home. That's the main reason given for hazing or initiation rituals. If you can keep your focus in the ring after having your head held in a toilet, you can keep your focus after anything.

You see, that's something people forget about this industry. It's a three-part genre. The title that we use to describe 2006 wrestling is "the Business of Sports Entertainment." Vince McMahon uses it all the time. When repeating it, people spout the whole phrase off in one breath as if it was a single statement. It's not.

It's so much more. It identifies three key elements that make up one industry. Each part is important. Each one plays a major role in shaping professional wrestling today.

BUSINESS (OFFICE): Contracts, legal issues, television deals, pay-per-view promotion, merchandising, accounting, live gates, advertising, publishing, music/film cross promotion, special appearances, autograph signings, production, editing, lighting, sound, venue scheduling, travel, human resources and public relations.

ENTERTAINMENT (WRITERS, BOOKERS, ROAD AGENTS, WRESTLERS): Storyline writing, script writing, character development, show planning, booking, creating match finishes, acting, public speaking and broadcasting.

SPORTS (WRESTLERS AND ANY OTHERS "IN THE LOCKER ROOM"): Physical strains associated with the actual professional wrestling performing, bleeding, conditioning, training, exercising, weight lifting, traveling, keeping a team attitude, trusting and liking those in the locker room.

It's three-fold. Sports is part of the title. Although it's often overlooked by most of us out of fear that someone might think that we think wrestling's real. (Which we don't. What? We don't?!)

The people who participate in this industry are athletes. You doubt it? Anyone can do it? Tell your fat Uncle Ralph to do a plancha after Thanksgiving dinner. Too tough? Too athletic? Not fair? Fine. Then just tell him to run around the house for ten minutes without stopping. After he passes out, wake him up and tell him to go hop on a plane to Detroit so he can do it all again tomorrow.

What about those big fat wrestlers? Well, there's big fat people in every industry. Baseball pitcher David Wells isn't the picture of perfection, is he? Didn't George Foreman roll all over the boxing ring in his 40s, yet still put up a fight? Every industry has large people. Not every athlete looks like an athlete.

In the case of wrestling, every athlete knows how to do three things:

> **1)** They know how to do a physical activity for prolonged periods without becoming fatigued to the point where they pass out.
> **2)** They're strong enough to hoist their own body weight into the air.
> **3)** They can do a flip and land on their back.

These three things have nothing to do with business or entertainment. They are three basic things that make wrestling a sport.

It's the basis of what makes these men athletes. Most of them are able to do millions of things beyond this list. Those are the good ones. Some other wrestlers can only do these three. They're not so good. But they all are athletes.

So here you are in a sports locker room unlike any other. The wrestlers not only have to travel together and like one another, they need to count on each other. How do they achieve this? They play pranks on one another and do things no different than a college fraternity or football locker room.

Problems arise when people like Amy Weber join the WWE locker room. Why should she have a hard time fitting in? This is entertainment, right? She's an entertainer.

Well, as we pointed out earlier, the locker room isn't about entertainers. It's a gritty backstage sweatfest that isn't the place for a woman who doesn't know what she's getting into. It's as if the Chicago Bears suddenly decided they were going to have female teammates in the locker room with them. No big deal? Well, the thing is that the female teammates don't actually play the game. In fact, they're not into sweating all that much. Oh, and they get paid more.

How long would that last? I'm sure the outcomes would be worse than what's happened in the wrestling industry so far. So, that's saying something. Unfortunately, it's something that's becoming the norm in World Wrestling Entertainment and it leads some doors to be opened that WWE should keep closed.

How do you deal with a company that encourages a boys-will-be-boys attitude backstage while trying to introduce untrained ladies into the lion's den? Talk about a conflict of interest. It's like they're begging for trouble.

> With the Divas, you're gonna invite the kind of people who come from modeling. They'll get some hot chicks and [Vince] might have to reprimand the guys and he might have to tell them "This is the way I want to run my business these days and I want you guys to act like corporate professionals." Well, OK. But you're gonna invite yourself into having average, I like to call them civilians, come in your business and be in your locker room. They're not gonna understand that this is not your average business. This is not a business like any other. It's not for

everybody. By doing this, I think you're opening yourself to a world of not just lawsuits but bullshit, heartache and horseshit that you just don't need . . . You're opening yourself up to chaos with a capital K . . . and I know it's spelled with a C, but I spell it with a fuckin' K.
— Tom Pritchard

We're not just talking about hazing in the sense of making newbies do your laundry either. World Wrestling Entertainment, together with the rest of the promotions in this business, fosters a self-policing locker room. Wrestlers are expected to carry out judgments and sentences on those who violate the sacred trust of those within the family.

Now the reason given by most wrestlers when asked about hazing is that it helps them establish and build trust. It's a valid point and something that seems to hold true in professional wrestling more than any other sport. After all, you're expecting a person to protect you in the ring. As opposed to football and other team sports where your teammates need to watch your back, in rasslin' your teammate can suddenly drop you on your head without notice. It's important to teach him respect for the biz so he remembers the grave nature of his role. Hazing exists so rookies remember to be professional and watch out for their opponent's well-being when the bell rings.

Now I don't doubt that most wrestlers genuinely feel this way. However, there's always a few "locker room leaders" who spring up in an environment like this. Usually, they're employees who've been on the payroll for a while. They watch over the hazing and the disagreements that come about from time to time.

They preside over things like "Wrestler Court," a self-policed trial of sorts meant to teach new guys with bad attitudes how to fit in with the boys. These locker room leaders get intricately involved in all aspects of backstage law enforcement. They do it because, above all else, they genuinely care about making sure newcomers hold the rules of the ring near and dear. The last thing any locker room leader wants is to see someone get hurt during the scripted wrestling exhibition.

Well, in honor of Rene Dupree, you have to excuse my French because that's bullshit. Who is Rene Dupree? Glad you asked.

Rene Dupree was a young WWE wrestler riding the wave of anti-

French sentiment all the way to the bank. Well, maybe not all the way to the bank. It was more like a quarter of the way to the bank. There was nothing spectacular about the way WWE presented him.

The thing about Rene is that he was young. By the age of 20, he had become the youngest WWE tag team Champion ever. The company publicized the fact that Dupree's first match had occurred at the age of 14. That was his thing. He was French. He was young. There wasn't much else.

As a youngster on the road, Dupree linked up with Bob "Hardcore" Holly. Bob was a throwback to a different time. He was a hard nosed, no-nonsense guy who enjoyed his status as a locker room leader. He earned his racing stripes, so to speak, by staying in WWE since the early 90s. Debuting under the name Thurman "Sparky" Plugg, Bob Howard played the role of a racecar driver. Vroom vroom! Right.

Eventually he became Bob "Spark Plug" Holly and later just Bob Holly or Hardcore Holly depending on the mood. All of this occurred over the period of about twelve years. Bob had seen it all.

Dupree hadn't seen squat. Nothing. He was in diapers when Bob was racing them crazy racecars. They were like a TV sitcom. The young flamboyant kid with the feminine French gimmick riding around the country with a grizzled bully who had to play a terrible gimmick for years. Fox should be all over this concept.

Take a wild stab in the dark at what happened next. Well, the young kid, who didn't "get" how to fit in so well yet, ends up pissing off the angry locker room leader. What a shocker.

The situation was simple enough. Rene borrowed Bob's rental car, got a ticket and then didn't pay the fine. It was behavior typical of Rene. It was also behavior that Bob Holly typically goes nuts over.

On the day that Holly had to take off and return to the city where this happened, Dupree said he would be there by his side. He wasn't. Basically, Renny was begging for a beating. These are things that would make a pacifist beat your ass, much less a wrestler with a chip on his shoulder. When you factor in that many wrestlers had issues with Dupe's backstage behavior and reputation for squealing to management, Rene's probability of getting beat up was pretty high.

So, that's that, right? Holly had to take this kid out back and toss him a good beatin', right? Beat him like he owes him money. Flatline him. You name it, he should do it. This kid needed to learn respect for his fellow wrestlers. If he didn't, then who could trust him in the ring?

After all, that's really what it's all about. Could this brash young man really hold up his end of the sacred trust in the ring? When a wrestler's trust is broken backstage, he must ensure that the trust won't be broken once the bell rings. Dupree had disregarded Bob when it came to his traffic ticket. What said he wouldn't decide to disregard Holly's safety in a match?

Something had to be done. It was important. Hardcore Holly had to teach this kid a lesson. If not, he might one day hurt someone in the ring. Guess how Bob taught him that lesson.

He hurt him . . . in the ring.

Yeah. After all this hazing, designed and defended under an inherently good premise of ensuring each other's protection in the ring, a guy like Bob Holly shot it all to shit and showed the world that it's nothing more than bullying for the sake of bullying — at least to him.

This wasn't new for Bob. He has the amazing distinction of actually beating up a wrestler in the ring before he even debuted. Now that's something special. During filming of *Tough Enough Season 3*, Holly brutally beat down eventual co-winner Matt Capotelli during a "fake" match because . . . well, no reason. He just beat him up.

Again, just for the sake of emphasis, Bob Holly wants to teach wrestlers respect.

He wants to teach them this respect because he needs to be able to count on them to adhere to the trust placed on their shoulders in the ring. So how does he teach them that? He violates their trust in the ring.

It's like saying, "I'm gonna teach my kid to not be violent by beating him with a hammer until he understands."

Better yet: "I'm gonna train my dog not to pee in the house by urinating on him in the living room when he has an accident."

Wait, here's the best one: "I'm gonna beat up the newbie during a match in order to ensure that he remembers the trust placed on him to protect his opponents during a match."

So it goes, Bob. You're in a grueling sport. The men are men and the testosterone flows freely (sometimes with extra help from "vitamins"). Just call a spade a spade, man. You beat them up because you're a bully. You're not trying to teach them a damn thing.

It's as if that kid in Junior High who would toss the nerds down the staircase said he was doing it to teach them how to properly walk down steps. Give me a break. The way you carry out your "teaching" is completely contradictory to the lesson you claim they will learn. Claiming that you're doing it out of love for the business is ridiculous. You're doing it because you're pissed off. You're doing it because it was done to you. Most importantly, you're doing it because you can.

Who are we kidding here?

What's funny is that management doesn't seem to care about this. Following the action, Triple H, the office version, told Michael Landsberg of *Off the Record* what his thoughts were on the issue. Why wasn't Bob punished?

> I think it was probably a "this is your last chance" warning. If that ever happens again, you'll be fired. I think that's inexcusable. We give each other our bodies in the ring and trust each other with our bodies. Anyone that takes a liberty with someone else is totally wrong.

Following this action, Bob went on to team with Charlie Haas and challenge for the Tag Team Titles, while Rene Dupree did nothing. When you consider that Holly beat up a *Tough Enough* student for absolutely no reason and the company allowed the segment to air on its MTV reality show, it makes you realize that maybe it's not so upset about stuff like this after all.

It encourages this type of self-policing. Hazing, wrestler court and in-ring lessons are all smiled upon. Why?

Well, maybe because wrestlers who are busy worrying about whether or not they shook hands with the veterans or sat in the right seat aren't worrying about other things . . . you know, like unionizing or getting health insurance.

CHAPTER 8

Trust No One

In college, I worked in the deli department of a local supermarket. When I first started, they took fifty bucks out of my paycheck for union dues. Whatever. No skin off my back. The way I saw it, the government takes a chunk of money out every week and I have no idea what it's for. State taxes? FICA? Formica? Who cares. At least I knew that this was going somewhere.

While there, I worked with someone named Dan. Dan was in his late 30s, had a mullet and sort of smelled. He was the most jovial guy in the place, although he came off a bit too friendly at times. He was the deli man that everyone knew, some tolerated and some were weirded out by.

> Mrs. Costa! Here on this fine morning to pick up some turkey from my deli? Hooray! I'll sing you a song while I slice it. Ohhhhhh . . . here's your tur-key, Miss-ess Cos-ta . . .

You know, that kind of stuff. His overbearing and sometimes unbearable personality shined through in everything he did. He still had a job, though. I guess it was because he didn't do anything wrong.

Well, that is until about three months into my time there. Dan was fired — out and out canned like Spam, ma'am. Why? Well, Danny had decided that the deli actually belonged to him. It was his to run around and eat through like a termite on crack. Salami, bologna, cheese and chicken wings, they were all fair game. One day, the manager saw him putting hams into his backpack. Hams? Yes, hams. He was fired.

After he was let go, I talked to another deli worker about it. This guy had worked for the supermarket since a year before God's parents were born. He seemed disgusted at the treatment his friend had received from the grocery store. He scoffed and said, "If they catch customers stealing, they don't do anything. If they catch employees stealing, they fire you. Hmmmph."

The first thing I thought was "They don't do anything if customers steal? Why didn't anyone tell me this while I was a customer?" The second thing was, "How can you defend that? It's wrong. He deserved to get fired."

Well, deserved or not, the firing had happened and that was that. Well, actually "that was that" for about two and a half weeks until Dan resurfaced in a deli apron, ready to accost Mrs. Costa and her turkey order once again.

What happened? Well, he called his union rep and made a big stink about it. Next thing you know, Dan is back. He's slicing. He's dicing. He's julienning. Oh, oh, and he's stealing too. Can't forget that.

At that moment, I realized the power that groups hold. The more together everyone is, the more likely the people are going to get what they want.

The problem is that companies lose power when dealing with unions. Think about it. It's easier to beat up a guy all by himself than him and a few thousand of his friends, right?

So what does management do? They create working conditions that keep everyone busy with other interests. No one is concerned about whether or not they get health insurance or stand up for people who are unfairly terminated. No. They're too busy worrying about things like putting their bags in the right area, shaking hands with the respected members of the locker room and making sure they keep out of "wrestler court."

See, the thing about hazing in the locker room isn't that it's brutal. I'm not concerned with safety or maturity or any of that. Wrestlers should develop a camaraderie. Groups use initiation rights all the time and I understand the need for it. When you have to see this new guy more than you see your own family, then you damn sure better do whatever you need to do to accept him. If that involves making him serve drinks on a plane or goofy crap like that, so be it. Serve your drinks and shut up.

Every group has hazing to a certain extent. There's football locker rooms. There's baseball locker rooms. There's hockey locker rooms. Hell, I bet Tiger Woods even plays pranks on the new golfers. It's life and it's understandable given the conditions in which athletes are asked to perform. Oh, there's only one small difference between wrestling and the sports mentioned above.

They all have unions!

> Once the office found out that people were trying to do unions, they'd get rid of those people who were trying to form it. The problem is that there's no competition. I mean, are you gonna start a union for the only company that offers wrestling? You do that and they fire you, where else are you gonna go? I mean, WWE pays you very well. They encourage you to think outside the WWE, invest your money and have other sources of income, you know? Most jobs you'd never get that unless you're playing professional football, baseball or hockey . . . but they do have unions in those other leagues. It would be great if they did have a union for a 401K or a pension plan for putting in your time. I could see that working out for them. In the NFL, you have to be playing for seven years to get that, so you'd have to play your cards right in WWE to where you wrestled for seven years. Then again, they do have insurance and take care of medical bills if you get hurt in the ring, so in that respect, they've come a long way. — **Charlie Haas**

The NFL, NBA and NHL all have initiation rights. We know that. They all have hazing to an extent. That's not the issue.

The issue isn't the hazing. The issue isn't the severity of it or its moral ramifications. The issue is management using it as a tool to keep their wrestlers busy and foster a juvenile environment so the "boys" don't realize that there's grown up stuff they should be working on first. Boys will be boys, all right. Management hopes it stays that way, that's why they ignore the Bob Hollys of the World and encourage a recess-like atmosphere.

> I'm a big conspiracy theory guy. I haven't heard that one, but I can see where that might happen. You get a locker room full of 70 guys, not everyone is gonna see eye to eye every time, you know? So I can kind of see that. The problem with the union is that, I know how dirty the business is, meaning the independent wrestling scene. You're not gonna find anyone more shady than some independent promoters. The problem is if 70 guys from WWE said "We're gonna form a union." I guarantee you that tomorrow, they'd find 70 more guys, you know. There'll always be someone there to cross the line, you know? — **Aaron "Jesus" Aguilera**

Aaron's not alone. Speak to nine out of ten wrestlers and you'll hear the same thing. The most prominent reason that you'll hear for not having a union is that there will always be more wrestlers to run in and take your place. Management will always be able to replace you.

That sounds a lot like something management would say, right? Weird to hear a world class wrestler devalue the job he can do. Anyone can do it? Anyone can step in and take away your spot? Wow. Imagine if every union said the same thing.

> A union? Come on! That'll never work. If I go on strike, they'll just find someone else to fix this elevator.

> What? Union? Give me a break. How hard can it be for the office to find someone else to operate a cash register? My training was ten minutes long. A union won't work.

You know what? The "anyone can do it" excuse seems to fit better for cash register handlers than it does with wrestlers. The weird thing . . . retail and department store people are in unions! Wrestlers aren't. Apparently anyone can step in and perform spectacular wrestling matches for sold-out arenas, but it takes someone special to print up a gift receipt.

There are lots of unions out there. Go to Unions.org and see for yourself. Farm workers have a union. Yes, farm workers. They live on a farm and do farm things, far removed from the business world, yet they have a union. Wrestlers, who are on television and travel to every place on the globe, don't. What the hell?

One of the most blatant showings of arrogance regarding McMahon's victory over his work force was the fact that he created a stable in the late 90s called "The Union." The group, headed by Mick Foley, came to the ring to a theme song that began with a group of people shouting "Union" followed by one of those Flintstones "Quittin' Time" horns.

Before you say it was just coincidental that Vince would create an on-air group that makes unions look silly and goofy, it wasn't. Nothing that gets on WWE TV is coincidental. Things are done for a reason. Characters with double meanings are meant to have those double meanings. If they didn't, they wouldn't have double meanings. They'd have single meanings.

That's all a red herring, though. The real question is how can an industry that's older than dirt evolve to the form of entertainment it's become today, lining the pockets of promoters with dollar amounts that they only dreamed of in the "good ol' days," yet the wrestlers are still being treated as second-class citizens. How could it be 2006 and there still be no union in place to protect the rights and needs of the backbone of professional wrestling — the performers?

Now look, I'm not claiming to have all the answers. I recognize the apprehension around forming a group to protect one another. I see the worry that people have. This entire industry has been built on the concept of "protect your spot or someone else will take it." Wrestlers have been ingrained with the notion that they can't fully trust anyone. Why do they feel that way? Because in many cases, they can't.

Maybe it's time to get away from that concept, though. Maybe it's time to help a new generation fix the problems of today for the wrestlers of tomorrow. Instead of forcing the young kids to shake hands with Bob Holly, wrestlers could force the young kids to understand what they could accomplish if they stick together. Maybe it's time to foster a feeling of camaraderie — tighter than that created through initiation rights — so strong in the next group of workers that it overtakes management, breeds genuine inter-employee trust and forces changes.

Wrestlers can make excuses for why unions would never work, but they have to understand that every time they repeat an excuse, they give management more creative control over them. It makes them powerless. It gives them no room to negotiate. At some point, some generation of performers has to stand up and say enough is enough. That's how other unions spring up. When will it be wrestling's turn?

How many more people have to be humiliated on-air for it to happen? How many more have to be "screwed" on pay-per-view before it happens? How many more people, including pregnant women and newlyweds, have to be fired for no reason before we make a change?

Think about how scary things could be without back-up. What if some crazy guy just suddenly showed up one day and forced every wrestler to dress the way he thought was appropriate. I'm not talking about at work, I'm talking about outside of work. The wrestlers would be unable to stop this. Even though they're technically "independent contractors," the lack of a union would force them to adhere to ridiculous rules that don't affect work at all.

Then again, no one would be so smug as to force these people to actually dress a certain way outside the arena, would they? With all the other issues plaguing the industry, how crazy would that be?

Well, grab your skateboard. Let me tell you about a Dynamic Dude named Johnny . . .

CHAPTER 9

The Legend of
Johnny Laryngitis

World Wrestling Entertainment isn't just about Vince McMahon and his family, although you might not know it from simply watching the programs. There's an entire group of producers, directors and other office workers who help shape the insanity that is WWE programming.

Once in a while, this network of names can find itself caught up in miscommunication. For example, there was the time when one of the producers was told to put together a commercial spot for the company's On-Demand 24/7 Wrestling Channel.

The promo was to feature Terry Spinski, better known to WWE fans as The Warlord. Terry had been a member of the tag team the Powers of Pain. He had wrestled for the company in the late 80s and early 90s. Spinski was a nostalgic figure to most and the company reasoned he'd captivate fans who've left the wrestling fold. His image would be invaluable for a 24/7 commercial. The order went out. Make a Warlord commercial for WWE 24/7 On Demand.

Well, there was one small problem with all of this. In the weeks prior to The Warlord commercial, WWE had been featuring lots of former stars on their shows. Marty Jannetty, Sensational Sherri and Jake "The Snake" Roberts had all made appearances on WWE programming. Therefore, it wasn't so far fetched for the producer in charge of creating the spot to think that The Warlord was actually making a return to *Raw*. This, of course, led to the order somehow being changed.

Basically, this misunderstanding led to one of the editors in WWE Headquarters being told to make an Entrance Video for The Warlord and have it ready to go by that night. They needed it for when Warlord "returned to *Raw*." Considering that *Raw* airs at 9 p.m. Monday and the order was sent out at 9 a.m. Monday, the editor had a daunting task.

He worked his fingers to the bone, searching high and low for any footage of Terry and his in-ring conquests that might exist on the shelves. Flipping through many videos, including the latest TNA pay-per-view tapes (which the company keeps on hand for employees to view), the editor was finally able to put something together. By 5 p.m. that day, the tape was ready to go and the young video editor braced himself for a chance to see Warlord's big return, along with the video he'd constructed, on that night's edition of *Raw*.

Sadly, that never happened. The Warlord didn't return. The entrance video was useless. The tape editor's entire day had been wasted.

Worst of all, he didn't find out until he watched *Raw* that night. The next day, when the word got out on the Internet that Warlord's tape had been made mistakenly, the office searched high and low for the mole. Weird that they would freak out and try to pinpoint the person leaking information, but they wouldn't freak out and try to identify the person who messed up the order and wasted a paid employee's day.

No biggie, though. Things like that happen a lot in any company. People have miscommunications all the time. Any seven-year-old who's ever played a game of "broken telephone" knows that by the time a message reaches the final listener, it can be changed drastically. You can start off by telling someone, "We need a Warlord 24/7 ad" and by the end of the day it's, "We need Warlord Underpants Dishwasher Cookiepuss." It's a fact of life.

That's why we need people like Johnny "Ace" Laurinaitis. One notch below the McMahons when it comes to dealing with on-air talent, Johnny is well known within the industry.

For starters, he was a Dynamic Dude. The Dudes were a tag team consisting of Johnny and "Hardcore Homecomer" Shane Douglas. The duo road skateboards to the ring and smiled a lot. They came off like a stereotype of what non-wrestling fans think pretty-boy wrestlers should be like.

Johnny Laryngitis, as he's called behind his back due to his raspy voice, has a history of dealing with office politics too. It was one of his last real chances at success. Why? Well, when your brother is wrestling legend Road Warrior Animal and you still can't get a top on-air spot in an American Wrestling promotion, perhaps you should turn your attention to doing behind-the-scenes stuff . . . in another country.

John did just that. He went to Japan and found himself working backstage. According to many of his detractors, Ace's Japanese successes can be attributed to schmoozing the right people, saying what those in charge want to hear and making googly eyes at the wife of promoter Giant Baba. However, those same detractors say that this isn't how he got his position as Vice President of Talent Relations in WWE.

No, not all. He didn't schmooze, kiss up and make goo-goo eyes at Mrs. Baba. No. He schmoozed, kissed up and made goo-goo eyes at Stephanie McMahon. (That's what the detractors say. Don't look my way. I ain't one to gossip, so you ain't heard that from me.)

Now, now, now, that's neither here nor there. People have to do things in order to reach positions of power all the time. Why? Well, because they have amazing ideas and strategies that might never see the light of day unless they butter up the right people. Johnny was no exception. He had things that he wanted to accomplish. In order to do that, he needed to get with the right people. Once that was done, he could finally put the wrong things right. Finally — yes, finally — Johnny Ace would fix the world of wrestling! Hallelujah! So, what were some of those things he wanted to do to make things better?

Was he intent on helping wrestlers get health insurance?

Was he set on fixing the drug and steroid problem that's prevalent in this business?

Was he here to institute some sort of creative input for wrestlers that are forever bogged down in nonsensical on-air stories?

Was he going to address the problem of wrestlers dying young and ensure that today's crop of superstars don't follow the same path?

No . . . none of those things. Johnny Ace was going to do something far more important. He was going to change the world.

Yes, Johnny Laurinaitis was going to dress everyone up in nice clothes.

You read that right — nice clothes. Ace decried that from this day forward, wrestlers were mandated to dress in professional attire. At the airport, on the way to the arena, at a restaurant or anywhere else wrestlers were, they were to be dressed up. They had jobs that were deemed important by the public. They might as well look the part, right? Dress 'em up! That'll be a great way to showcase your employees, huh? Ugh.

Now, let's forget for a moment that no one really gives a damn what wrestlers are wearing when they see them in public. Sports entertainers walking down the street are viewed one of two ways. Fans freak out and rush them for autographs, whether they're wearing a suit, a fanny pack, a sombrero or a pair of Mork and Mindy suspenders. Non-fans walk right by, never even realizing who this person is supposed to be. So, in that sense, it doesn't matter.

What makes things worse is that WWE wrestlers are not employees. The company has long classified them as "independent contractors." It's an easy way to get around things like health insurance, retirement planning and other unpleasant subjects. However, for some reason, these independently contracted employees can be told by World Wrestling Entertainment what to wear to and from events. Wrap your head around that one. How can that be?

Oh yeah. Almost forgot. No union. (Hee hee — Union. What a funny theme song they had. *Toot toot! Union!* Ahhh. Oh Vince, you slay me.)

Well, OK. I get the idea here, sort of. Johnny Ace's reasoning was that wrestlers in suits are looked at as stars. If you run into Chris Jericho on the street, you'll see him as more successful if he's dressed up — or something like that. Whatever. That's all well and good. There's only one problem with all that.

These men, in their suits, are wedged into the coach section of airplanes during flights. Why coach?

Well, in January 2005, World Wrestling Entertainment, these proprietors of prestige, decided to cut costs by disallowing wrestlers to fly in business class, even on international flights. I'm not kidding. They're in business attire and they can't fly in business class! Are you people reading this? It's almost as if Johnny was getting some perverse pleasure out of torturing the employees. It made no sense at all. You have a tired, sweaty and uncomfortable 250-pound man in a suit crammed into a seat next to his fan. What kind of lasting impression is *that* gonna leave on fans?

> Wow! Chris Jericho! I'm such a huge fan! I'm so amazed that I got to meet you! You look so important in your suit. Can I trouble you for two small things? First, can I have your autograph, you suit-wearing wrestling God? Secondly, can you move over a bit so I can use the armrest?

Crazy, right? Let's forget the business class ban. This suit rule was implemented before John snatched away business seating. But even then, wrestlers couldn't fly in style while wearing their nice clothes. They've long since been barred from flying first class, even if they pay for it themselves. Why? Well, locker room etiquette dictates that you're not allowed to. The reason is . . . well, there is no reason. It's just the way things are. You don't question it or else you'll end up in wrestler court or some other self-policing situation that WWE bestows upon the "boys."

So management makes the wrestlers uncomfortable and then lets the wrestlers haze each other in order to ensure that everyone's even more uncomfortable. Hate to sound like a broken record here, but if the wrestlers stopped worrying about who was upgrading plane tickets and started worrying about their employers overstepping their bounds in the workplace, this wouldn't be going on at all.

So, you tell me, what will a fan think when he sees a wrestler wearing a suit, but in ghetto airline seating? Seems counterproductive, no? I guess projecting the right image is only important when it inconveniences the employees and doesn't cost the company a dime.

To make sure everyone knew he was serious, John took swift

action against those who stood in the way of his dress code. When 5'4" high flying wrestler Rey Mysterio failed to comply with Ace's demands, he was promptly fined. Nice! Serves him right, that friggin' midget. They're always causing problems. I wish there was something we could do about them short people. Hey Johnny, any ideas?

Funny you should ask. The next order of business for Laryngitis following Dress-Up Day was to insist that all wrestlers promoted to the main WWE roster be over 6'4". No joke. No kidding. Wrestling skills, interview skills, charisma and character development be damned. It was all about height. That was the big problem with World Wrestling Entertainment . . . well, besides the clothing.

This decision was nuts. Now, I'm not saying that because I think smaller wrestlers are better than bigger ones. In fact, this policy would be just as wrong in reverse. It sets limits on who you look at to bring up to your main roster. The reason why it's nuts is that it cuts WWE's choices for future stars down tremendously. It decreases the numbers in the potential talent pool and leaves the company with fewer to choose from. It's not about personal preference. It's about limiting the choices. It's about taking the variety out of what should be a variety show.

To me, with wrestling, it depends what they want to do, what they feel is right – the company. Some big people got in their position because [the company will] push them so much that the fans end up liking them. To me, they can do the same thing with Cruiserweights if that's the direction they want to go. Like you have some people like Rey [Mysterio], who's one of the smallest guys in the business, but he's phenomenal. You see him do things that, he'll go out there and do things that make sense. You have some small people that do amazing things in wrestling. You're like "There's no way this little person is gonna beat this big person." But once you see the story start to unfold and make sense, they have you believing, "Well, he can beat him. Wait a minute, he did beat him!" So it all depends on how you put it together. — **Elix Skipper**

The humor of all this is that Vince McMahon has forever been known as a fan of the "larger than life" wrestlers. Hell, it even got him indicted once. Strange that the new deputy in town would immediately go to work and create a rule that coincides 100% with what his boss had always wanted. Weird, huh? It's almost as if he did it to garner favor with the owner rather than because he thought it was good for business. At least, it seems that way. (Again, I'm not one to gossip.)

That, right there, is the main problem. Rather than keeping keen eyes around him to serve as checks and balances to his power, Vince McMahon chooses yes-men and others that tell him what he wants to hear. Laurinaitis is not alone. There's a million of them just like him, who dress like him. Walk, talk and act like him. I say this because you find yourself asking if the real Vince McMahon can please stand up. Why? It's because it's hard to distinguish the chairman from those that shadow him, echoing his thoughts and desires.

It's an issue. In fact, it's probably become World Wrestling Entertainment's most prevalent issue. Mr. McMahon, free from worry that a competitor can come and gobble him whole, has the luxury of paying people to laugh at his jokes, believe his beliefs and give him a hearty thumbs up even if he doesn't deserve it.

That must stroke his ego pretty nicely. I can't imagine that it would make him any money. Then again, that's not what it's all about, right?

One of Vinnie Mac's most trusted aids, Pat Patterson, was brought out of semi-retirement in 2004 to help him decipher what was wrong with the on-air product. Perplexed by waning fan interest and unable to get a straight answer from the corporate robots, Mac turned to a man who'd never thought twice about giving him an honest answer.

After spending some time examining the company, Pat came back with theory. Perhaps it was Triple H and the fact that he eats every opponent he meets that has stunted the company's ability to create new stars. Patterson reasoned that Helmsley's character could be scaled back, allowing others to shine in his absence. That would solve most of the problems right there.

Sounds good, right? After all, that's what sane people had been saying for years. That's what the yes-men couldn't tell the chairman. Thank God for Pat. Thank God for cooler heads. At least now Vince could do something to correct this problem. Finally, he could get rid of the problem.

He did just that. A month later, WWE wished Pat Patterson a fond farewell as he tendered his resignation and settled into retirement.

Now you tell me, if your boss canned the one guy who told him the truth about his company's woes, would you do what you could to make him see the errors in his decisions? Something tells me "no." Dumb question. Sorry, nevermind.

What I meant to ask was this: Would you remain a yes-man, knowing that you'd be out of work if you didn't? Would you do everything you could do to agree with Vince's ego-driven insane decisions? Would you watch him dance and play the fiddle while his empire burned around him? Think about it. Would you?

I believe the answer you're looking for is, "Yes sir, Mr. McMahon."

> Vince McMahon has very much the [Sylvester] Stallone syndrome about him. The Stallone Syndrome goes back to when I was in Paradise Alley years ago. Sly would do a scene that he wrote. At the end of the scene, everyone would say "That was great. That was academy." A scene would go by that he directed and they'd say "That was great. That was academy." Everybody would applaud. "Oh man, that couldn't have been better." At the end of the movie, it was, "How was the movie?" "Oh, it was the greatest I've ever seen." Because that's what you get whenever you're the king, the boss, or the head of a corporate system. You get the accolades when they're not due. — **Terry Funk**

Eventually good sense prevailed and this Bag-the-Big-Guys policy didn't last. It was bound to happen. Larger than life characters like Gene Snitsky didn't amount to a hill of beans without proper character development anyway. Size doesn't really mean all that much in a scripted world of sports entertainment.

It doesn't matter how big you are. You can be the Incredible Hulk. If the writers give you storylines that make you look like the Jolly Green Giant, you're not making any money. Size is immaterial. Before Kevin Nash hit pay dirt with the N.W.O., he played throwaway characters like Oz and Vinnie Vegas. Just because you're big, that doesn't mean you can be interesting. In 2006, only those who are scripting your journey can make you that. It didn't used to be like that. 'Tis now, though.

> Come on, James. So Johnny brought up some big guys. They're big. How bad can their characters be? How bad are the gimmicks on this show? How can writers fuck up a huge strongman with a look that screams money?

You don't know? Oh man. Throw out your milk cartons and grab a mat, kids. It's story time.

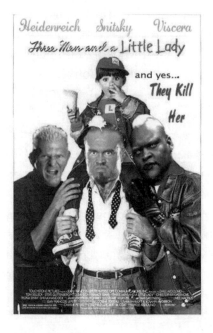

CHAPTER 10

Perverts, Racism
and Other Funny Concepts

The writers at World Wrestling Entertainment can make or break anyone. With so many wrestlers being cut loose at any moment, wwe gives them all a common reason. According to the company, "creative has nothing for you."

Thanks to this scapegoat, wwe can now feel free to release anyone they see fit to at any time. There are no limitations on who could go. It's a buyer's market and Mr. McMonopoly has no one to compete with. He can cut loose any employee he wants. He can make a game out of it.

What messed up stuff could he do? Hmmm. Could you imagine if he fired a married couple on the same day? Actually, I should say, could you imagine if he made John Laurinaitis fire a married couple on the same day? Wow. Think about that for a second. A man and a woman both work for the promotion and both lose their jobs on the same exact day. That must be horrible. Even wwe couldn't be that cold.

Guess again. They not only did that, they did that . . . twice! They did it to two separate couples. In the case of Charlie and Jackie Haas, they got the axe less than a month after their wedding. That's gotta sting, don't you think?

> First we found out from John Laurinaitis, who called us and told us that WWE creative could not find anything to do with us. They couldn't find the right character or gimmick to put on me. So the first thing that went through my mind was when they say "for better or for worse" at weddings, they're not kidding. We got the worst right off the bat. Not only did I lose my job, but so did my wife. So both sources of income were cut off completely two weeks after we're married. But what won't kill you will make you stronger. — **Charlie Haas**

Just hearing that is enough to make you think that the newly formed Haas Family was a headache in the locker room, right? After all, in any other line of work, firing a husband and wife on the same day would be considered, I don't know, a punishment or something. It seems like the type of thing done to send a message.

Sorry. Not in wwe's world. Around here, it's done because it's business. What's more, it's done because it can always be blamed on the creative team. The wrestlers don't really fail or succeed on their own merit anymore. They fail and succeed based on what's written for them by people who don't know much about the wrestling industry. That's got to be scary. Essentially, you trust your career to a writer who's never wrestled and, in many cases, can barely write.

> That's frustrating. Back in '98 and '99, when wrestling was on top and there was competition between WCW and WWF, they were firing writers left and right for not coming up with storylines for everybody. That's what was different with the WWE of the late 90s compared to today. They had a storyline for everybody. From the beginning of the show to the end. From Crash Holly all the way to Stone Cold Steve Austin. Everybody had a storyline and I think that's what drew in the fan base they had at the time. Because maybe Stone Cold wasn't someone's favorite wrestler, maybe Crash Holly was or Bob Holly was. The fans wanted to see their favorite wrestler and everyone had a storyline. Back then, if they didn't have a storyline for everyone, they'd fire writers and keep the wrestlers. Now they're firing the wrestlers and keeping the same writers who aren't doing their job. Like Dave Lagana, you know, who has no idea about wrestling. Here he is, he thinks he can dictate to someone who's worked their ass off and sacrificed broken bones,

torn ligaments, blood, sweat and tears to get to where they are. . . . He can dictate someone's life. "Oh, we can't come up with a character for you." Yeah, well if he's the one who's the creative mind, supposedly speaking, then they should fire him. — **Charlie Haas**

Charlie's right in that respect. What's funny though is that while performers like him and his wife caused the writing team to draw blanks, they have no problem firing away countless horrible ideas for some other larger-than-life performers. How does that work?

That brings us to the scariest part of World Wrestling Entertainment's creative team. We've watched their stories unfold on TV. We've seen their visions. Well, you know what? When viewing the world through their eyes, it looks pretty friggin' disturbing. If their art imitates their lives, then they live in a place where all ethnicities are accentuated to the umph degree and big men are creepy rapists who get the girl in the end. That's the world they live in. Every big guy likes forced sex. There are no exceptions.

I'm not kidding. In the span of two years, WWE has portrayed a stream of wrestlers as disturbing sexual deviants. They were all fairly big and they all required a strong gimmick in order to take the focus off any deficiencies within the ring. It's understood. What's really frightening is the all the insane skits and segments, especially when you look at them all together.

"The Big Red Machine" Kane forced Lita to have sex with him in exchange for leaving her boyfriend Matt Hardy alone. She complied. She got pregnant. He forced her to marry him. They fell in love after she lost the child in a tragic circumstance that's so familiar to many out there. It was the ol' "Husband gets hit with a chair and falls on the mother's stomach during a TV broadcast" story. You may also know Kane as the guy who hooked Shane McMahon's testicles to a car battery on *Raw* a few years ago. One thing is certain. Big Red likes his ladies and he likes his ballgames.

Eventually Lita turned on the Monster. He then treated us to an on-air crying session. It works, right? Don't you remember the *Friday the 13th* where Jason Voorhees bawled and slobbered all over his hockey mask out of anguish? You don't? Me neither. That's probably because it never happened.

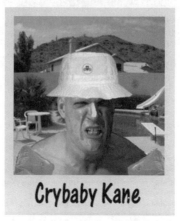

Crybaby Kane

Then you have Gene Snitsky. Snits is the guy that hit Kane with the chair into Lita. Boo on you, Gene. That would be a fine gimmick. He could be a heartless thug with no regard for life. However, after his first promo yielded unintentionally hilarious results, WWE creative saw his true potential. He basically became a goofy nutcase. They shot segments of him punting a baby doll into the audience and imitating its cries. About a year later, when Lita turned on her "husband" Kane, she thanked Snits for killing her baby and kissed him.

> Now James, you're nitpicking. It sounds ridiculous, but as you clearly pointed out earlier, Leets didn't want to have a demon baby. No one wanted her to! She should be thankful that the baby's not here to terrorize the world. We all should be.

You're right. It does make sense for Gene to be the good guy who saved the world from the destruction of the anti-Christ. She should do more than kiss him. He's a hero! Go Gene! Thank God she escaped the evil monster who forced her to bear his seed. Boo Kane!

The problem is that Lita and Snitsky were the bad guys. Kane, the monster rapist, was the good guy. There. Wrap your head around that one. Next.

One of Gene-o's most memorable moments occurred with the next wrestler on the list, John Heidenreich. John began his run in World Wrestling Entertainment as a deranged giant of a man who asked anyone he could for a job. He showed up on *Raw* and begged

Steve Austin to give him an opportunity. That's fine. Nothing wrong there. Oh, he also apparently talked to his penis as if it were alive. Yup. He had a friend named "Little Johnny." We never learned the identity before Heidenreich took hiatus. It was pretty obvious, though. Weird. Hey, look at the bright side. At least he'd come back with something better, right? Ah ha ha ha.

He returned to WWE and started breaking heads on *Smackdown*. He was managed by the David Koresh of Philadelphia, Paul Heyman. Paul E. brought Big John back to the fold by repeating his last name over and over in vignettes.

> Ready, Paul? One, two, three . . . action!
> Hei-den-reich! Hei-den-reich!
> Cut! Beautiful, Paulie. Alright, kid loop that video 19 times and replay it on *Smackdown* for three weeks.

Also, when the giant returned to the ring, he wore little boxing gloves. Honestly. He wore little red boxing gloves. It looked like someone was trying to prevent him from scratching himself or something. Little boxing gloves? What's the worst he could do? Fight in a little boxing match? Big deal. Well, not so fast. There's a whole lotta bad stuff he could do. He could yell at old people. He could spit on the ground. He could rape WWE announcer Michael Cole. He can . . . wait, what?

Yup. You read that right. He raped Michael Cole.

OK, he didn't actually rape him. He just kidnapped him and slammed his hips into the announcer's back from a locked room hidden away in the arena. The camera was conveniently positioned from the waist up. Afterwards, the Little Boxer read Cole a poem and then asked him to say "thank you." Michael complied. I have no idea why. I wouldn't say "thank you." At that point, what can he do to you worse than what he just did? Once you've been dry humped by a large man in little boxing gloves on broadcast television, you have nothing else to fear.

Based loosely on the poetry gimmick of "The Genius" Lanny Poffo in the 80s and 90s, Heidenreich was no Lanny. Instead of writing his poetry on Frisbees and tossing them into the crowd, he wrote them on a piece of paper and tossed little Johnny around.

Good ol' nutty Heidenreich. Well, as we said earlier, John caught up to Gene Snitsky at both the 2004 Survivor Series and 2005 Royal Rumble. Both skits were truly insane. They both involved Snits and Heidy grunting and groaning in way that makes you feel icky. Their first meeting went like this:

Snitsky: I like your poetry.

Heidenriech: I like what you do to babies.

Yeah. "I like what you do to babies." Crazy. On their next meeting, both men declared their fondness for one another. We all thought we'd get a chance to see Team Poetic Baby Killing Sodomy at *WrestleMania* that year, but it never happened. In fact, neither man ended up wrestling on the biggest show of the year at all. Wow. I'm so glad we spent so much time following them and their propensity for baby killing and deviant sex around. Even WWE must have realized that it didn't want WM, its yearly time capsule, to feature such insane characters. I wish it felt the same way about their TV shows.

The irony of John Heidenreich is that his gimmick eventually got mangled so much that no one had any idea what the point of it was. He went from threatening to have sex with other men to beating up fake fans, wearing a straight jacket, hanging out with children and looking for friends. Considering that WWE fires people all the time because the writers have no ideas for them, it's amazing that they can come up with a never ending stream of bad gimmicks for a guy who, well, can't wrestle all that well.

Then you have Viscera. Having been portrayed as a rap star and demon, WWE was almost out of ideas. After all, in the World Wrestling World, there's only so many ways you can promote a 500-pound black man. Oh wait . . . that's it. How about a Barry White–inspired rapist! It's different than Kane and Heidenreich because . . . well, he's inspired by Barry White.

Vis got a monster push in 2005 as an oversized soulful lover with a blonde Mohawk. Apparently he enjoyed eating and sex. I'm not making a joke. That was the gimmick. He would make inappropriate sexual remarks to women like ring announcer Lillian Garcia and then call for food to be taken from fans and given to him. Vis summed it up best on the May 23, 2005 edition of *Raw*:

> Yeah, you always gotta have a good meal with romance. You know that don't you? Always have to have a good meal, baby. Yeah, come on in here with that hotdog, girl. Yeah, I got a hot dog for you too. Yeah.

Creepy. Oh, also, he liked to hump men from behind. Anyone was fair game. If Viscera got you on your belly, he'd climb on top and plow away. No joke. It was one of his specialty moves and it was called the Visagra. He was Bubba the Butt Bumper. That was the gimmick. While the segments were enough to draw curious channel switchers to stop and see what was going on, it was also a vindication to those who don't watch wrestling anymore. Sadly, the V Man was just one of many WWE superstars with a bizarre sexual appetite. They weren't all large in stature either, but they all had strange fetishes when it came to getting it on. At the end of the day, that's what it's all about. The name on the marquee is *Sexual Perversion*. Come on. You know that.

You had Dave Batista defeating then–World Tag Team Champions La Résistance all at once and then planting a flagpole in them as they lay in a heap. The visual was that of Tista sodomizing them with it, an act he threatened to do to them earlier in the night. Threatening to shove a flag up a guy's ass is something a tough guy would do. Actually shoving that flag up his ass is something a bizarre gay rapist would do. There's a fine line between bad-ass and grab-ass, Dave.

Of course, there's resident Olympic gold medallist Kurt Angle telling Booker T that he desires "dirty" sex with his wife. While that would be strange enough, it didn't stop there. According to the Olympian, he wanted to have "bestiality sex" with her. Now either no one in WWE knows what the term "bestiality" means, or else they all think that Booker married a goat. You make the call. On a side note, when you're a professional wrestling company that employs an actual Olympic gold medal winner in wrestling and the best thing you can think of for him to do is threaten to have animal sex with someone's wife on TV, you're in bad shape.

There was Tyson Tomko's match against Steven Richards at *Unforgiven 2004*. Richards, dressed in drag, was savagely beaten on pay-per-view while Tomko screamed out "He's a faggot" as loud as can be. Tyson wanted to make that point clear just in case anyone doubted that they were actually witnessing a hate crime. Ironically, the next week would be the week that Heidenreich "raped" *Smackdown* announcer Michael Cole. Ah, autumn. The leaves change colors and everyone is perverted. La la la.

Two weeks after that, wrestling legend and 55-year-old man Ric Flair, in an effort to sell his match against Randy Orton at the *Taboo Tuesday* pay show, reminded the live cable audience of his sexual prowess by making an analogy between Orton and virgins. According to Naitch . . . well, he said this:

> So in my eyes, in my eyes, you look at me and say Legend. I look at you and say virgin. You are a virgin at killing legends. And you know how many virgins I have made holler, scream and bleed all night long? God!

Ick. It's like your grandfather telling you — in graphic detail — about all the women he got with. Good plan, WWE. Make the fans throw up and they'll surely order the show!

Flair is also famous for having a conversation on *Raw* with Gene Snitsky while staring deeply into his nipples the entire time. Ric has salivated over Batista's arms and gotten on his knees and bowed in front of Triple H. The next year, Ric would threaten to grab Kurt Angle's testicles in a match. Later that night, he would make good on that threat. All things considered, the virgin line took the cake. Something must have been in the air around that Tuesday. Talk about Taboo.

When *Taboo Tuesday* finally did roll around a few weeks later, it was fellow WWE 55-year-old Jerry Lawler's turn to be skeevy. During a schoolgirl battle royal, Lawler, on commentary, told co-host Jim

Ross that he wished he was in grammar school again so he could see girls in schoolgirl outfits. Grammar school graduates are around 12 years old. Jerry Lawler has major issues.

This is the same company that featured Mark Henry receiving oral sex from a transvestite on a *Raw* broadcast in the late 90s, Dennis "Mideon" Knight in a flesh-colored body suit under the name "Naked Mideon," and 60s sitcom parody Beaver Cleavage salivating over his mother's . . . well, cleavage. Sex is always a good hook when looking to enrage those high moral watchdog groups. After all, business booms when programming is deemed offensive by pundits. It makes Vince out to be the bad guy. As we mentioned earlier, he likes that.

Even more disturbing with gimmicks like this is that WWE writers seem to feel that women enjoy being physically intimidated, raped or kidnapped. After all, it happens a lot and the women always end up in love. In real life, that doesn't happen.

Critics say that things like this should make us wonder if the WWE writing team members have ever dated a woman. Not me. I say that things like this should make us wonder if WWE writing team members have ever met a woman. You don't need to be a sex expert like Dr. Ruth to understand that forcing women to have intercourse with you doesn't equal love. Even if it does once in a while, it doesn't happen all the time. In the World of Wrestling Entertainment, it does.

I don't think that the writers or the creative team as a whole understand how to write or present a serious angle in a way that the powers that be, who put the final stamp on it, would understand or agree with it. Because to get that serious angle, you have to have some sort of believability in it. You have to suspend everybody's disbelief. I don't know if they understand how to get back to that or even go there. They may think they're going there or getting back to that, but it's pretty evident that some has humor in it. How many times can you hit someone in the head with a sledgehammer before they die? You know? Is that serious? Someone will look at that and say "I'll give him the benefit of the doubt," but there's only so many times people will believe you can take a sledgehammer out there and hit they guy in the head and he's

It's not just about sex, though. Seriously. There's so much more to it than that. It's about pushing buttons. It's about going to the offensive well so many times that the bucket's breaking. It's about searching for attention in a mainstream world where no one will give it. If we can't hook them in with entertainment, we'll force them in with offensive material! That's the WWE way.

Muhammad Hassan and Khrosow Daivari were introduced to *Raw* fans in 2004. The duo, billed as Arab-Americans from Detroit, were not terrorists. They were, in fact, citizens of Detroit. What was their gimmick? They were so upset about being prejudged by Americans because of their nationality, that they have decided to make America pay. Now there's a lesson. "Any Arab, American or otherwise, is inherently bad. Even those who are good will turn against America after a while. Praise George W. Amen."

WWE insisted that this characterization was "sophisticated." It was deep and more than a black or white, good guy versus bad guy issue. Many of WWE's fans understood the "sophisticated" nature of these characters and acted accordingly. They held up signs that read "7-Eleven is hiring" and "I lent Daivari my Carpet."

Oh, and World Wrestling Entertainment showed those signs on TV. Now, that's some sophisticated stuff there, Scooter.

Oh, oh, hold on. I almost forgot. Prior to Daivari and Hassan debuting on *Monday Night Raw*, WWE Diva/Crazy Lady Ivory asked her *Sunday Night Heat* co-host Todd Grisham how he'd be getting to Huntsville for Monday's show. Todd responded that he was driving. To this, Ivory replied on-air, "Good, because I don't want you to be flying, if you get my drift." Wow. This whole thing is so sophisticated I could throw up.

Then again, those weren't racial slurs. They were in poor taste, but nothing offensive. Even WWE will draw the line now and then.

Oh . . . oh, on the June 13, 2005 *Raw*, WWE good guy, Stone Cold Steve Austin joined them for an in-ring showdown. When they arrived, he said, "I see sand people." Scratch what I said about drawing a line.

By July of 2005, both Muhammad and Daivari were members of *Smackdown*. They taped a segment that depicted the two of them leading a group of thugs, complete with black hoods, into the ring to beat up The Undertaker. Taker had just crushed Khrosow Daivari, who was serving "a greater purpose." Muhammad stood tall while the hooded assassins, obviously based on all those bad guys from the beheading videos, bowed to him. They finished the segment with the evil group carrying the beaten Khrosow from the ring. The announcers pointed out that they were carrying him away "like a martyr."

Wow. As if that wasn't bad enough, the segment was taped on Tuesday, July 5 and then set to air on that Thursday. When Thursday morning rolled around, something came up. London's subway system was hit by a terrorist attack. Over 50 people died. 700 were wounded.

This was the morning that the show was supposed to air. Crazy, right? So I guess you're figuring that the Hassan angle never aired on television. Wrong. It did. When? Well, it aired that night . . . the night of the London bombings.

They had a full day to edit the tape. In fact, WWE actually aired a scrolling graphic at the bottom of the screen that urged "parental discretion" for those watching. They had the time to write up a warning and edit it in, but not enough time to cut that part out of the show and replace it with a music video for the next pay-per-view? Hell, replace it with ten minutes of hair care tips by Triple H. Replace it with anything.

They didn't, though. It was an absolute lowlight for World Wrestling Entertainment. To showcase this story on the same night that so many people were affected by a tragedy was both tasteless and classless.

Had Vince McMahon been a grown up who realized the gravity of the situation, he could have swayed the collective opinions of countless fans. Many would have rallied behind Big Mac if he had started off that night's *Smackdown* with a statement like this:

> We here at World Wrestling Entertainment are in the business of entertaining our audience. In light of this morning's tragedy in London, we felt that one of our stories might be less entertaining than it was

originally intended. Because of the timing and out of reverence for those lost and affected by this event, we are editing this segment from our show. We hope you enjoy our program and thank you for tuning in.

Who wouldn't forgive WWE's indiscretions after that? People would say, "You know, this gimmick may be offensive, but at least WWE realizes that it's based on something real. They respect those that have died. They respect something."

Instead they ran a quick crawling disclaimer at the bottom of the screen. It was the same type of thing they used to do to advertise local house shows. It was a shameful and disgusting decision. It was one of the times in my life that I truly regretted watching the WWE product. I was ashamed of the company. I was sad for the industry. It was clear that WWE realized the gimmick was based on something real, yet it had no respect for anyone who had been so recently affected. They respected nothing.

Their disrespect for everything was so out-in-the-open that World Wrestling Entertainment even printed the negative newspaper articles on their website, promising that Hassan would "answer his critics" on *Smackdown*. Notice they said "his" critics. There was no mention of how it was WWE's fault for airing the segment, not the actor for playing a role. That would make them WWE's critics, not Muhammad's. This is all semantics, though. UPN stepped in and told the company that it would not broadcast a Hassan segment on that week's *Smackdown*. Apparently, UPN felt the segment was in bad taste.

Keep in mind, this is UPN. I once watched a guy lick a woman he had just met during an episode of *Blind Date* on UPN. Apparently, it thinks that WWE is in bad taste. Wow. It's hearing things like that that makes you think, Holy Cow, what the hell am I watching?

Funny enough, the day before that on the 4th of July, WWE also shot an episode of *Raw*. On that show, Chavo Guerrero Junior arrived and denounced his Hispanic heritage. He asked that everyone now refer to him as Kerwin White. He wore a sweater around his neck and embraced the white bread lifestyle. Sometimes I wonder if it would be easier for WWE to just put a little graphic in the bottom corner of the screen that says "Not white? Stop watching."

Ethnic stereotypes are a classic staple of this business. In fact, it's saved me a hell of a lot of time when meeting people. I just take out my WWE inspired Profile Card and see what I should expect from them.

BLACK

Most likely a rap star, racist, sex addict, All-American Athlete or animal of some sort.

Enjoys hip hop music.

Had a troubled youth.

Has made or will make unwanted sexual advances on white women. When denied, he will challenge her boyfriend to a fight and then lose.

May enjoy working as a servant for rich white people until he feels oppressed. Then he will revolt. Following the revolt, he gets beat up weekly by his old rich white master.

Loves his mama.

MEXICAN

Lies, cheats and steals.

Use the terms "vato, esse, loco, holmes and ona le." Also a big fan of the word "ariba."

May be seen wearing sombreros from time to time.

Drives a bouncy car.

Has a huge family that all work in the same profession he does. They often end up getting into fist-fights with each other though. Then they make up. Then they fight again. This goes on and on.

Refers to everyone from Mexico as his family. After saying "family," he follows it up with "familgia" for no apparent reason (example: "Carlos and the boy, they are my family — my familgia, holmes!").

Wears a mask. If you rip it off his head, you humiliate him far worse than you could ever imagine.

Footnote: Mexicans are interchangeable with Spanish, Brazilian, Latino, Chicano and dark skinned Italians.

JEWISH

Not too much to go on here. There were only two Jewish wrestlers to be featured prominently with their religions in the forefront. One was Barry Horowitz. The other was Bill Goldberg. There were probably many others, but these are the first two that would spring to anyone's mind. Goldberg was an ass-kicking monster. Horowitz wore sparkly suspenders, patted himself on the back and came to the ring with "Hava Nagila" as his theme. Oy vei.

So, there you have it. Jewish people are either brutal powerhouses or weird guys in sparkly suspenders. Your call.

AMERICAN INDIAN

Headdress, facepaint, tomahawk. No exceptions.

GAY

Prances. Always prances.

Wears eye makeup. You can't spot a gay man without the bright blue or purple eye make up. Otherwise, how would you know?

Wears a neck scarf. A feather boa could qualify, too. Then again, Hulk Hogan and Jesse Ventura used boas and they're not. What? They're not.

Kisses opponents during competitions. If they'll do it in a wrestling ring, they'll do it on the golf course. You just know it!

Wears ladies underwear under regular clothes. If you catch one and strip him naked, you'll find panties. Go on. Catch one. You'll see.

JAPANESE

Knows karate and specifically enjoys kicks.

Doesn't speak English, although attempts to through weekly skits that have him misusing words in a hilarious manner. (Ah! Ha ha! He called him "Miss" instead of "Mister!" Aha ha ahah!)

Spits a blinding green mist from his mouth and no one finds it odd. It's seen by observers as if he was just using some sort of weapon. "Oh

look! He just spit that blinding green mist into his opponent's eyes!"
Instead, they should be saying, "Holy fuck! Why is his phlegm green!?
Why is his phlegm green! Oh the horror! Help us all, Lord! Ahhhhhhh!"

Bows constantly.

May or may not wear a mask. He's not as attached to it as the
Mexicans are, but if you tear it, you still piss him off a little.

Throws salt. It's not as visually stunning as the green phlegm, but
it's cool.

Footnote: Japanese rules apply to Chinese, Korean, Vietnamese or
any other nationality WWE deems "Easy Peasy Japanesey."

MIDGETS

Funny. They're just so funny. Go find a midget and poke him with a
stick. That's so funny! They're just like real people only funnier!

Can be hired to impersonate your enemy as an attempt to anger
him. Price of a facemask in your enemy's likeness for said midget to
wear is not included in his asking price.

During a competition, will most likely bite the referee or
umpire's ass.

Has the word "little" somewhere in his name. It can be his first
name as in "Little Rambo." It can be his middle name as in "Larry
Little Feather." It can be his last name as in "Larry Rambo Little."
Then again, it doesn't matter because they're just so damn funny.
Who cares what their names are? Why are you still reading? Go find
one and poke him with that stick already!

BRITISH

Drinks tea. Drinks it all the time. Some of them drink it so much
that they carry a pot with them everywhere they go.

Likes only one type of music — classic British music. Favorite
songs include "God Save the Queen" and "God Save the Queen."

Makes a face as if he just smelled something disgusting.

Likes to wear a frilly dickie under his jacket.

May walk with one arm bent behind his back.

Says "bloody" instead of "fuckin." (Example — I'm gonna kick your bloody ass!) Not all rules apply. For example, the term "Mother Bloody" is not accepted.

Is presently wearing, or at one time has worn, the Union Jack on a pair of short shorts.

When not wearing frilly scarves or the flag on his underpants, he's in a suit.

CUBAN/PUERTO RICAN

Lucky with the ladies.
Violent with the ladies.
Bites fruit and then spits it at people.
Says "chico," "chica," and "ju" instead of "you."
Doesn't button his short sleeved Hawaiian shirt.
May drive a bouncy car. (See Mexican.)

ITALIAN

Gangster. Not a scary gangster. More like a comical gangster. He has two bumbling sidekicks and they eat a lot of spaghetti.
"Fuhgedaboutit."
Does the "screw you" motion of the hand flick from under the chin.
Smokes cigars. Actually, he chews on cigars. He probably wears a leather jacket too.
Eatsa pizza pie! Mama mia!

OLD

Crazy. Old people are crazy.

Likes to get naked for no reason. May scream and start stripping at any moment.

Drinks a lot.

May jump you suddenly and initiate a sexual act against your will.

WOMEN

Wants to show me her puppies.

If you force her to have sex with you, she'll eventually fall in love with you.

She's constantly being bombarded with chants of "Slut! Slut! Slut! Slut!"

Has pillow fights with her girlfriends. They wrestle around in lingerie and end up tearing each other's clothes off. In the end, they all hug — except for one crazy chick who goes nuts and beats them all up.

Likes the guy who abuses her.

Turns on the guy who's nice to her.

Will now or at sometime during her life make out with Vince McMahon.

MIDDLE EASTERN

Hates America.

Has facial hair.

Wears a turban and pointy shoes.

Does the Camel Clutch. Even if this person isn't a wrestler, he likes to do the Camel Clutch. Every Middle Eastern person likes the Camel Clutch.

Bad guy. Always a bad guy. Even if he's a good guy, he'll become bad because he feels discriminated against.

Footnote: Anyone can play a Middle Eastern. If you're a white guy with a good tan, you can be Middle Eastern too.

FRENCH/FRENCH CANADIAN/PIRATE

Makes a face as if they just smelled something disgusting. (Similar to British face, but less nasally.)

Carries a Quebec flag with him everywhere.

Insults the U.S., but not with the same fervor of the Russians or Iranians. They use phrases like "USA is Not OK." To back up these claims, they carry around a sign on a stick.

Has a poodle. Fluffs its fur until it looks as fruity as possible. The dog's name is Fifi.

Fifi may also be a maid. If it is a maid, she will most likely come off as if she's dumber than the dog Fifi. She doesn't speak English at all.

Steals. Likes buried treasure and earthquakes.

If they say they love the United States, their sentiments will most likely not be genuine.

Likes to wear a frilly dickie under his jacket. (See British.)

ISLAND PEOPLE (HAWAIIAN, TONGAN, TAHITIAN, ETC.)

Flies through the air with ease. After all, he's from an island, right? He's almost a monkey.

Eats coconuts. Mmmm. Monkey love coconut.

Hates shoes.

Has a tough time keeping his wavy, greasy, black hair out of his eyes.

Wears a Sarong.

UGANDAN/BOTSWANAN/SAMOAN/MONGOLIAN

Eats people.

Eats live animals.

Moans and screams.

Has no idea what's going on . . . ever. Always needs a handler around to toss him a fish or a chicken to destroy.

Hates shoes.

CANADIAN

Hates Shawn Michaels. He hates him. Boo! Hates him!

Has probably lived in Stu Hart's basement at some point.

Has appeared on TSN's *Off the Record*.

Sings in a band.

Has a U.S. residence that he claims to be from when working in the States.

Shiny clothes. Gotta have the shiny clothes.

Is a Bizarro person. So bizarre. Mr. Canadian Bizarro here boos the good guys and cheers the bad guys! What's up with that? Maybe it's because WWE created a storyline in 1997 that was made to start a mini-war between the U.S. and Canada. They encouraged Canadians to cheer and boo in the opposite way that U.S. fans do. They created this monster and now, because the Canadians liked the idea, they're called bizarre by the World Wrestling Entertainment announcers. That sucks, doesn't it?

CHAPTER 11

Smart Marks Work the Kayfabed Babyfaced Heel Heat

Stereotypes, sexual deviancy and bizarre feuds have all become common place in today's WWE. They mean more to the company than simply giving fans a wrestling match. In fact, often times these strange soap opera things don't even build towards a match at all. Storylines like Viscera's love affair with Lillian Garcia, Al Wilson's on-air marriage and murder at the hands of Dawn Marie and Kane's barbecuing of Jim Ross were all moments that the company centered around at one point. Sadly, they were then dropped, never used to try to sell the fans a match. It makes no sense. That's how you make money. That's how you get people to buy pay-per-views.

It's kind of like the deal with Championships. Often overlooked or given to improper performers, the titles have all but become worthless pieces of gold. To many of those writing the shows, these belts and their history mean nothing.

Look, I know it's silly to debate the tarnished image of championships in professional wrestling. In the grand scheme of things, titles themselves mean nothing. The history of any championships is subjective and based on whoever is writing the history book at the time. In this entertainment industry, title belts are seen almost as archaic by some. They're nothing more than throwbacks to the day when promoters and carnies would try to fool the marks in the audience into thinking that the staged performances were real.

That's the mentality and it rears its ugly head quite often. The most repeated quote is something usually attributed to former WWE writer and WCW wrecker Vince Russo. In a nutshell, wrestling championships mean nothing. They're merely "props."

That term sends wrestling purists up a wall. How dare you call the championship a prop?! It's much more than that! It's sunshine. It's jellybeans. It's teddybears. It's love. It is *not* a prop.

Sadly, it *is* a prop. It always has been. I agree with this whole-heartedly. Professional wrestling is a scripted form of entertainment and everything involved with it is a prop. The ring announcer's microphone is a prop. So are Ric Flair's robes, Jerry Lawler's crown, Triple H's sledgehammer, Captain Lou Albano's rubber bands and everything else on the screen. They're all props.

Here's the thing, though. Championships may be props, but they are *the main* props. While still looking at them for what they realistically are, titles should also be treated with the utmost respect. Without them, your show makes no sense.

> It seems like now titles are just props. Whatever happened to the day where two guys fought for a championship and the winner got paid more money? Now you gotta sleep with somebody's sister's cousin's brother's uncle to get a title shot. You know, people always said, "The emotion you showed when you won a title looked real." That's because it was real. Because in the grand scheme of things, I was a mark that got to live out his dream to be a wrestler and here I was winning championships and going down in history in the profession of which I really admired. Holding championships meant a tremendous amount to me in terms of how I wanted to act and how I wanted to portray myself as a champion. — **D-Lo Brown**

Wrestling is called a soap opera. It's a male soap opera. That's the catch phrase that all the fly-by-night fans from the late 90s repeated over and over. It's like *General Hospital* with a shot of testosterone. It's *90210* with muscle heads and implants. It's a soap opera.

Fine. Accepted. It's actually much more than that, but for the sake of time, let's say that's true. However, it's a soap opera set in a wrestling company. That's the premise. Just like *ER* is a show set in a hospital that follows around the lives of doctors, WWE is a show set in a wrestling arena that follows around the lives of wrestlers. There's no debating here. That's that. It's a soap opera about wrestling.

Therefore, in the scripted world of wrestling soap opera, titles mean everything. It's why these wrestlers come to work. It's the motivation behind their characters. Imagine if Angela Lansbury didn't solve any crimes on *Murder She Wrote*. Why should she? The murders aren't real. The dead bodies are just "props."

Yes. Titles are props. Just like Rocky Balboa's title was a prop. Just like the Hill Valley Trophy in *The Karate Kid* was a prop. Just like the Batmobile was a prop. They're all props. The only difference is that Batman never peed on his car.

WWE does that to its titles all the time (figuratively, of course). It misuses its championships, misusing its contenders in the process. When the Cruiserweight Title is mistreated, the wrestlers in the Cruiserweight division are indirectly misused too.

How so? Well, imagine your name is Nunzio. You're a small performer who can all but give up your World Title hopes in the land of giants. With Johnny Ace and the McMahons salivating over big men, your chances of landing the lead prop are pretty weak.

So, you have a title like the Cruiserweight Championship to shoot for. That's why you come to work. Your best shot at anything is to win the Cruiserweight Title. It's your goal.

Now let me ask you something. Would the Cruiserweight Title seem all that impressive if it was held by a 55-year-old comedy champion? Would it be that great if it were then captured by a 5'2" woman? The belt would seem almost comedic, right? It would make anyone striving to attain it seem like a tool, right?

That's what happened. Fifty-year-old Chavo Guerrero Senior captured the strap. Shortly thereafter, Jacqueline was crowned Champion. Some prize, huh? The biggest goal of a guy like Nunzio is nothing more than a joke prop to be given to a retired star and a female performer. Some goals, Nunzy. Some goals. Your dream title is handed out to random names all for the sake of comedy. Gee. I wonder why no one cares about the Cruiserweight Division.

I'm sure WWE finds all these random champs humorous, but that's not what it should be looking for in its title holders. Prop or not, it should still make sure its champions have credibility in the fantasy wrestling world. Why?

Well, it's as if Rocky was chasing a title not worn by Apollo Creed but by Lassie. Come on. That would be funny, right? Lassie! It's random. It's humorous. Why wouldn't that work? Maybe because Lassie is a dead dog that has no credibility as a boxer. So what? She doesn't need to be a boxer. It's all fake. The title's only a prop! See the insanity of that statement?

This isn't the first time this has happened. If anything, WWE specializes in damaging its roster because it doesn't fully grasp the importance of lending credibility to its titles. As mentioned in the Hunter chapter, WWE absorbed the Intercontinental Championship into its World Title in 2002. In one match, Triple H (surprise, surprise) became a double champion and the IC belt was no more. For the next six months, no one cared about the mid-carders on *Raw*. Why? Maybe because they had no reason to be on the show. The only title that they could possibly have a chance of winning was gone. How wonderful.

Then again, maybe WWE knew what they were doing. Nah. They ended up bringing the strap back to *Raw* six months later.

So what? Titles imply that the wrestling matches are important. To WWE, they're not. If they could, they would yank the ring out of the arena and fill 90% of the show with women stripping.

Want proof? In August of 2003, Vince McMahon was backstage at a house show (a non-televised wrestling card). On that show, Tajiri wrestled Rhyno. It was a mid-level match that wasn't meant to bring the house down, so road agent Dean Malenko told them to "slow down the pace of the match." They did.

After they exchanged headlocks for some time, the crowd became restless. Once the boring chants started, Vince lost it. He marched out to the ring, called off the match and gave the fans what they wanted — a bikini contest!

Yeah. Could you imagine if you were at work and your boss told you to slow down your presentation? Then, as you're explaining your new product line in a more pronounced manner, the CEO marches in, tells you you're boring and then introduces a strip tease from Julie in Human Resources?

Not only that, but what kind of insane rationale goes into confirming to your audience that wrestling is boring. Better to ignore them and let the match come to a close before confronting Rhyno and Tajiri backstage. Why? Because Vince McMahon is in the wrestling business! You don't crap on your main product in front of your customers. The Billionaire Promoter King needs to be told this?

Look. No matter what he says, it's about wrestling. You can have a wrestling show without bikinis. You can't have it without wrestling. It's the one constant. It's the one thing that can't change. I'm not saying that McMahon should base his whole company around wrestling. But he should present it in the best light possible because it's his main product.

It's like MTV. While MTV likes to have its reality shows and top 10 things, it's still "Music Television." It might not primarily focus on music anymore, but Kurt Loder never went to the MTV Beachhouse and called music "boring." Why not? Because it's where MTV's bread is buttered and it knows it. I wish I could say the same thing about Vinnie Mac.

That's the thing about WWE that always amazed me. It's so embarrassed to admit to being a wrestling company. All it wants to do is call itself entertainment. It has strived for years to branch out and get away from what made WWE famous — the wrestling.

> They're forgetting how they got to the dance. I understand that people want to be entertained and times change, people want to see something different. Different can be talking on the mic a little bit then going out there and doing something. But when there's a two-hour show and you only get five matches, there's a problem. Because wrestling is what got everyone to where they are. Everyone made all the money they made. It's what they did in the ring. We can go to an arena and take this away. We can take that away. They can take everything out of that whole arena. Everything. They can still have that wrestling match. But if they move that ring or take out that ring, they can't have a show. They need to remember how they got to the dance.

People love to see a little bit of drama, but they love to see the wrestling. I know I want to see the wrestling. Sometimes it can be the funny wrestling. Sometimes it can be the serious wrestling. Sometimes it can be the back and forth, it's all different types of wrestling. But wrestling is what got us to the dance. Everyone needs to remember that. — **Elix Skipper**

Notice that neither I or Elix is saying that WWE needs to have two guys trade headlocks for an hour. That's not the issue. I'll be the first to admit that prolonged wrestling matches are something that some people just aren't into. If they are, chances are they watch wrestling anyway. The objective of promoters is to reach out to a new audience and expose them to this wonderful magical world of rasslin' that so many people look down on.

So what does WWE do? It goes out of its way to be something else. WWE has tried to be a football company. It's tried to be a bodybuilding federation. It's made work-out supplements. It's had reality competitions. Don't worry if you're into the wrestling, though. It's still there. You're just not supposed to like it.

Even the term "wrestler" has been dropped from WWE's vernacular, replaced by "sports entertainers." Wrestler is a bad word. Don't believe me? Well listen to this.

WWE hands out a form to all of its new announcers. Entitled "WWE Announcing/On Camera Notes," this sheet documents what should and shouldn't be said on air by the announce team. The first thing that struck me funny when viewing this sheet is that certain commentators have done nothing more than repeat the examples that the company has written. Things like "Undertaker demands respect and will stop at nothing to get it," is not just a one-liner thought up by an announcer. It's a sample sentence on the sheet. They just repeat it.

Another funny announce team rule tells them to "don't call a move before it happens." What kind of people are they hiring here? How brain dead do you have to be that you need to be told that? It's like saying "Don't tell the fans that this is all fake bullshit."

That's just the tip of the iceberg when it comes to on-air notes for commentators. Some, like the one that tells announcers to not say exact dates, are explained like this: "Nobody knows dates. Everybody knows when 'in two weeks,' 'tomorrow,' etc. is." Others, like the words that will follow, are simply listed.

These are the words that WWE prohibits its announcers from saying on the air. They are specifically listed on the sheet and tell you volumes about how the company looks at its product. They are:

Belt, strap
Feud
Backstage
Acrobatics
Me, I
War
Inside Terms (Blown Up, Shoot, Rib, etc.)
Performance, Choreograph
International
Interesting
House Show
"Shots" (no title shots)
Pro Wrestling
Pro Wrestler

There you have it. That's what announcers can't say. There are two things I love about that list. The first is that after listing "belt, strap" they go off about how they don't have "belts" but "championships." It's explained that WWE titles "represent something." Considering all you read in the last four pages or so, that's pretty funny.

What really struck me were the final words. Pro wrestling and pro wrestler are both banned terms for those that call the action. Makes sense. After all, this isn't a wrestling show, right? It's World . . . uh, mumble mumble . . . Entertainment. You know that.

It's not just announcers, though. Fans are expected to forget about wrestling too. In fact, wrestling fanatics who call for more actual wrestling on the shows are scoffed at. It's not about the wrestling. You should know that. If you're into the wrestling you're a . . . mark!

Oh no! Mark! For those that don't know, "mark" is to wrestling fans as "comic book geek" is to comic book fans. It's a delicate balance for some fans of the industry. They like to follow the business, but they can't be too into the wrestling matches. If that's the case, they're one of *them*. They're a lowly mark. Wrestling is for dorky marks. The cool people watch wrestling for the reality show competitions and bikini contests. Right.

The thing that always got me was the misuse of the word "mark." People tend to think that if they like wrestling too much, they're a mark. No. No, you're not. If we're getting technical, mark is someone that a grifter, or con-artist, targets to fool and get money from. It's not just a word exclusive to wrestling. It's a term used whenever the carnies come to town. They trick you. They take your money. They bet you that they can say your name without even knowing it. You agree. They say "Your Name." You give them ten bucks. That's being a mark. When the circus glued the horn on that goat and called it a Unicorn in the mid-8os, the people who went to see it were marks.

According to the *Merriam-Webster Dictionary*, the definition of "mark" in this context is "a victim or prospective victim of a swindle."

There's no mention of liking technical wrestling too much. I don't see "hardcore fan of specific entertainment genre" included either.

Mark is only a bad term in that you don't want to be tricked out of your money. No one wants to be considered gullible. However, the term has evolved for a number of reasons. Most prominently because wrestling isn't about tricking you anymore.

They admit it's fake. Wrestling's fake. There. I wrote it. Wrestling's fake. Look, I wrote it again. Had this been forty years ago, a big guy with a baseball bat would have taken my kneecaps out or something like that. Not anymore, though. Even according to WWE owner Vince McMahon, there's probably only about 2% of the population who think it's real anymore. (Something tells me that those 2% must be friggin' wild to party with.)

So it's not trickery anymore. People know it's "phony baloney." If we all know it's not real, what does mark mean? What's left?

Giving up money — that's what. A mark is a wrestling fan who spends money on the product. Nothing more, nothing less. If you buy

WWE merchandise, you're a mark. That's all there is to it. The spending money part is the only part of the term still truly applicable.

Mark doesn't mean "cheer," either. A lot of people will say "When so-and-so returned to *Raw*, I marked out!" Well, unless you started throwing quarters at your television, you didn't.

Marks aren't even wrestling fanatics. If you're a hardcore fan who can't afford to spend money on pay-per-views or T-shirts, you're not a mark. Sorry. You aren't really considered in WWE's plan. You are simply a follower of the industry who doesn't put money in their pockets. Its job is to get you to fork over your money. When you do, you'll be a mark.

So it seems like some people go through much trouble to avoid being called a term that doesn't even mean what they think it does. If you like the wrestling but don't pay for it, you're not a mark. You're a fan. You know what? Even if you *are* a mark, so what? Why shouldn't you be?

People buy what they like. Under this rationale, I'm a Sierra Mist mark. I drink that soda all the time. I'm a DVD mark. I'm a video game mark. I wear Calvin Klein cologne, so that would make me a CK Mark.

Why shouldn't you spend money on the things you like? You gonna take it with you? You want *WrestleMania*? Buy the pay-per-view. Go ahead, you big mark. No one's looking.

In many ways, it seems less logical to *not be* a mark than to be one. Why watch the show for free on television and then never get a pay-per-view show, featuring the payoffs to the television stories? How many weeks of your life do you have to waste 4–8 hours at a time before you finally plop down a dollar? It's weird to watch *Raw*, *Smackdown*, or whatever else and never once get a video game, ice cream bar, magazine or action figure.

It makes sense to buy things associated with World Wrestling Entertainment. Even if you haven't bought something directly from them, you've probably patronized their advertisers. At one point or another, we're all marks. All of us.

The term is used a lot, though. Some people are referred to as "marks for themselves." This is just another way of saying someone is arrogant and affected by their self-appointed fame. I had a drama teacher in high school who was full of himself and egotistical. We didn't call him a "mark." We called him a "dick."

It's the twisting and turning of terms like heat, kayfabe, turn, eep-opp-ork-ah-ah and whatever else we used to say when this business was a huge work on the American people that has led to the fans' self-conscious efforts to avoid being marked as marks. All these terms were supposed to be kept private. If you're in the industry, you know what it means in context. It's like waiters knowing that "spinart" is "spinach artichoke dip." It's part of the job description. They have to know. The customer doesn't.

This brings us back to the wrestling thing. Many people think that mark means "wrestling geek." It doesn't. Chances are, if you're watching WWE during its lean times, you're a die-hard fan. That means that while you like other aspects of the show, you probably like wrestling. If you hate wrestling intensely but can't stop watching because you think that the WWE has some amazingly acted and produced Oscar-worthy backstage skits, then you're either drunk or insane . . . or insanely drunk.

> In The Depression, hobos would put a mark on the house where they got employment and a meal or whatever. Since a hobo needs work and a bum won't work, I don't think it was originally designed to be a negative term. He's a "mark" meant he would employ you for a price. Later it got to mean "he's a sucker." P.T. Barnum said one was born

every minute so it became negative. I go to Broadway plays. Am I a mark? No, I just like Broadway plays. If you like wrestling and can afford it, why are you a "mark" and I'm a "patron to the arts"? Do what you want to do while you can. Don't worry about what people think or say. Otherwise, you're a REAL mark! — **Lanny Poffo**

Better yet is when WWE and its mouthpieces try to attack the diehard fans for being so damn diehard. They mock them for having the nerve to judge their performances without ever performing themselves. How the hell can a mere fan possibly have something to say about the way a wrestler took a bump or sold a move? It's not his job!

I've heard all the snide remarks from those who jump on the audience.

How was your last match? How was your last promo? If you can't answer that because you never wrestled, then you can't comment on my in-ring showcase. Besides, diehard fans just like to complain.

Fine. So you mean to tell me that no wrestler has ever complained to the manager of a restaurant?

Oh, I'm sorry sir. Your food wasn't out fast enough? I'm sorry, Mr. Rassler. Let me ask you one question . . . are you the waiter? No. No you're not. How was the last meal you served? Was it good? Oh, wait. I'm sorry. You didn't serve a meal because you're not the waiter! You want to complain about my performance? Well screw you! You'll complain about anything! Also, stop using the term "spinart," you mark.

Crazy, right? I know the argument you have now:

But James, waiters are performing a service. You pay them money and they do it. It's not the same thing.

Yeah, when wrestlers start wrestling in my backyard for free then it's not the same thing. The day that Roddy Piper shows up in my kitchen with the set of his *Piper's Pit* talk show and introduces his special guest, Hulk Hogan, who's sitting in my driveway, then it won't be the same thing. Until then, it is. We pay to watch wrestling in some way.

Either you get the pay shows or cable or buy some advertised product or something. You pay money for this stuff. You have a right to complain about it. Pro baseball players are criticized by non-ball players. Same goes for every other sport, branch of government, form of entertainment or . . . hell, every damn profession takes criticism from people who never did their job.

Some of my old teachers sucked. I can say that even though I never taught a class. The dentist I used to use was a schmuck. Again, I'm not a dentist but I can say that because he always messed up. The new kid at Starbucks leaves too much room in my coffee for milk. I end up getting a cup that's about three quarters filled. Even though I never ground a bean for Mr. Bucks, I feel secure in my right to critique him.

You can't blame the fans for using the terminology. For the past decade or so, they've been encouraged to look at this industry without blinders on. The fanatics of the business have not only been let behind the curtain but they've been told all the secret words.

As opposed to the "olden days," the secrets of professional wrestling are now on the table for anyone to see. Prominent documentaries like the *Unreal Story of Pro Wrestling*, *Beyond the Mat*, *Southern Discomfort*, *Wrestling With Shadows* and a ton of others have all done their fair share to let the fans know what the sports entertainment business is all about.

Making matters stranger is that all these videos include athletes within the business telling the audience how things work behind the scenes. Rather than implying the backstage stories, they're all being told to the fans point blank. The mystery has been lifted and the crowd is now in on the joke.

That must be why WWE's performers routinely grow frustrated with the "smartness level" of its fan base. With all these documentaries being shot, fans now know too much. It must be annoying to hear wrestling fans using terminology that you use on videotapes that are sold to them. I can understand.

Check out this 2004 quote from Ric Flair. It's from an interview conducted by Silvervision UK, WWE's DVD company in Great Britain. The interviewer asked Ric if he preferred to work as a heel or babyface. He answered but then explained why he took issue with such a question.

> Well fans who use terms like that I have no respect for, because they're not wrestlers. That's a wrestler's terminology. See that's inside talk — I don't like outsiders using inside talk — I have no respect for it whatsoever. Everybody wants to think that they're a wrestler.

Look at that, folks. It's 1983 and it's Georgia. The Nature Boy is going wild and this time the fans are playing the role of Dusty Rhodes, if you will. Slick Ric is gonna style and profile all night. Whooo! Blah. Come on, Ric. Give me a break.

So now the man — "Nature Boy" Ric Flair — is enraged over this widespread use of insider jargon by non-rasslers. These fans sure have some nerve! It's not WWE's fault that they know these terms. It's the fault of the tell-all videos, Internet newsletters and writers.

Oh . . . oh, but wait. It's also the fault of World Wrestling Entertainment. We'd be remiss to not point a finger at them too. You have terms like "babyface" and "heel" being used to distinguish between heroes and villains in WWE video games. There's tell-all WWE DVDs and TV programs. We have countless books by past and present wrestlers featuring "real life stories from the road." It's a different world now.

Well, that doesn't mean that Ric Flair has to like it, dammit! The on-air manager of Triple H expressed his disgust over this practice and it's his right to do so. His sentiments, often echoing those of McMahon's son-in-law Hunter, are certainly valid. Poor Ric spends so much time trying to protect the top-secret terminology of this industry, yet WWE just splashes it onto every piece of media they put out.

Actually, there's the fact that Mr. Secret Codeword himself, Ric Flair, has appeared on many of these DVDs and programs. In WWE's *Greatest Stars of the 80s* DVD, Naitch told us all that Ricky Steamboat couldn't be regarded as the best wrestler of all time because he "never worked heel." As the DVD progressed, Ric told stories about working with his opponents throughout time. These were the opponents who he was supposed to have deep-rooted hatred for back then. Nowadays, they're looked back on fondly by Flair as he talks about the "chemistry" they had together. Sounds pretty insider to me.

> Come on, James. Get real. Ric can say those things because he's an actual wrestler. Didn't you see the quote?

Sure, but who does he think is buying this DVD? If he hates fans using terms like babyface and heel because it's his widdle special thing, why use them on a product that will be purchased by fans? Seems counterproductive to me. If I don't want America's youth saying bad words, I'm not about to say "Fucky Fuck Fuck Fuck" on a *Sesame Street* home video. See my point?

I guess I'm overreacting. That was just an offhanded comment on a WWE video. Normally Flair would fight to the death to protect his secrets, stories and secret language. It's no big deal. It's not like the guy wrote a book or anything.

Oh, but he did write a book. In it, he gave away a ton of backstage info about the good ol' days of the business. How could someone so adamant against fans knowing the insider terminology put out a book filled with it and lend his likeness to home videos that feature him explaining things to the audience that he believes shouldn't be explained?

Terminology, eh? Here's a sampling of terms that Naitch included in his tell-all book:

> Get Juice, Crowd Psychology, Booker, Booking, Worker, Broadway, Draw, Stroke, Angle, Storyline, Turn, Sell.

If he hates the fact that fans know and understand that top secret Captain Crunch Decoder Ring jargon, then why use it in his book? Did he think that only wrestlers would read it? Did I miss the sticker that told me to not spend $26 on his memoir because it's only for wrestlers?

(By the way, *everyone* is allowed to buy my book. The more people the better. In fact, you should go out and buy another one. Can't have too many.)

Nothing like watching wrestlers blame the audience for problems that they and their company help to foster. If performers don't want fans to use the insider terms from wrestling's brotherhood, then they shouldn't use them when speaking publicly about the industry. Keep kayfabe and those who follow you will too.

It's like any other fraternity or sorority. You're told the ritual and all the top secret handshakes and words. It's a big secret. If you don't want the rest of your college campus to know these secret things, you don't talk about them in public. If you do, you have to deal with what you get.

Hey, I wish I could go out drinking with you guys tonight, but I have a fraternity meeting. We're going to open the meeting with a smoking candle and two bibles. Then we all do our secret handshake with four fingers extended and end with our top secret word – booboobo.

Oh . . . OK. We'll miss you tonight, man. Have fun at your meeting. So, booboobo, huh? That's your secret word?

Oh my God! How dare you use the booboobo word! You're not in the frat! That's disrespectful!

Uh . . . but you just told me about it. Remember? You just said you had a candle and two bibles . . .

Oh no, no, no. You didn't! You know about the candle and bibles too? That's it. Put up your hands. It's go time.

Are you completely insane?

There's man-on-man rape, necrophilia and general perversion cluttering up professional wrestling's on-air product and the biggest problem that WWE can reach for is the fact that you, the customer, refer to a heel instead of "bad guy." Now those are some crazy ass priorities.

CHAPTER 12

What I'm Trying
to Say Is . . .

As you've read through this book, you've been exposed to some of the horrors that exist within the world of professional wrestling. You've heard about the scorn that non-fans cast upon the industry and the industry casts on its diehard fans. You examined the nepotism and poor storytelling that plague World Wrestling Entertainment's product. You were even exposed to the egos and the power plays that take a part in slowly eating away the entire wrestling genre. It's all been laid out on the table for you. Nothing has been McMahonitized for your protection. It's all there in plain sight.

So, after reading all that, one question must be sticking in your mind.

> James, if all this is true, why do you watch it? Why do you still watch wrestling?

The answer to that is simple. I don't have to think twice about it. I love the wrestling industry. I always have. I always will.

I'm not afraid to say it. I'm not embarrassed to let it be known. This business has been a part of my life for as long as I can remember and it'll be there for years to come. I grew up with it and I'll grow old with it. That I know. That I accept.

As a little kid, when other boys and girls were watching Punky Brewster chase her stupid dog around, I was watching Roddy Piper smash a coconut over the head of Jimmy Snuka.

When I was angry at a teacher in Junior High, I'd flip on the television and let Jake "The Snake" Roberts land a DDT for me. It was Jake who did my dirty work and living vicariously through him, I could imagine it was I slamming my earth science professor's bald head into the canvas.

The Thursday before my wedding, when everyone was running crazy and finalizing plans, I made certain to sneak away and catch *Smackdown*. When I remember getting a chance to step back and reflect on things before the big day, I remember seeing the debut of the tag team, MNM.

Wrestling's a part of me. That's it. Just like a diehard football fan can remember points in his life based on Superbowls and season tickets, I have pro wrestling to help mark off points in my own life. The only difference is that no one condemns football fans. They're allowed to be who they are. Wrestling fans? We get mocked by everyone.

I love it when I get a funny glare about the fact that I like wrestling from someone who watches *The OC* religiously. At what point do we accept that each one of us enjoys some form of entertainment that others might not? To snicker at someone for liking professional wrestling is like snickering at someone because they like country music. What's the point? You don't have to like it. No one asked if you did.

In some ways, I'm glad that everyone doesn't like it. I know that's a no-no to say because we're supposed to pray everyday that the whole world will start tuning in again, but I don't care. I said it and I stand by it. I'm glad that there are people out there who don't understand why I like wrestling. It means that this industry is everything I know it to be. It's not for everyone. If it were, I probably wouldn't like it as much.

It's an intricate form of entertainment mixed with sports and business to create a performance that can't be duplicated anywhere else. It's not like a movie. It's not like a sitcom. It's not like a sporting event. It's its own thing. I've never seen anything like it.

It's the appreciation of all this that makes someone a wrestling fan. You don't have to like the actual wrestling. You don't have to like the promos. You don't even have to like the storylines. All you have to do is appreciate the art of this business. Strip away all the bells, whistles and bullshit and you have something special. A wrestling fan realizes and respects that.

What keeps me going is my love of wrestling's basic message. That's what saves me from the Katie Vick stories and the Triple H squash jobs. That's why I keep watching. It's because, at the base, this industry is the greatest form of entertainment that I've ever been exposed to. No other program or film has ever been able to evoke the type of emotions from me that professional wrestling has. Others who don't watch wrestling may mock this. That's fine. It's fine because they never felt that way from watching a match. I'm sort of glad they didn't, actually. If everyone did, it wouldn't be as special.

All that aside, this industry is also wonderful in the sense that, when done right, everyone makes money off everyone else. In a perfect world, the promoter makes money off the ticket sales. The wrestlers make money off their characters. As for the fans, well they're happy to toss their cash at any exciting company.

That's the funny part. Wrestling fans want to spend money. Many of them would love nothing more than to get that excited feeling every time they tune into *Raw*. Many of them desire nothing more than to toss buckets of greenbacks at Vince McMahon, if only he'd give them something good to purchase. Like any other diehard fan of a form of entertainment, wrestling fans want to get excited and spend money. All the promoters have to do is give them something worth buying.

That's when things break down. As you read through this book, you may have noticed that the industry isn't so much about making money anymore. In a world where one promoter reigns supreme, taking in revenue has been placed on the back burner in favor of revenge and ego. The fans, dying to be inspired and excited by WWE programming, are left watching McMahon home movies as they fall

all over themselves trying to rewrite history and bury those who might challenge their power. Where's the fun in that?

If we're shooing straight here, I'd be remiss not to condemn the McMahons for what they've been slowly turning the wrestling business into. This industry, which all of us know can be so amazing, has frequently been used as the toy for a victorious owner. It's almost painful to watch.

> Come on, James. Shut up. Stop whining. If you don't like it, watch something else.

Well , that's the problem. I can't watch anything else. Know why? Because Vince McMahon bought everything else!

You see, Vince's purchase of wcw in 2001 was more than just some corporate buyout. What Mac failed to realize is that he was taking the burden of carrying a piece of American culture on his shoulders. By taking away any viable alternative that fans could have to his own product, vkm essentially accepted the responsibility for providing the only stream of large-scale televised wrestling in the country. It's all him. He wanted the industry. He got it.

Now that he has it, it's not so much fun anymore. It's not fun for him. It's not fun for us.

He's used it to get even with the people he wanted to. For example, there was Superstar Billy Graham. In 1992, the former WWE Champion tore McMahon apart on *The Donahue Show* and alleged that he was in on the big steroid conspiracy. BG was quite vocal about it. The most ironic statement of Graham's career actually occurred during a stint with the World Wrestling Federation in the 1980s. He was calling commentary on the 1988 *WrestleFest* Event. During the opening match, Superstar started to talk about the extra body weight that had been put on by the Killer Bees tag team. Billy said this:

> It appears that way, Lord Alfred Hayes. Maybe, uh, they need that extra body weight for leverage. It's obvious in the World Wrestling Federation, brother, you got to have power, mass, intensity, strength and body weight to go anywhere in the World Wrestling Federation.

There was no denying that Graham, sporting a fake hip thanks to steroids, was onto something with his accusations. Many rallied behind him, supportive of his anti-drugs in wrestling message. Sadly, he admitted to lying about all of his WWE accusations in 2003. Coincidentally, his admission occurred two years after Vince had become sole owner of the wrestling business. It also occurred right before Graham was inducted into World Wrestling Entertainment's "Hall of Fame."

Things like that have made this monopoly-like purchase fun for the Big Mac. He doesn't have to put up with anyone talking bad about him. Most people wouldn't dare anymore. It's their choice. They can have their pride or they can have their legacy. Which is it, guys? You can't have both. The man who owns the video library writes the history. You want to be his friend or his enemy? Be careful what you choose. It could mean the difference between being trashed on a DVD or getting a place in the non-existent McMahon-created Hall of Fame. All of this is growing old pretty quick and the more that the company is used for childish storylines and personal grudges, the more it strays away from what it's meant to be.

"Meant to be." That's an important phrase. That's what keeps wrestling fans going. It's what will always keep us going. No matter how bad the product on television is, no matter how stupid the stories become, we know what the wrestling industry is meant to be. We know what it could be. We know what it should be. We know what we want from it.

We want to be entertained. That's it. Wrestling promoters and bookers slam their heads into the wall trying to get into the brain of an average fan. What do they want? Do they want blood and guts? Do they want soap operas? Do they want comedy? What do they want?

Actually, they want all of those. It doesn't matter what form it comes in, good wrestling is good wrestling. That's the beauty of it. If it's creative and portrayed well, it's good. Whether it's funny or serious makes no difference. It's whether or not it's entertaining that really matters.

Wrestling fans shouldn't have to tell that to the promoters. They should know that. Actually, I'm dancing around the subject. Forget "promoters," I should say that wrestling fans shouldn't have to tell that to the *McMahon Family*. They should know it.

They should know it because they're the ones who took control of the entire industry and chose to be the only show in town. That's their choice. I'm not taking that away from them. It was Vince's victory and one that he should relish in. The only thing is that if he's going to accept the duty of being the only major proprietor of professional wrestling in the United States, he should at least know what his fans want and not blame them when he can't figure it out.

Even if he doesn't know what the fans want, he should at least know what they don't want. After all, it's just common sense. No one enjoys storyline logic holes, overpushed family members, false history lessons, bitter backstage politics and on-air revenge. They enjoy creativity. It's all they want, yet they don't get it. Why? Why then does WWE continue to give the fans the same things they don't want each week, yet expect different results? Hey, isn't that the definition of insanity?

Well, yes. I guess it is. Phew. Boy, did I pick the right title or what?

Insanity Extras

(The following pieces appeared online between 2002 and 2005.)

'Twas the month before Christmas and numbers were bleak,
Not a ticket was selling, and business was weak.
The stock prices were falling, investors were scared,
So Vince got a raise to keep them all there.
The wrestlers were dressed up in nice formal clothes,
Cause Johnny Ace said to — the Dynamic Dude knows,
Though a murdering rapist, Kane was a face,
While Hassan and Daivari were heels based on race . . .
Then out in the ring there arose such a clatter,
That the road agents ran to see what was the matter.
Rene Dupree flew from the match like the wind,
Chased by Bob Holly, who was usually pinned.
The anger Bob had, most understand,
So he beat Rene senseless, in front of the fans,
Bobby just laughed. Then what should appear?
But a big bad-ass sleigh, and eight angry reindeer,
With a little old driver — who Holly made sick.
"Enough of this garbage!" screamed good ol' St. Nick.

More rabid than Benoit, the deer were not tame,
Claus whistled, and shouted, and called them by name:
"Now Vader, now Gayda, now Savage and Stinger,

On Maven! On Raven! On Hogan and Swinger!
To the top of card! To the end of the line!
Now run away, Sparky. Cause your ass is mine!"
As Bob tried to run, without annoying this guy,
Santa reached out and grabbed him and spit in his eye,
Tossed ol' Bob in the sleigh, and kicked in his face,
Then drove away fast, like a real NASCAR Race.
And then, in a twinkling, Holly let out a cry.
Begging Kris Kringle to please tell him why.
He spoke not a word, but went straight to his work
Plotting some punishment for this sad mid-card jerk.
Holly's head was all busted, he was covered in soot,
And his ass had the imprint of Ol' St. Nick's foot.
Bob claimed to have reasons for hurting Rene,
"There's the Rental Car thing . . . plus his trunks are so gay!"
Santa just laughed, and said, "Yes, Bob, I know.
But why not just fight him after the show?
This isn't the first time you flipped your lid,
Did you also loan your car to that *Tough Enough* kid?
Oh no. You just did that for fun, I forgot.
And to make the boys say, 'What big balls you've got.'
You could have had grace. You could have had class.
But you didn't, so now I'll be kicking your ass."

Although chubby and plump, he's a powerful elf,
Santa said, "I'll be Lesnar and put Bob on the shelf."
A wink of his eye and a vicious right hand,
He whaled on poor Holly, so he'd understand.
"I don't normally do this," Santa yelled so we'd hear,
"But apparently, this is how we teach lessons 'round here."
Then he swung a steel chair and hit Bob in the head,
Causing the locker room cop to fall from the sled,
Bob quickly dropped to the Earth like a missile,
Then he hit with a splat while Santa let out a whistle
And I heard him exclaim as he raised his eyebrow
"Merry Christmas, you bully. How do you like *me* now?"

Spiro Agnew Elementary School — Sometime In The Future . . . (7/25/05)

Principal Jenkins: Gather around children. We're all very blessed here today. As we just found out, one of our students, Arnold, comes from a very famous family. His mommy and daddy own the World Wrestling Federation. They write all the stories you see on the TV shows. Well, they've agreed to help us out here today by writing and directing our third grade school play. Let's bring in Arnold's mommy and daddy, Stephanie and Paul McMahon.

Triple H: Levesque.

Jenkins: Gesundheit. Take it away, folks. These little bastards are all yours.

Stephanie: OK, children. Paul and I are very excited about directing this play. Paul's coming around with some dittos of the scripts for all of you to take. We're going to do a read through. Are you all ready? Yes, little boy?

Billy (holding his hand in the air): I have to make pee pees.

Hunter: You want to go to the bathroom? Don't you have any dedication? That's why you'll never draw any money. You won't sell any tickets. People won't come to this play to see you! They won't! You have no heart! You hear me? No heart!

Billy: What?

Stephanie: Let's just take it from the top. (Pointing) You, little black girl, you're the narrator. Read the title page.

Brian (looking around): Me? I'm a boy . . . and I'm white.

Hunter: Just shut up and read, Nappy.

Brian: OK. Whatever. (Clears throat) "Eye Scream Balls" by Stephanie and Paul Le . . . Le . . . Lev-eck. Our story opens with Chris Cocker. He's looking for the love of his life.

Billy: Hello everyone. My name is Chris Cocker. Where is my lovely girlfriend? Lovely girlfriend? Yoo hoo?

Brian: Jennifer enters the scene. She has pay . . . uh . . . pay . . . uh . . . pay-st-ies on and a hotdog in her ear.

Joanna: I am Jennifer. I don't love you. Look at my puppies.

Hunter: OK, kid. Now you're supposed to grab your puppies.

Stephanie (annoyed): She doesn't have puppies, stupid. She's eight.

Joanna: I have two puppies at home.

Hunter: Now Steph, isn't this a problem we can correct?

Stephanie: You don't mean . . . ?

Hunter (smirking): Yes. Oh yes. Say, Joanna. How'd you like to get two new puppies?

Joanna: OK!

Hunter: You got it. First thing Monday, you get a fresh set. See, Steph. Bam! That'll sell some tickets. You hear me? Bam! Mo money! Mo money! That's what people buy tickets for. Unlike pee-boy over there.

Billy (frowning): I had an accident.

Stephanie (screeching): Shut up! Ahhh! OK. OK. Sorry about that, Shaniqua. You go on. Read.

Brian: My name isn't Shaniqua! I'm not a black girl! My name is Brian!

Stephanie (rolling her eyes): OK. OK. Word up, homeslice. Now just read.

Brian: After grabbing her puppies, Jennifer is grabbed by Chris Cocker and whisked away.

Hunter: Ha ha. Cocker. I love it.

Billy: You are my girlfriend now, Jennifer. Come here you, uh, uh, gutt-er slut. You are my woo . . . woo . . . woman now.

Brian: Suddenly, Ach-mad Sandperson arrives.

Timmy: I am Ach-mad! I am a terror symp-athizer. I will sue . . . a . . . suicide bomb everyone. (Out of character) Uh, directors? I don't feel right saying this. I don't want to be a terrorist.

Stephanie: You're not a terrorist. You're a terror sympathizer. See the difference? It's like crossing the line, only not. We almost cross the boundary of good taste, but leave enough rope to climb back onto the safe side if it becomes a serious issue.

Hunter (sweating): God, you make me friggin' hot when you talk like that.

Timmy: But, it's kind of like the same thing. I don't know. My daddy is a firefighter and I think he would be upset.

Hunter: That's perfect, kid. You say it and your dad can get really mad. You'll get heat. It'll be like a worked shoot.

Timmy: What's a worked shoot?

Stephanie: That's when you say things about your real life while you play a scripted character.

Timmy: Huh? That's stupid. If you're scripting something, you shouldn't say things about your real life. That's not entertainment. That's confusing and dumb. I'm in third grade and even I know that.

(Stephanie and Hunter stare blankly.)

Hunter: Whatever. Up yours, you mark. Now . . . take it away, black girl.

Brian: We rejoin Jennifer and Chris Cocker. Jennifer is freshly raped and now in love with Chris.

Joanna (confused): What's raped?

Hunter: It's forced sex. He made you have sex with him. Now you love him. That's how the real world works.

Billy (jumping for joy): It does? Hell yeah!

Stephanie: Nice going, stupid. Now you f**ked him up for life.

Hunter: Yeah? Yeah? Well . . . uh, look at my crazy facial hair.

Stephanie: That's your answer to everything. Forget you. Keep reading, girlfriend.

Brian: We rejoin Ach-mad . . . (looking up) Uh, Mrs. McMahon, what about Jennifer and Chris Cocker?

Stephanie (grinning): Hee hee — Cocker. Yeah, well, we're done with them. Their story is over.

Brian: But it doesn't have an end? That's weird.

Stephanie (sternly): Johnny Ace warned me about you, little girl. He said you weren't tall enough for this play. Let's just skip ahead and cut to the final scene. Everyone turn to page nine.

(Everyone pages ahead and skims the scene.)

Billy (looking up at Hunter): Hey! It says you kill us.

Hunter: Yup. I kill all of you with my light saber.

Brian: Screw you! You're not in our play!

Hunter: You listen here, Tracy Chapman . . .

Principal Jenkins (returning to the auditorium): Excuse me. Excuse me! Mr. and Mrs. McMahon? I just went back to the main office and it's come to our attention that we don't have an Arnold McMahon or Helmsley or Levesque enrolled at this school at all. In fact, we did a quick check with our database and couldn't find any record of you two having any child whatsoever. Would you mind telling me why you called my office claiming to be a parent of a non-existent student so that you could write and direct our third grade play?

Awkward pause.

Hunter: Well, you see. Uh . . . ha ha. Well, when Batista and I went to Hell, it was a Cell. I made Evolution and this business is the Game. Uh, I am Game. That's because, uh. Hey what's that over there? . . . Run, Steph! Run!

McMahon's Petty Grudges Have Ruined the Magic (10/11/02)

> I'm tired of Generation X getting a bad rap. Are you a degenerate? I'm positive I'm one. — **Shawn Michaels, October 13, 1997**

I guess I'm a slacker. I am a card-carrying, tried and true Generation X slacker. I can argue against this stigma, but a part of me knows that I won't convince people otherwise — and another part knows it's true. You see, there are a number of stereotypes associated with my age group. The one thing that plagues us is the word "cynical." In fact, wrestling fans of the Internet generation have been written off as "cynical" for years. But why are we cynical? Who is to blame? Why are we so unimpressed by what generations before us applauded?

I read an online article recently that dealt with the issue of Jimmy Snuka's out-of-ring behavior. He wrote of the violence that has plagued Jimmy's personal life and made him undesirable to be around outside the confines of the ring. According to many, Jimmy's propensity for violence against women is almost legendary. Jimmy Snuka is a flawed man. He has his drawbacks and he is not the type of man that I would want to sit next to at Thanksgiving.

But "The Superfly" was — and still is — a God.

You see, I knew about Jimmy's personal problems years ago. I made the decision to read about it in newsletters and on the Internet. I know about what wrestlers do backstage because it was my prerogative to find this out. Vince McMahon never told me about it. It was never splashed across the TV screens of WWF Superstars and Prime Time Wrestling in the 1980s. Even after Snuka left (took his ball and went home?), Vince allowed us to keep the memory of the Superfly's athleticism inside the ring. When I think of Jimmy "Superfly" Snuka, I don't think of him tossing a frail woman to the floor of a hotel room. I think of his bare feet springing him off the top of a steel cage at Madison Square Garden. I think of him sailing across the ring as if he could fly. I think of a super hero.

What do you think of when you think of Hulk Hogan?

It all started with Hulk. In 1995, Vince McMahon took it upon himself to let us know the shortcomings of his performers behind the scenes. Do you remember when Hogan jumped to wcw? He had been plagued with bad publicity. There was an appearance on *Arsenio Hall* where he danced around the subject of steroids. There was bad press on *Larry King* and *Donahue* that paraded out Billy Graham and Bruno Sammartino as if they were the grainy Zapruder film, showing Hogan's weaknesses like it was the Kennedy Assassination. But it was my choice whether or not I tuned into to hear these allegations. I watched wwF programming regularly. *Larry King* was not in the rotation.

Then in 1995, Vince McMahon figured he would make things easier for me. He proceeded to lambaste Hogan on *Raw* — constantly. We watched as Jim Cornette referred to Hulk's match with Roddy Piper at wcw's pay-per-view as "Age in the Cage." We bore witness to an old man playing the role of "The Huckster" — flexing his pale, aged arms and repeating the catch phrases of "Hulkamania" as if it was a punch line for a joke that I didn't find funny. We were even told of Hulk's promise to pay Vince back for any money that he lost making the 1989 film *No Hold Barred*. What was once kept silent and allowed to seep into the minds of his fans from other avenues had been plastered all over wwF-sponsored television. I couldn't watch Hogan anymore. The man who he stood side by side with and made more money than I'll ever see was telling me that his time was done. So I accepted it. Who needed Hogan? He was the "old generation." We had the "new generation" — we had Bret Hart. He was safe. He could do no wrong.

What do you think of when you think of Bret Hart?

You think of the 1997 *Survivor Series*. By November of 1997, the "New Generation" campaign had run out of steam. Vince saw Bret as more of a liability than an asset. Bret was told that he could explore other employment options. All of this was done professionally and, for the most part, behind the scenes. But the problem surfaced when disagreements arose surrounding the loss of Bret's title. Vince made the executive decision to declare Shawn Michaels the submission winner of their main event match at the *Survivor Series*. Bret was upset, and a number of unpleasantries were played out for all to see. We were told: "Bret screwed Bret." Everything from Bret's charisma to his dedication to the industry was assassinated publicly each week. There was no need for *Donahue* anymore. Vince had his employees keep us updated as to the situation backstage. There was no need to be concerned. Who needs Bret Hart? We have Steve Austin.

"Stone Cold" Steve Austin was the "icon" of the company. That is, until earlier this year when he walked out. Vince told us all about it. We knew all of Steve's shortcomings and problems. But who needs Steve? We have Hulk Hogan. Hulk Hogan? Wait a minute? Isn't that where all this started?

Vince McMahon has slowly but surely destroyed the magic that makes this business great. It's as if David Copperfield showed us intricately how he performs each trick and then wondered why we don't want to watch him do them. I watch professional wrestling for the escape from reality that it offers (or at least used to offer). The characters were larger than life. Your friends had flaws, your family may have come up short, but the Superstars of the WWF were super-heroes. They took whatever problems you had each week and made them disappear for one hour at a time. No one worries about paying bills or working overtime when they are watching Ricky Steamboat and Randy Savage put on a classic. There was something magical there. Where's my magic, Vince?

My generation has no magic. We've seen it all and we know it all. While the mainstream was wondering if the XFL would succeed, I didn't wonder — I knew it would fail. Why? I saw the debacle that was Vince's WBF (World Bodybuilding Federation). While casual fans called McMahon a genius for developing the Rock and Austin, I remembered T.L. Hopper and the Gobblygooker. I know where WWE is heading before they even start the trip. I'm two steps ahead of you, Vince. Nothing surprises me anymore. You say we're the generation of "Crash TV." The quick MTV shock value TV production was your idea. You don't want to write dramatic or intelligent programming, so you try to shock us. We're the generation that tuned into pay-per-view and watched the cameras pan a stunned arena watching Owen Hart fall to his death — yeah, I'm really shocked by Billy and Chuck.

They call us "smart marks" or "smarts." The term is used to refer to fans that follow the business closely. It's almost a tongue-in-cheek insult. The term "smart" is not used to describe our intellect, but to poke fun at us for thinking we are intelligent. I suppose I'm not that intelligent. Maybe I'm kept in the dark about most backstage situations. I only know half the story — I only know the parts that Vince tells me.

Every star that I have ever cheered was eventually buried in the long run. I supported Hulk, Bret, Steve, The Ultimate Warrior, Randy Savage and countless others, only to have the company that took my money while they pushed them laugh at me for supporting them once they were gone. Bret Hart was the leader of the New Generation? Until he left — then we were told he had no charisma. I guess I'm stupid. Can I have back the ticket money I spent to see him? Maybe that's why you can't get the fans to support your stars anymore. What's the point? Cheer for Kurt Angle, Brock Lesnar, Rob Van Dam and Chris Jericho — the first time things go sour in their relationship with Vince, we'll know everything they ever did to anyone and we'll be made out to be idiots for ever putting a dollar on the table to see them.

These men are not characters anymore, they are mere men. The reality based programming of the late 90s killed any "larger than life" feeling there was surrounding them. Storylines are interweaved between their on-air characters and their real life situations. Maybe the reason why no one can figure out why Steve "Austin" Williams' domestic issues do not affect "Stone Cold" Steve Austin's stance in his dispute with Vince McMahon is because we've never been told they were two different men. Steve Williams never gave anyone a Stunner. Steve Austin opened up a "can of whoop ass" on a weekly basis.

A few weeks ago, WWE did an angle on *Raw* where Jimmy "Superfly" Snuka was given a lifetime achievement award. When his music hit, the arena exploded. People rose to their feet and applauded. Jimmy Snuka may have fallen on tough times lately. He may have a checkered past, and for all I know he might just be a downright terrible human being. But the Superfly was honored as a hero that night by all who came to the arena. It must be nice to still be able to cherish your memories. I wish I could look back on those who have put their bodies on the line for my entertainment and support their characters. I wish I could still have heroes.

But what do I know? I'm just a cynic.

The Legend of the Legend Killer's Killers (2/10/05)

After the 2004 Presidential elections, people were offering up a bevy of excuses about why the Democrats were unable to defeat George W. Bush. While the issues factored heavily into the outcome, one of the most cited reasons for Bush's victory was that people just didn't want to back John Kerry. The exact statement was that Kerry's campaign focused more on why Bush was a bad president, rather than why John would be a good one.

It's pretty hard to exist as a politician, or anything for that matter, when your biggest appeal is that you're not someone else. Yay, John Kerry's not George Bush. Let's vote for him! Then again, *I'm* not George Bush. Vote for me. Heck, under that rationale, anyone can be president. That's a big issue that many people had with electing Kerry into the highest office in the land. If your biggest selling point is that you're not the other guy, you are setting yourself up for a bumpy road.

There's another person besides John F. Kerry that knows how true this is. He didn't win any Purple Hearts. He wasn't in Vietnam and he doesn't get free ketchup. Hell, Randy Orton doesn't get much of anything these days. The only real similarity he has to the swift boat veteran is that the basis of his entire persona for the last six months has been that he's not someone else. The whole selling point behind him is that he's not the Champion that came before him.

Randy Orton's entire persona was based on the fact that he wasn't Triple H.

Ort came up through the ranks quicker than a firecracker or hiccup or whatever they say. He stood alongside his Evolutionary buddies and pushed their agenda. With a smug look and an arrogant swagger, the Legend Killer had the attitude that any young heel should. He knew when to be cowardly. He knew when to get intense. He knew how to push buttons and he knew how to get under the collective skins of those that bought a ticket.

That's why people were excited about his victory over Chris Benoit for the World Title. Randy had risen up the ladder and seemingly shattered the glass ceiling that so many of the Hunter Hearst Haters claim exists on *Raw*. He was the top star on the show and he had the arrogance of a world-class bad guy going for him.

So immediately, WWE turned him into a hero. They had him leave Evolution. Well, that's not entirely true. It's more appropriate to say that they had Evolution beat him like a stray dog. Because of his World Title victory, Orton found himself punked out by the H Man and his backup dancers.

Randall had the Championship, but he had no allies. In fact, he had no character anymore. The problem with Orton was that he wasn't built for a babyface run. The reason he had risen up the ranks so quickly was because he was a strong villain. He had never constructed any in-ring mannerisms that could appeal to the audience. He never had any real altercations with Trips that could be used to serve as a backstory for his eventual split. In essence, the day he fell from Batista's shoulders on *Monday Night Raw* was the day he fell from the top of WWE's mountain.

The biggest complaint that I had about his journey to the side of good was that it wasn't a turn worthy of someone in his position. There's nothing overly heroic about being beaten up by your friends. In fact, in the storyline world of *Raw*, had Hunter not pummeled him, Ort would have remained within his group. It made fans question why he should be cheered. He deserves applause because his friends hate him? He should be cheered because he got beaten up by people he had trusted? At most, people might feel bad for him. Then again, this is the same guy that had been bragging weekly about his skills. We're supposed to feel bad for him now because he has no friends? There's plenty of shut-ins in the world who have no friends. We don't run around cheering for them.

Randy's Evolution departure was more on par with a mid-carder being dumped by the N.W.O. It was far from the type of angle worthy of a World Champion severing ties with a team. He had no reason to leave the stable other than that the remaining members wanted him gone. He had nothing to offer eager fans other than the same old smug smile and the fact that he's not the Game. Let the good times roll. His career took a nosedive and he's been trying to climb back up a ladder coated in grease for half a year. After all that, the best option he has now is to play off his new head trauma gimmick, lose his memory and hit the reset button. That's got to be a disappointment. If you had to deal with Orton's situation, you'd have headaches too.

This brings us to Dave Batista. Dave isn't going to be surprised when his Evolution departure comes. His weekly struggle with the overbearing leader of *Raw*, Triple H, has been well documented. When he turns babyface, it'll seem to be a product of an internal rivalry between him and his teammates, rather than a case of him being dropped by his friends. He'll have credibility with the audience and play the role that a hero is supposed to play. He'll be a babyface that should be cheered for holding on to his convictions and following his dream, rather than a hero that should be cheered out of pity.

Barring any insane creative decisions, Tista is on the fast track to a solid spot in the main event. His turn, character and following have all been handled well by WWE. They've gauged his audience reaction. They've planted seeds to show his anger with his group. They've made fans eager for him to turn, rather than setting them up to be surprised by it. With the build he's been given, Dave could excel where Orton failed. It shows how if WWE pays attention to small details, it can change an entire situation.

For former Evolution members, it can mean the difference between taking the World Title and taking Tylenol Migraine.

Raising Kane — Filling the Logic Holes of The Big Red Machine's Life (07/16/03)

I hate inconsistencies. I always have. The only way to make your way through them in the world of professional wrestling is to try to explain them.

This past Monday, WWE went full steam ahead on Operation Rebuild Kane. A sit-down interview with Jim Ross showcased a stunning revelation that The Big Red Machine is not burned. But that explanation brought with it new holes to fill in. So let's do this. Let's piece together the life and times of a man called Kane and think of how everything in his life could be possible when everything seems so damn contradictory.

***

Undertaker sets fire to his childhood home with his parents and younger brother, Kane, inside. The wreckage from the fire is so intense that it's nearly impossible to recognize any of the charred remains. Officials assume that Kane has burnt to death like his parents.

Fearing that the young Red Machine will be placed into foster care, his secret birth father, Paul Bearer, decides to raise the boy as his own. However Bearer's questionable past and unwillingness to step forward with his affair, causing a scandal in the town and angering the arson-setting Taker, forces him to keep his son's existence a secret. Bearer keeps the boy locked away and tells him that he's horribly disfigured. Despite obviously having no burns, Kane comes to accept his appearance as that of a freak. It's the only reality he knows from a young age.

To show his son that he genuinely cares about his well-being, Paul takes him to out-of-state doctors for evaluation. However he cautions him *not* to remove his mask. The doctors, having met Bearer, are skeptical of the injuries. They suspect that the boy's father may be a crackpot and push Kane to remove his mask so as that they can assess the damage. Out of fear, he refuses and lashes out.

As young Red Machine gets older, Paul begins to manage The Undertaker in the WWF. Seeing the success of the Taker, Bearer realizes that his own offspring may have some of the genes that made his brother a superstar. Paul makes brief exceptions to his rule and allows his son to leave the basement and train to become a professional wrestler.

Showing up at the school, Kane still refuses to remove his mask. Since professional wrestlers with strange quirks are nothing new, the school allows it. The Monster demonstrates great ability and for the first time ever is accepted by those around him. This is where he meets Katie Vick.

Katie is the object of Kane's desire. After being kept away from the outside world, The Machine latches on to the first sign of female interest. The two become friends and she listens to him tell the tale of his horrible accident. He refuses to remove the mask the entire time they know one another.

Deciding to cast his fears aside and let his true feelings be known, Kane makes a pass at Vick and is refused. Unable to understand that she simply does not have any romantic interest in him, Kane believes that her rejections are due to his "burns." He becomes irate and proceeds to end her life before satisfying himself with her prone corpse.

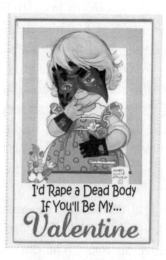

I'd Rape a Dead Body If You'll Be My... *Valentine*

Having been trained adequately and growing in size each day, Kane becomes the apple of his father's eye. On screen, Bearer begins to tire of The Undertaker, finally turning on him in a brutal and unexpected attack. He proceeds to blackmail The Taker with the story of the fire and his brother's death, before finally screaming out that Kane is alive. Undertaker is shocked. That shock turns to anger when Kane makes his debut at *Bad Blood*, attacking him.

Prior to his debut, Bearer informs his son that the people are all against him. He must make sure that no one sees his charred body. Kane is covered almost entirely by his wrestling attire and Paul tells him to smear black face paint on under is mask, just in case he loses it. Paul's rationale is that if a competitor *does* remove his mask, the paint would shield the audience from the disfigured face beneath. It also serves to hide any skin around the eyes that can be seen through the holes.

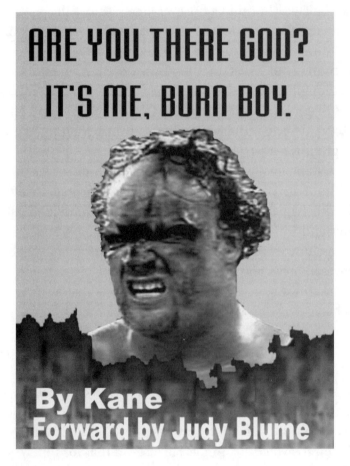

As time progresses, Kane convinces himself that his body may be scarred but the worst part of him is his face. He decides to change his outfit and show his burnt arms and chest to the world. His outfit evolves, but his mask remains. The world could deal with scarred limbs and such, but the face would be too much to bear. Was the fact that although we could all see Kane's unburned flesh while he still continued his claims to be scarred our first glimpse of his mental issues?

Throughout his time in the promotion, many try to take his mask and get a glimpse of his face. When Pat Patterson and Jerry Brisco *do* remove his mask and snap a photo, they are repulsed. Rather than realizing that Kane's pre-match ritual involved the smearing of black face paint, they assume it is rotting flesh. Having thought, like all of us, that Kane was burnt in a fire everyone assumes the picture is that of a decaying accident victim rather than a sick man intent on keeping his "scars" hidden underneath make-up.

He confides to X-Pac that his entire body is burnt. His former friend, though never seeing it, tells his former manager Torri and all the fans that it is true. Having had a strictly professional relationship with Torri, despite innuendo to the contrary, she too believes that Kane's groin is deep fried.

When Kane finally loses his mask on *Raw*, we see what he looked like without it. With the black face paint smeared following his match with Triple H, Kane looks right into the camera. We all see the monster and immediately react the way Patterson and Brisco did. We too assume it is scars. But to Kane, the scars are hidden beneath. He shaves his head and forgoes the face paint from that point on. He wants the crowd to get a good look at the freak that he believes himself to be.

***

There you go — Kane in a nutshell. I'm not saying that this is what happened, I'm just saying that this *could* be what happened. I'm sure wwe will do something different. You know, like nothing.

Oh and the voice box thing? He just did that for fun.

Snitsky and Heidenreich do Vaudeville (11/15/04)

Forget Abbott and Costello. Throw away Laurel and Hardy. Screw Burns and Allen. Now for the first time ever, you can own the complete collection of the funniest moments from the Greatest Vaudeville Act of All Time – Snitsky and Heidenreich. You saw their dramatic reunion at the Survivor Series, but now you can relive the magic and moments from their hilarious routines and second-to-none stage show. When you order this four-DVD set, you'll get it all . . . including this famous skit . . .

WHO'S THE BABY'S MOTHER?

Gene Snitsky: Hey there! You know, John, being on *Raw* sure is a lot of fun. I get to do these wild and cah-razy angles where I kill babies. In fact, I'm getting set to do another baby-killing angle.

John Heidenreich: Why how grand! Tell me, Gene, what are the names of the players in this storyline?

Snitsky: Well, John, nowadays the bookers give these characters some pretty crazy names, I tell ya. Who's the mother. What's the baby. I Don't Know's the father.

Heidenreich: Who's the mother?

Snitsky: Yes.

Heidenreich: The baby's mother.

Snitsky: Who.

Heidenreich: The mother of the baby.

Snitsky: Who.

Heidenreich: Look, all I wanna know is . . . What is name of the baby's mother?

Snitsky: What is the name of the baby!

Heidenreich: I'm not asking you who's the baby!

Snitsky: Who's the mother.

Heidenreich: What are you asking me for?

Snitsky: I'm not asking you, I'm telling you. Who is the mother.

Heidenreich: I don't know.

Snitsky: He's the father. We're not talking about him.

Heidenreich: Argh! Listen. You kill a baby?

Snitsky: Certainly.

Heidenreich: What is the name of the baby you killed?

Snitsky: Exactly.

Heidenreich: What's the baby's name?

Snitsky: Exactly.

Heidenreich: So, you killed Exactly.

Snitsky: No, I killed What.

Heidenreich: You killed what?

Snitsky: Damn straight. Bashed his head in.

Heidenreich: You bashed in whose head?

Snitsky: No, I bashed in What's head. Who watched.

Heidenreich: I don't know.

Snitsky: He wasn't there. I put him in the hospital.

Heidenreich: Look, when the parents go to the cemetery to see the baby you killed, what's the name on the grave?

Snitsky: Yes.

Heidenreich: The baby's name on the grave.

Snitsky: What.

Heidenreich: Can't you hear me? Who's the baby?

Snitsky: No, no, no. Who's the mother.

Heidenreich: I'm not asking what's the mother's name!

Snitsky: No, no. What's the baby's name.

Heidenreich: I don't know!

Snitsky: That's the father! Aren't you listening?

Heidenreich: Hmmm, hmmm! I'm a ba-a-ad boy.

Act now and receive so much more! Listen fondly to some of Gene and John's melodic music from their amazing stage show. Featuring such grunting and groaning timeless classics as: She'll Be Coming 'Round The Mountain, Then I'll Kill Her Baby . . . 50 Ways to Rape Announcers . . . Little Johnny's Coming to Town . . . It's Not My Fault (The DJ Scratchy Woovy Berserk Re-Mega-Ultra Mix).

Plus Much More!

Don't be left out in the cold. Be a part of the magic and misery that is Snitsky and Heidenreich. Supplies are limited, so order your DVD set today . . . before the WWE office wakes up and these guys get released!

Insanity Contributors

Dr. Tom Prichard worked at WWE for over a decade. He served as a wrestler, trainer and internet columnist with the company up until 2004. He stays active in the industry, working as a trainer and performer. He also continues to look closely at the industry and write about it online. His work can be found at www.WorldWrestling-Insanity.com.

Former NWA Champion **Terry Funk** is a true legend in the wrestling business. Serving as an active performer since 1965, Terrible Terry has wrestled for WWE, WCW, ECW and every other promotion he could find. A member of the famous Funk family, Terry has appeared in such films as *Roadhouse, Over the Top* and *Paradise Alley.*

D-Lo Brown debuted with WWE in 1997 and remained with the company until 2003. His time there included numerous title reigns, including a double championship run with both the Intercontinental and European Titles. You can find him online at www.d-lobrown.com.

Debuting for WWE as one half of the World's Greatest Tag Team,

Charlie Haas was a member of the *Smackdown* roster for two years. His run included a diverse selection of storylines ranging from his partership with Shelton Benjamin to Rico. Charlie's website can be found at www.haasofpain.com.

Former WWE developmental performer **Elix Skipper** has appeared in WCW and TNA. A former Team Canada member in World Championship Wrestling, Skipper took TNA fans' breath away with a top of the cage Hurricanrana at 2004's Turning Point pay-per-view. You can read more about Elix at www.primetimeelix-skipper.com.

Voted the Greatest WWE Intercontinental Champion of all time by the fans, the **Honky Tonk Man** is still very active in the wrestling business. He does speaking engagements, corporate events, golf outings and, of course, wrestling events. HTM can be reached at www.the honkytonkman.com.

Missy Hyatt has worked for WCW, WWE and other wrestling promotions. She invites you to check out the "1st Wrestling Reality Website" for the first time. The First Lady of Wrestling Missy Hyatt teams up with The Queen of Extreme Francine. They are uncut and uncensored with behind the scenes footage from the road. New stuff uploaded daily at www.missyhyattandfrancinetv.com.

Aaron Aguilera, formerly "Jesus" on WWE's *Smackdown*, can be found online at AaronAguilera.com. Best known for his role as Carlito Caribbean Cool's bodyguard, he also appeared on WWE's PPV *Armageddon*, wrestling John Cena.

Lanny Poffo wrestled for WWE during most of the 1980s. Most famous as the evil and poetic "Genius," Lanny focuses his time now on writing and teaching kids the dangers of smoking. Leaping Lanny can be found online at at www.LannyPoffo.com.

The Ugandan Giant **Kamala** worked for WWE on and off for over ten years. He appeared as recently as the 2005 WWE *Taboo Tuesday* pay-per-view. Today, Kamala enjoys focusing on his blues and R&B music. His website is www.thegiantkamala.com.

Amy Weber participated in WWE as both a 2004 Diva Search Contestant and on-air manager for JBL. Amy has appeared in a number of movies and TV shows including CSI, *Melrose Place* and *Son of the Beach*. You can find her online at www.AmyWeber.net.